# Keeping faith?

## Channel Four and its audience

# Keeping faith?

## Channel Four and its audience

David Docherty, David E Morrison, Michael Tracey

John Libbey
LONDON · PARIS

BROADCASTING RESEARCH UNIT

**British Library Cataloguing in Publication Data**
Docherty, David, *1956-*
    Keeping faith? : Channel 4 and its audience.
    1. Great Britain. Commercial television
    services : Channel Four
    I. Title   II. Morrison, David, *1944-*
    III. Tracey, Michael
    384.55′4′0941

    ISBN 0-86196-158-7

Published by
**John Libbey & Company Ltd**
80/84 Bondway, London SW8 1SF, England (01) 582 5266
**John Libbey Eurotext Ltd**
6 rue Blanche, 92120 Montrouge, France (1) 47 35 85 52

Typesetting in Century by E E Owens & Co Ltd., London SE15 4AZ
Printed in Great Britain by Whitstable Litho Ltd, Whitstable, Kent

# Foreword

Channel Four commissioned the BRU to undertake a research project to investigate public attitudes towards the channel and specifically to assess how far the channel was perceived as fulfilling its distinctive remit under the Broadcasting Act. The result of their work is *KEEPING FAITH? Channel Four and its Audience*, based on an extensive series of group discussions around the country and a major national survey. The analysis of the evidence concerning public attitudes forms the essence of the book, and provides revealing insights into attitudes not just towards the channel, but towards many of the most contentious issues affecting broadcasting on all TV.

As they considered how best to address the channel's brief, the BRU decided that it was sensible to speak with those whose job it is to translate the formal codes of a mandate into programmes, the commissioning editors. This book reflects the views of the BRU.

# Acknowledgements

We would like to thank all those who helped in the preparation of this book. In particular, we are grateful to Sophie O'Neill who worked extremely hard in preparing valuable briefing papers: she was especially influential in laying down some of the initial intellectual framework for the study. Many busy people gave of their time to be interviewed for this book and we are grateful for their attention: John Cummins, Farrukh Dhondy, Alan Fountain, Michael Kustow, Adrian Metcalfe, Gwynn Pritchard, John Ranelagh, Robert Towler, Peter Ansorge, Elizabeth Forgan, Mike Bolland, Seamus Cassidy, David Rose, Naomi Sargant, Caroline Thomson, David Lloyd, Nick Hart-Williams, Sue Stoessl, Jeremy Isaacs, Edmund Dell, Anthony Smith, Lord William Whitelaw, David Graham, Mark Lucas, Joan Shenton, Peter Montagnon, Rob Burkitt, Alan Lovell, Don Coutts, Sebastiane Cody, Ann Skinner, Michael Darlow, Paul Styles, John Ellis, Colin Shaw and Chris Rowley. We are grateful to Stephen Hearst and Nick Garnham of the BRU Executive Committee who read and commented helpfully on the manuscript. Anna Noble, Shivaun Meehan, Cynthia Brown, Alison Joseph, Kirstie Morrison and Jim McDonnell helped prepare the manuscript for publication. Paul Lott and Alison Lyon, of N.O.P. were immensely helpful with the discussion groups, and Nick Moon (also of N.O.P.) was, as ever, invaluable with the survey. Finally, we would like to thank John Libbey who bore more of a burden than a publisher should.

# Contents

# Introduction

At the end of his account of the conception of Channel Four, Stephen Lambert comments: 'The one group who have notably not featured in the story of Channel Four are the people who will now judge its performance — the TV viewing public. Despite attempts to excite public interest in the subject there has been no widespread public demand for a fourth channel and the long debate over its allocation has been conducted almost solely by professional broadcasters and film-makers, politicians and civil servants, advertisers and academics.... If Channel Four succeeds in achieving its aim to be engagingly different, to cater for particular audiences traditionally neglected, it will be popular. A channel for "all the people — some of the time", it hopes to reach 80% of the population over the course of a complete week.' (1)

The channel opened without fanfare on November 2nd 1982. Five years on its share of television audience hovers around 8 per cent and it reaches between 70 per cent and 80 per cent of the viewing public in any given week. It has, however, taken on the mantle of a monumentally important symbol for how future television might be organised and produced. Other countries look to it for the lessons they might learn, and for clues on how to replace the traditional, centralised and monolithic structures of public broadcasting while retaining the public service ideal.

The successful incorporation of independent production into the channel's output has created an idea which now washes across the whole surface of British broadcasting. The BBC and ITV companies rush to include 'independent producers' in their production cycle as the government moves from requesting to demanding that they do so. Its first Chief Executive, Jeremy Isaacs, has emerged as one of the most charismatic and influential figure of his generation; a man of vision and adventure unfortunately ill-suited to the

1

present. (It is said that at his interview for the Director Generalship of the BBC he gathered only one vote from the twelve BBC Governors. It is also said that during the course of that interview Sir John Boyd observed: 'Mr Isaacs, you don't seem to me like a man that will take very kindly to discipline'. He saw Isaacs smile at this, and uttered further: 'Now you may take that as a compliment but others of us in here would take that as a criticism: what have you to say to that?' Here was the endless, centuries old dialogue of British life between those who want to say something, and those who want to stop things being said because they think that it is their job to stop things being said. He felt, he says, that 'the whole thrust of what I was asked was "how do we stop things". It wasn't "how do we get good things on the air", it was "how do we stop bad things on the air".'

The very success of the channel poses its own problems. There are many changes being mooted about the channel and its future. Should it sell its own airtime? Should it be removed from the IBA and 'privatised'? Should it be made into a trust? To cap the heady atmosphere of change, Isaacs retired early in 1988, and was succeeded by Michael Grade as the Chief Executive.

As part of the stock-taking associated with the channel's fifth anniversary, Channel Four asked the Broadcasting Research Unit to evaluate the success of the station – particularly its relationship with the public. This research began with a basic concern: there have been persistent accusations over the past five years that Channel Four has been irresponsible in attitudes to the depiction of sex and violence, and biased toward the left in its political attitudes. We set out to discover the public's views concerning these accusations. In particular, we wanted to know whether the audience demanded or tolerated a different type of television from C4 than from the other three channels. Does it think that the channel has a special mandate to allow for the expression of different voices on television? Is it prepared to accept polemical television which differs substantially from traditional current affairs? Is minority television acceptable to the majority? Or does the public want Channel Four to be 'just another button', as *The Times* put it in the week of the launch? On the basis of a national survey of public attitudes and forty-four in-depth discussion groups we can say that the answer to all of these is a qualified yes.

This is essentially a study of public reaction to Channel Four, not of its reach or audience share, but of the kinds of judgements which the public-as-audience, or rather as a series of audiences, has begun to make. It is based on both quantitative and qualitative evidence, digging beneath the surface of the public mind, rather than just offering a snapshot of the surface. The rationale behind such research is that one can strip away layers of superficial responses and begin to peer into the more complex, certainly more subtle, not always consistent construction of the public mind. We did not, therefore, merely go into the groups or the survey simply to ask: Do you like/dislike the channel? As a result we discovered that the channel has the support of the public, but the terms and conditions of that support are, as we shall see later, extremely complicated.

As well as exploring the channel's public image we sought to understand the channel's self-image. What did the founders think they were going to achieve? Did they think that it had been successful? Had the commissioning editors changed their minds over the years about how to achieve breakthroughs in television? And, finally, what were the views of the people whose work had helped the channel succeed — the independent producers? To this end we conducted long interviews with most of the main intellectual and political founders of the channel, as well as every commissioning editor, and a number of independent producers.

This is not a history of Channel Four. Dorothy Hobson has been the official historian of the channel since its very early days, and her work, which will be a detailed analysis of the problems and successes of Channel Four, will appear at some later date. Neither have we undertaken an organisational study of how the Channel Four commissioning process works, nor of how Jeremy Isaacs' regime operates, nor of the related finances and structure of Channel Four. Our primary concern has been with the channel's remit from Parliament, the Independent Broadcasting Authority, and from the mass of opinions articulated by some of the groups and individuals over ten years or more, prior to the start of the channel. We were particularly interested in what we take to be the most challenging aspect of this mandate: that it serve special interests and minorities, and give a voice to those who previously had not had access to television.

The interviews with the channel's founders in Chapter One and the commissioning editors in Chapter Two should be regarded as clarifications of the channel's remit. The first two chapters tease out the ways in which the mandate was developed and interpreted, but make no attempt to judge the channel's structure. For instance, we take as given the government's decision to establish an editorial channel under the IBA, rather than an access channel under a new broadcasting authority. We are more interested in clarifying the reasons and implications of this decision than in going over old ground in criticising it. The first two chapters define the mandate. In Chapter Three, however, on the basis of the public's complex and sophisticated understanding of the mandate, we make our own evaluation of how the channel has fitted into the changing political and cultural moods of the 1980s.

We were particularly interested in the public's concern with programme balance. The concept is used here not in the traditional and simple sense of a proper, occasionally obsessive, weighing of competing political, ie parliamentary, standpoints, but in the broader sense of the position of the channel vis-à-vis consensual values within British society, and the extent to which C4's evocation of different 'voices' — political, cultural, moral, sexual — becomes not the fulfilling of a mandate to extend the range of British television, but

3

rather something which corrupts that consensus and therefore the social order of which it is a product.

We interpreted the issue of 'balance' as suggesting a wider question: that of what the proper intellectual location of the channel within the general provision of broadcasting in Britain should be and what the responses of the public to that location were. Given that it had a clear mandate to introduce new voices it is hardly surprising that for Channel Four the issues of balance and bias exist, not in relation to some internal aspect of a programme, or programme strand, but in terms of its relationship to more consensual values within Britain. A sharpness is given to this problem by the fact that 'imbalance' – a basket concept for a knot of related anxieties and concerns – is often, one might say largely, not an objective condition but something which lies subjectively in the eye of the beholder. The sharper the self-conscious adherence to those values, the sharper the likely sense of there being an imbalance in Channel Four output. The paradox which Channel Four faces is that the more it fulfills its mandate the more it will enrage particular individuals and constituents and the more its mandate is potentially called into question. The following chapters attempt to tell the story of the channel from these various points of view. First, though, we explore the expectations raised by what the ITV companies responding to the Annan Report called 'the empty room of British broadcasting'.

# Chapter One

# Channel Four: Theory and Promise

## (1) The Promise

There can be few developments anywhere in the history of broadcasting whose birth was accompanied by such heady expectation and detailed intent. In the first instance, then, we must spend some time sketching in just what it was the channel was supposed to do.

At the Edinburgh International TV Festival in 1979 Jeremy Isaacs offered his view of what should be the organisation and purpose of the new channel. It was a view as much of the strategic organisation of the new channel, particularly in relation to the thorny question of the balance between the existing ITV companies and the independent sector, as of the programme content. On the latter Isaacs argued that the channel should aim at a variety of audiences and at a 10 per cent share of the total TV audience. He wished the channel to cater for substantial minorities neglected by the other parts of the television industry without walling up such programme slots into ghettos: 'I hope in the eighties to see more black Britons on our screens in programmes of particular appeal to them and aimed at us; more programmes made by women for women which men will watch; more programmes for the young, for the age group that watches television least partly because so little television speaks to them.'

In the lecture he referred to actuality programmes which would embrace a complete spectrum of political attitude and opinion while also serving, however informally, education. Above all the channel would 'somehow be different' but 'not that different'. He continued: 'We want a fourth channel that will neither simply compete with ITV1 nor merely be complementary to it. We want a fourth channel that everyone will watch some of the time and no one will watch all of the time.'

To anyone aware of the history of the BBC, which had long pursued an all-things-to-all-men philosophy, there was much that was familiar in this statement. Public service broadcasting in Britain has long worked on the assumption that the audience for broadcasting did not constitute a single mass. Rather, the audience was seen as a whole network of groupings formed through taste, class, interest and so on — in fact that whole galaxy of motivations which go to make up social life. The purpose of public broadcasting was to serve and articulate those interests, to make a virtue of their difference, and occasionally to bring them together. The new channel was therefore very much part of a tradition, while being in effect asked to provide a final net to catch all those minorities — of mind, mood and matter — which somehow slipped through the public service net provided by the duopoly of the BBC and ITV.

Jeremy Isaacs has become so closely identified with Channel Four that a conception has arisen that it was from him, through utterances such as the Mac Taggart lecture, that the direction and character of the new channel were shaped. The reality — and to be fair, Isaacs is the first to point this out — is longer and more complex than that. The channel is, in fact, the child of many parents. In 1971 the ITCA requested control of the fourth TV channel which was available, and this is generally considered to be the start of the debate leading to the creation of the new channel in 1982. Behind the rhetoric of their request the prime impulse of the ITCA companies rested on the simple, if powerful, belief that there was an awful lot of money to be made by using the new outlet. The only real voices of dissent to this came from representatives of the independent producers and the broadcasting trade unions. The Independent Film-Makers' Association argued forcefully: 'The case for a fourth channel has always been the case for a different channel, for a different approach to both scheduling and programme making. It is based positively on the need for diversity and innovation and negatively on a recognition and critique of the inadequacies of the current three channels. More of the same is a disheartening prospect (indeed it's a persuasive argument against another channel); more difference (in programme forms, in personnel, in audience, in financing and in administration) is an exciting one.'

The very idea of the fourth channel immediately raised the whole question of what its audience would be and what the ramifications would be for the existing relationship between the BBC and ITV. Brian Young, then Director General of the IBA, suggested in a speech in the summer of 1979 that the fourth channel would aim at attracting 15 to 20 per cent of the audience, and that TV4 together with the rest of the ITV network would claim a total of 60 per cent. Such talk immediately sent nervous shivers down the spines of BBC executives who saw a ratings war develop as they tried to maintain the 50-50 split of the audience. Since the late 1950s it has been an orthodoxy within the Corporation that without such a division of the audience the very existence of the BBC would be called into question, as more and more viewers failed to see the point of paying a fee for a service which they less and less used.

Alasdair Milne, the BBC's Managing Director of Television at the time of Young's speech, was quick to warn of this.

The beginning of the definition of the nature and purpose of the channel is contained within an article written by a former BBC producer, Tony Smith, in the *Guardian* in April 1972, which was developed and submitted as evidence to the Annan Committee in December 1974. He put forward a plan for a National Television Foundation which would 'publish' programmes by 'authors' who would work from outside the Foundation. As such it would stimulate, encourage and provide work for all those talents camped outside the walls of the existing broadcasting organisations: 'It would supplement existing broadcasting by broadening the input, by allowing anyone to bring a project to it, whether an independent programme-maker with a finely worked out plan, neatly costed, or a firm, organisation or individual with merely a well argued complaint that some issue was failing to get across to the public. The foundation would then play a kind of impressario role, merely by allocating resources to some, but fitting producers, writers, technicians to others who arrived only with an idea, a grievance, a cause.'

Isaacs recognises the importance of Smith's thinking: 'I think that one should take one's hat off in a very, very big way to Anthony Smith, who more than any other single individual, and certainly more than I, enunciated a philosophy which contributed to the practice of this channel.' Another index of the intellectual significance of Smith's ideas is that they were included in a memo prepared by Colin Shaw, then a senior figure in the BBC, and submitted to the Annan Committee. That memo was in part a spoiling tactic by the BBC – the last thing they wanted to be confronted by was ITV2 – but also a genuine nod in the direction of a new and interesting idea.

The Annan Report, published in 1977, argued that an ITV2 would create a stultifying four-channel system obsessed by ratings. It recommended that the fourth channel be allocated to an Open Broadcasting Authority: 'Unlike the existing Authorities, who are required to take editorial responsibility for all their programmes in order to ensure a proper balance and wide range of subject matter in their programming and due impartiality in the treatment of controversial matters, the OBA would operate more as a publisher of programme material provided by others.' Those 'others' would include both the existing ITV companies as well as 'a variety of independent producers' who would be encouraged to offer 'productions which say something new in new ways'. The Labour Government was disposed to accept these proposals. The Conservative Government, which came to power in 1979, was not, and quickly revoked them, making it clear that the IBA should be given responsibility for the new channel 'subject to strict safeguards'.

It has to be said that there were serious and justified reservations about the financial viability of both the Foundation and the OBA. As an idea the 'publishing' analogy was deeply attractive to many people. The idea of funding from various sources – sponsorship, advertising, donations from public bodies and Foundations – which had been espoused by Smith and accepted by Annan, was to more sober eyes a fiscal dog's dinner. The task, post-1979, was clear: to retain the brilliance of the 'publishing' role for the new channel and marry it to a structure and form of finance which would give it sustainable viability.

Once the government had made it clear that the IBA would be the major actor in creating the new channel, the ITCA companies, independent producers and the Channel Four Group all began to lobby an Authority which was giving only the barest indications of its plans. Initially the ITV companies' claim rested on the argument that it was 'unfair' for them to have to compete against two BBC channels, that their production facilities were underused and their creative staff increasingly frustrated. Once it was clear that the companies more than matched the BBC for audiences and that the spare studio capacity no longer existed, they shifted their arguments. The new rationale was for 'complementary scheduling', the argument being that if the new channel's programmes were not to clash with those of ITV1 then they were best generated from the same source.

An important assumption made by the ITCA, and one that carried a lot of influence with the IBA, was that only they could realistically keep the fourth channel on air. Colin Shaw, by this time the Director of Television at the IBA and a key figure in the Authority's thinking, made it clear that he did not think that the independent sector would be able to provide anywhere near the amount of programming which a new channel would require. The only detailed prospectus for the channel saw it operating in tandem with the current ITV system both for reasons of complementary scheduling and for the financial support it would need to draw from ITV in order to survive in the early years. The IBA proposed that 55 per cent of the new channel's programming would come from the ITCA companies, news and sport would get 10 to 15 per cent, education programmes would have a similar allocation and 15 per cent would come from independent producers, the latter being crucially defined as a proportion which 'should be regarded essentially as an entitlement'.

Though this commitment to guarantee the airtime available to independent productions seemed to be a major development, the way it was stated avoided the problem that not all independent productions are of the same nature. At one end of the spectrum were independent producers making programmes which, though fashioned ouside the controls of the major companies, were nevertheless no more than versions of the kinds of programmes already being produced within the companies. The forms of TV remained unchanged. At the other end of the independent spectrum were programme makers who saw themselves as challenging accepted notions of TV content, experimenting with the nature of the medium and trying to extend its boundaries. The Independent Film-Makers' Association argued: 'As potential programme makers, we are not interested only in getting a share of the airtime and a share of the audience, necessary though these are. We are interested in achieving a different approach to scheduling, to programme making and selection, and, more important of all to the audience ... a determination to welcome the controversial, the committed and the unfamiliar, beyond the dead grip of the consensus. Minority interest should mean more than minority leisure pursuit or pastime.' It was basically then a call for the pursuit of the unfashionable, the unconventional, the challenging; a call however whose pretensions were much clearer than the ways in which they would be achieved.

The Channel Four Group called for a rejection of ITCA control or domination of the new channel, and for the creation of an OBA within the IBA, with its own controller and a scheduling committee representing all those providing programmes. This position was supported by the Incorporated Society of British Advertisers (ISBA) in the belief that this would not only create more airtime for advertising but would also break the price control exerted by the monopoly of the ITV companies. Similarly the main craft union, the ACTT, came out in opposition to ITV2 and in favour of the plan from the Channel Four Group.

The Channel Four Group plan did not avoid the problem which dogged the original OBA plan, that no one could quite see how it was going to establish financial viability *and* retain its cultural and political independence. The whole debate was inhabited by a fear that the ITCA would inevitably dominate the channel to the detriment of the independents and, therefore, to the detriment of experiment and imagination.

In a speech in September 1979 in Cambridge, William Whitelaw, the Home Secretary, outlined how his Government saw the future of television in Britain. He buried forever the idea of an OBA and confirmed that the IBA would be the statutory body responsible for the new channel. The source of finance for the channel he said would be 'spot advertising, though block advertising and perhaps sponsorship may be permitted'. He then moved on to the question of the 'strict safeguards' referred to in the Queen's Speech. He observed: 'Our whole tradition, whether in the BBC's Charter or in legislation for the control of independent television, and most would agree that this is a tradition which has proved basically sound, has been to entrust a wide measure of discretion to the broadcasting authorities. There are good reasons for this. No person or body of persons, not even Parliament in its collective wisdom, can foresee the future with absolute certainty. What are seen as obvious problems today or obvious dangers to be guarded against may assume less significance as social and technological conditions change and others may, and almost certainly will, arise whose precise form at any rate cannot be foreseen, so that great detail in legislation may prove misconceived and actually hinder in the future the broad objectives sought. Yet, on the other hand, an injunction to do good, so general as to be

9

platitudinous, would rightly not satisfy either Parliament or the public; and could be a positive embarrassment to the authority which is entitled to a reasonably clear indication of what it is that the law expects of it. A middle way must and can be found, and one which enables Parliament and the public to form a judgement on how far our intentions are being realised in the event. Full and regular reports on how the fourth channel is operating, including financial matters, the types of programmes broadcast and the like, ought to be required and given publicity.'

Whitelaw believed that 'what we are looking for is a fourth channel offering a distinctive service of its own', a single national programme service without regional variations, except for Welsh language broadcasts, with programmes that were 'appealing to and, we hope, stimulating tastes and interests not adequately provided for on existing channels'. He suggested, for example, that there be new approaches to news, wider political coverage and 'far more extended treatment of news and current affairs which is excluded from TV simply by the limited time at present available'. He also had in mind developments in educational programmes, both 'structured and more informal'. The source of these programmes he saw as being the network ITV companies, the regional companies and independent producers, though he refused to be drawn on what the various proportions would be. Neither would he be drawn on the detailed description of the structure and organisational arrangements for the new channel, other than to indicate that they would be distinct from those of ITV2. He then summed up the implications of the government's approach for the new channel:

> The IBA will be expected to develop a distinctive service on the fourth channel, subject to similar general statutory provisions as now exist on programme content — for example, the avoidance of offence against good taste and decency and the like — in a way which is designed to give new opportunities to creative people in British television and to add different and greater satisfactions to those now available to the viewer. It will be expected to extend the range of programmes available to the public, to find new ways of serving minority and specialised audiences and to give due place to innovation. It will be expected not to allow rivalry for ratings between the two channels for which it has statutory responsibility nor to allow scheduling designed to obtain for each of those services the largest possible audience over the week. It will be expected to make arrangements for the largest practicable proportion of programmes on the fourth channel to be supplied by organisations and persons other than the companies contracted to provide programmes on ITV1. It will be expected to increase the number of programmes shown which are originated by the regional ITV companies and ITN and, in consequence, to ensure that those companies which have networking rights on ITV1 have much less time on the fourth channel. It will be expected to provide an allotment of time for educational programmes, both structured and informal, on the

fourth channel, and for Welsh language programmes on the fourth channel in Wales. It will be expected to ensure that the arrangements for planning and scheduling of the fourth channel service are not dominated by the programme companies contracted to provide programmes on ITV1, especially the network companies, that the budget for the fourth channel is adequate to achieve the sort of service I have described and that a fair payment is made to all contributors on the channel.

Whitelaw provided the political weight to give life to the new channel. Had he been of a different disposition the story of the channel would have been utterly altered. In his own mind, in those months after the election, his immediate feeling was that they had to fill the new channel with something: 'I think that the first problem we faced was whether to fill the fourth channel at all. There were quite a large number of people at the time who said don't use it at all, keep it open and see what's going to happen. It seemed to me at the time that increasingly in people's minds [they thought] I have bought a television set which has got four channels, why am I not allowed to use it.' Whitelaw therefore began with the simple but important feeling that they had to do something. What though? 'I thought it right to put it out under the umbrella of the IBA because I thought the first thing was, if, as many people advocated, it was to be different and have rather different priorities, quality was still very important, and therefore some overall check of how it was going on was equally necessary. Indeed, in my discussions with my colleagues if I had just said, I'm going to set up a fourth channel which is going to have no responsibility to any broadcasting authority, they would have said no. And I think very reasonably said no. So that was how it led to the second [conclusion], it should be under the IBA. Then came the question: what was its purpose? And basically the idea was that it should be a channel used more for the smaller interest groups, that it should be a channel used more by independent producers and thirdly it should have a somewhat distinctive approach to many different subjects. Then came the question: how was it going to be financed? Here of course the IBA came into it because [it would be] financed by advertising, and indeed now that would seem to have been quite a considerable success. But at the time there were a great many Jeremiahs who said — oh no, it won't work, and if you say it's got to have the independent producers and distinctive programmes and giving the right amount of access to minority groups, then of course that will make it more certain than ever that people won't advertise.'

One senior IBA official closely involved with the channel's development described Whitelaw as 'a good man, a big man who is broad in his sympathies', particularly towards minorities. Whitelaw himself recognises an almost sentimental attachment to those needs, though he argues this with a fair dose of realism: 'If you are Home Secretary in any government, you are going to take the view that there are a lot of minority interests in this country, [for example] different races. If they don't get some outlet for their activities you are going to run yourself into much more trouble. I just thought it's right that they should have some chance. I just wanted to open the thing out rather more broadly than it had been before, a channel that was somewhat different, but not too different. If you wanted it to be very different you would have struck it away from the IBA altogether. I think one always had that sort of safeguard at the back of one's mind.'

Whitelaw's significance, however, lay not only in his acceptance that the channel should be different, with a particular responsibility to minorities within society. Nor in his acceptance of the argument that the IBA should finally be responsible for its supervision. His significance lies also in his having had the political clout to convince the other members of the government, and the Treasury in particular, of how the channel should be funded.

The gestation of what emerged as the triangular relationship between the IBA, ITV and Channel Four was within a series of intense discussions which took place within the IBA in the closing years of the 1970s. The dramatis personae of this were the Director General, Brian Young; Colin Shaw, Director of Television; and Chris Rowley, TV Schedules Officer and as such one of the principal links to thinking inside the ITV companies. Their feeling was that if the fourth channel was used to establish a 'third force' in British broadcasting, the possibility of cooperation with the ITV system would be lost, and with it the possibilities of such practical but vital considerations as common junctions in schedules, complementary scheduling and so on, all of which might reasonably have been held to be serving the interests of the viewer, and without which life could be made extremely difficult for the new channel. There was some doubt inside the Authority, and throughout ITV, of the ability of the independent sector fully to programme a whole new channel, and so again cooperation with an ITV which could feed in its own ideas for programmes that fitted the new channel's likely mandate seemed to make sense. There was also some expectation within this group that the development of the new independent sector in the wake of the opportunities afforded by the new channel would trigger some useful competition with the ITV companies, both editorially and in terms of the financial efficiency of the rich companies.

Perhaps the most powerful father to the thought, however, was the recognition that if the new channel was not somehow linked into the interests and perceptions of the ITV companies then they would simply kill it off. Young, Shaw and Rowley felt that if ITV had a financial stake in the channel they would be less interested in strangling the interloper at birth and indeed could be led to nurture it through such simple means as common junctions, on-air promotions and so on. Out of this sequence of thought emerged the ingenious idea that the channel should be funded by a subscription from the ITV companies, who would then be given the right to raise revenue by selling advertising time on the channel. The only worry they had was that the Treasury might see that they would be losing out since at least in the first instance the amount of money produced for its coffers from the ITV levy would inevitably be reduced. The argument was made to the Home Office, for the Home Secretary's ears, that this would only be a temporary phenomenon, and as we have seen Whitelaw was clearly in the frame of mind to be convinced of the power of that argument. The final piece in the puzzle was the proposal that the IBA would be the honest broker in setting the level of the subscription which would be made over to C4. It did not harm the ability of the IBA, in making this case to the companies, that their franchises were up for renewal at more or less the same time. (We need only add that if the process is put into reverse gear, for example by removing the companies' financial interests in the channel, then the consequences which the IBA trio were seeking to avoid might well be something more than a theoretical possibility, ie that the Channel will have its throat cut.)

In a note written to Brian Young in mid-1978, Chris Rowley summarised thinking about the new Channel:

## THE FOURTH CHANNEL

*What is wanted from the fourth channel:-*

1. A 'third force', (as described by Annan), to encourage innovation and to allow for an alternative source for such areas as news.

2. A channel that is neither controlled by the present ITV companies: nor run by the IBA — whose role means they must be one step removed from the programme-making process.

3. A structure that is practical — that can ensure that there is enough money and a consistent production level.

4. A schedule that is complementary, consistently offering viewers alternative programmes to ITV.

5. A wide ranging selection of programming that is concentrated mainly on specialised interests but not to the complete exclusion of some general interest and some popular programmes.

*How to get the above*

1. The IBA would appoint a Director of the fourth channel, who would have his own staff — a head of drama commissioning, a head of factual programme commissioning, and so on, as well as the necessary financial/administrative expertise. An associated development could be that extra members of the IBA could be appointed to be concerned exclusively with the fourth channel. There is no reason why this fourth

channel body should not be known as the Open Broadcasting Agency or Corporation.

2. The fourth channel would be entirely separate from both the ITV companies and the IBA, commissioning programmes from whatever source it wanted. The ITV companies would obviously be the primary suppliers, particulary to start with, but the programmes would also come from abroad, from educational sources and, increasingly, as they gradually developed as contributors to British TV, from independent producers.

3. The IBA would give the fourth channel an annual budget, which would be taken from the companies in the form of a special 'rental'.

4. The ITV companies would collect all the advertising revenue for the fourth channel, using existing spot advertising but some experimental advertising ideas. (The companies would therefore have an interest in producing good programmes because they would be obtaining the revenue.)

5. The fourth channel would compile its own schedule but would have to submit it to the Authority for approval in the same way as the ITV companies. The Authority would ensure that the fourth channel provided a variety of primarily minority interest programmes in a package which gave viewers a properly balanced alternative to ITV, allowing for such things as common junctions.

In order to obtain a fourth channel that is practical and that really will give viewers a sensible alternative to ITV, it is necessary to have some kind of overall supervision of both channels. A new organisation can be set up by the IBA that will not be dominated by the ITV companies and that will provide the stimulus that British television needs. That triangular relationship was a brilliant device since it guaranteed both the intellectual and creative ambitions of the channel and its finance, a truly imaginative extension of the principles and financial logics of public service broadcasting.

The neatest description of public service broadcasting holds that it is a means of ensuring that resources flow in directions in which given other political arrangements – for example, state controlled or solely commercial systems – they would not. This is simply a way of saying that in the allocation of programme resources to match programme ideas the need to take on board other, non-programme considerations was, if not eradicated, at least muted. Thus was created the necessary environment in which money could be spent on the new, the bold and the different, as well as the old, the comfortable and the familiar.

Support for this way of doing broadcasting has come traditionally, in Britain at least, from a number of constitutional and financial devices. The BBC owes its existence to a Royal Charter and therefore, technically, to the Crown and not the government. The Governors who *are* in the BBC in law are, technically, appointees of the Crown and not the government, and therefore can only be removed by the Monarch. The Corporation has therefore been cocooned within the trappings of a constitutional monarchy and within, for much of its history, the broad consensus of opinion in Parliament. It is true that of late a certain erosion of that consensus has taken place with, in some eyes, attempts to nominate to the Crown only those who are of the same mood and manner as the government. It is equally true that the process of 'politicisation' of the Governors has not gone as far as that of the public boards controlling broadcasting in West Germany. The licence and agree-ment to transmit, which the BBC has from the government, is far from being a massively inhibiting or demanding document. True it contains the power of veto, a power hardly ever contemplated and never used. (Even in the *Real Lives* case, the Home Secretary, Leon Brittan, suggested rather than demanded that the programme should be withdrawn.) The only prescriptions cover such relatively innocuous issues as the demand that the BBC cover Parliament and that there be space made available for 'ministerial broad-casts'. The almost total demise of the latter is revealing. The condition was that such broadcasts be non-controversial. When they became such, a right of reply was granted to the official opposition, a fact which displeased Ministers and quickly led to the declining use of such mandatory opportunities to broadcast.

The archstone for this whole structure, however, was the licence fee, which is paid for the privilege of owning a receiving set, not as a subscription to the BBC. The net effect of this licence fee mechanism was to distance the BBC from having to pursue, in any grubbing sense, state funding or commercial revenues.

Equally clever, however, in creating an environment within which resources would be spent creatively, was the mixing of public regulation and private commerce in the IBA–ITV system. The granting of monopoly business rights to a franchisee − ie the sole right to sell air-time in a given region − was intended by Parliament to be totally dependent on the demand that the franchise is not treated as *only* a business. The social and creative purpose has also to be recognised in the allocation of programme resources, and where it is not, the removal of the franchise as a consequence.

And then we have perhaps the finest, perhaps final, flowering of this way of doing broadcasting: Channel Four. Just consider what that channel is: a body which is given a large sum of money, to fulfill a mandate laid down by Parliament that it be different, innovative, serve minorities, give voice to the voiceless, and not to worry about too large an audience or where its money

15

is coming from − the former is not necessary and the latter guaranteed. And from where is the money to come − from the rich part of the IBA−ITV system, the companies whose monopoly rests on their involuntary munificence and their further right to sell airtime on Channel Four.

Perhaps the neatest part of a neat system, the final guarantor is that the two parts of the total system − the licence-funded BBC and the advertising-supported IBA−ITV−C4 structure − do not compete for the same revenue. It goes without saying that the proposals for change − introducing advertising or subscription to the BBC, selling the franchises for ITV rather than granting the conditional monopoly, making C4 raise its own revenue − have serious implications. Public service broadcasting would become not a robust structure but a delicately balanced house of cards.

In November 1979 the blueprint for the Channel Four Television Company was published by the IBA. Inevitably it was to prove to be close to the thinking within the Broadcasting Bill published three months later. On programming policy, the Authority said that the Fourth Channel was to have 'its own distinct character' complementing the service provided by ITV without necessarily pursuing a majority of the audience. The Authority stated: 'The consequence will be that programmes, while still intended to appeal to as many viewers as their individual terms of reference allow, can address themselves to particular interests or concerns and adopt new approaches far more freely than at present. Our wish is that Channel Four will take particular advantage of this freedom, and that enterprise and experiments will flourish. It must provide opportunities for talents which have previously not been fully used, for needs to be served which have not yet been fully defined, and for the evolution of ideas which, for whatever reason − personal, structural, institutional − have yet to be revealed. But it would be quite wrong on at least two counts to deny to the new channel programmes likely to draw very large audiences. First, it would be fatal if the broad public, the sum of countless special interests, were to feel that it was somehow not for them. Even if, by its nature, the Fourth Channel will be a service visited from time to time rather than watched constantly, as BBC1 and ITV1 have tended to be by significant parts of their audiences, it must remain in the public's mind accessible. Secondly, there is a need to present the work of independent producers within a popular context rather than simply as a fringe activity. We would not intend therefore to make the Fourth Channel wholly a "minority" service; nor would we want the present blend of the first independent channel to change in the direction of an unrestrained search for popularity. Rather, we would see the present 'mix' on ITV's single channel continuing, while the Fourth Channel roughly reversed that 'mix' with about two-thirds of its programmes addressing sections of the audience who want something particular or who want something different. In the remaining one-third there would be programmes intended to appeal to larger audiences, though often in a style different from that of some popular programmes now seen.'

The actual legislation establishing the channel referred to the duty of the Authority 'to ensure that the programmes contain a suitable proportion of matter calculated to appeal to tastes and interests not generally catered for by ITV'; to ensure that a suitable proportion were of an educational nature; 'to encourage innovation and experiment'.

 The individuals who came together in early 1980 as 'consultants', until such time as they could legally became directors of the new channel, had to translate this history of discussion and expectation into a clear mandate. At one of their first meetings, as recalled by Edmund Dell, the first chairman, Tony Smith argued that they needed something more detailed and polished than the guidelines which had so far been provided by the IBA. They called for a programme policy statement, which was duly drafted by Colin Shaw. This spoke of the channel having 'as a particular charge the service of special interests and concerns for which television has until now lacked adequate time. The Fourth Channel is expected, by providing a favoured place for the untried, to foster the new and experimental in television.' The channel was intended, the statement continued, 'to complement and to be complemented by the present ITV service.' The needs and interests of the audience 'should be served not only by programmes directed to minorities but also by some aiming to attract larger numbers.' In an important paragraph, it added: 'The additional hours of broadcasting made available by the Fourth Channel increase opportunities for programmes directed to different kinds of minority groups within the community, whether ethnic, cultural, or occupational distinctions mark them off from their neighbours.' The document reaffirmed the importance of the independent production sector in achieving their goals.

It is clear, then, that by the time of the appointment of Jeremy Isaacs as Chief Executive in September 1980, the details of the channel's mandate were clear in the minds of Government, Authority and Board. Indeed, when he was appointed Chairman, Edmund Dell had not even heard of Isaacs nor, in the course of the appointment, did he think he was the only outstanding candidate. Dell had read carefully Jeremy Isaacs' Mac Taggart lecture, which at the time had been viewed almost universally as the most eloquent and public job application in the history of television. Dell commented:

> There are two things in that lecture which I didn't particularly like. I knew nothing about television, but what I did know was that there wasn't much on television that I actually liked, and therefore I wanted it to be different. Jeremy told me two things in the Mac Taggart lecture: different but not too different, and ITV2 not Channel Four. Now to me the key things were, Channel Four, because that was symbolic and the second is that I did want it to be distinctive. So as far as I was concerned the Mac Taggart lecture was dissuasive not persuasive.

In the end the choice of Chief Executive became one between Isaacs and John Birt, then of LWT, who was felt to have made a particulary excellent

17

application. In fact there were two other figures whom some would have wished to see applying. One was Charles Denton, then Director of Programmes at Central, and the other Brian Wenham, Controller, BBC2, of whom Dell says 'If he had applied he might easily have got it.'

When Jeremy Isaacs took up his position as Chief Executive his immediate task was to organise a structure to translate into the hard reality of programming the creative ambitions of so many people over the previous twenty years as well as the more formal prescriptions of the government and the IBA. Isaacs did not arrive simply to impress his own seal on the softwax of a vague idea. He is, however, nothing if not a powerful, charismatic figure who had spelled out his own vision for the channel on more than one occasion. In his position as Chief Executive there would obviously be ample opportunity to influence the channel, if only through intrinsically malleable operational practices. It is important therefore in understanding the purpose of the channel to pin down the elements of Isaacs' own thinking about the opportunities it afforded, and the differences between the channel and the rest of the public service broadcasting system.

Isaacs is a broadcaster with a memory, and as he embarked on his application for the position of Chief Executive he looked back on the previous fifteen to twenty years of British broadcasting not as a golden period but as one in which the full potentiality of broadcasting had not been reached, as one of missed opportunities. He saw, as did others, wonderful programmes, but also gaps, inadequacies, angles of vision which were not employed, perceptions of, and dialogue with, the audience smothered beneath, for example, the high mandarin style of BBC2. He felt that the atmosphere, the mood, of the 1970s was wrong − the product of what he calls 'a sort of cozy consensus in broadcasting. You were aware as a programme maker in ITV of endless battles with the IBA for programmes that could express any opinion at all.' And he felt that television, particularly in the post-Greene BBC, had lost the capacity 'of annoying people'. In an article written in the early 1970s he argued that television should allow all kinds of people to put their point of view. A few days after this piece appeared he received an applauding letter from Kenneth Alsop who told of how he, Alsop, had just been scolded by Grace Wyndham Goldie, ex-Head of Current Affairs at the BBC, for an overly-opinionated piece about South Africa.

Isaacs' commitment to allowing all kinds of people to put their point of view on television was sorely tried during the early days of the channel. He recalls 'an absolute run-in' with Norman Tebbit at an embassy dinner party shortly after Channel Four went on the air. Tebbit told him: 'You've got it completely wrong. When the Act said 'cater for interests not catered for by ITV, or be a distinctive service', we didn't mean you to put on left-wingers, or put on homosexuals, or put on trade unions, or put on any of those things. What you should be doing are programmes for yachtsmen and golfers.' Now to be fair to Isaacs he spoke of the conversation in a way which indicated that he felt that Tebbit had a point, and that the difference resided in his own very different perspectives and interests. 'I think that maybe in twenty years' time, when two or three people have run this channel after me, it will be seen that what has characterised my regime has been an interest in ideas and attitudes and opinions that will not necessarily be shown by my successors, whoever they'll turn out to be, because you can interpret the remit in different ways.' He adds: 'My view of what a liberal society is all about [is that] you tolerate people's activities as long as they don't harm you.' And here he brought the question of the mandate right back to its birth: 'What Willie Whitelaw understands is the need for a tolerant society, to have broadcasting that allows all sorts of opinions and attitudes.'

The immediate problem that faced Isaacs and his colleagues was whether Channel Four could uncouple the viewing public from their ingrained habits – which had not been challenged since the start of BBC2, 18 years earlier. It had, however, one immediate advantage over the birth of BBC2. In 1964 BBC2 was Britain's first TV channel designed for colour and as such was transmitted on UHF. New transmitters and new sets were required. By 1969 there were still only 30.8 per cent of TV homes capable of receiving BBC2, and it was not until well into the 1970s that it was nationally available and therefore a force within the overall ratings game. In November 1982 C4 was already receivable by 82 per cent of TV homes, and by 1984 by 97 per cent of TV homes, therefore having effective parity with the other channels. In a spirit of generosity to the newcomer, Brian Wenham is quoted as saying: 'Jeremy hopes to reach double figures by the end of three years. I'd say that was a decently ambitious target. For Channel Four to get 10 per cent regularly within 12 months would mean that they've had more than their fair share of correct guesses. I'd be surprised by under 4 per cent or over 12 per cent.' (*Observer* 31.10.82)

From the standpoint of the ambition which lay behind the creation of the channel, any judgement of success or failure would finally have to rest on the *kinds* of people who made up those figures and the character of their response to the programmes they were watching. Isaacs commented: 'A lot of sterile debate hangs on the opposition between the audience or no audience. People are much choosier now. You have to stop thinking about the viewers as an undifferentiated mass or as a series of nuclear families.' There was no obvious empirical basis behind this statement, although it could be taken as a perfectly respectable theoretical ambition. There was however another vein of thought behind his conceptualisation of the audience and its relationship to television.

This was the view which had been most forcefully espoused by Sir William Haley, who had retired as DG of the BBC in 1952, and was the last of the Reithians. Haley thought that TV could be used to create the 'active' society. Isaacs' own views seemed to reflect something of this thinking: 'I certainly don't think that television is good *per se*. I think it is entirely a question of what it replaces in people's lives. We are going to do sports programmes which will encourage people to engage in their outdoor activities, putting the emphasis on participation not just on professional competitive success. We are going to do a book programme which will encourage people to read books. We are going to do a news programme which will encourage people to think.' Another familiar echo of the idea of television as the glue of public life could be heard in the statement that one of its important functions was its ability to unite the nation during events which people feel they want to share 'like Royal Weddings and Cup Finals'.

Running throughout all discussion of television in Britain is the tradition of TV as a social force, the notion that by mixing together programming of a certain stamp with particular reactions from the audience one could induce not just emotive or intellectual response, but social change and enhancement. One can see quite clearly within the demands of at least parts of the independent sector that their kinds of programming, free as it would be of the repressive bureaucracies and debased values of the BBC-ITCA axis, would touch new areas of national life and provide that social chemistry which fuels social change. One can see, for example, this particular line of thought in the channel's educational output. Naomi Sargant, the Commissioning Editor for Education in the channel's early years, told the *Times Educational Supplement* that television has a 'responsibility' to the viewer. In particular, she added, it had an ability to expand the viewer's outlook and make available 'an array of richness'. She spoke of the majority of the programmes commissioned by her as not being clones of Open University output, but rather as programmes which 'aim to encourage, stimulate, open the eyes and increase the curiosity in viewers who are then offered ways of pursuing those stimuli if they wish.' (*TES* 31.05.1985)

As we have seen Channel Four was born out of a mixture of ideas, ideals, bureaucratic genius and political commitment. Not everyone was happy, however, as the following section demonstrates.

## (2) Channel Four and its Critics

The imminent arrival of the new channel triggered heady expectation and ambition among many, tinged with a familiar leftish cynicism which effectively implied that if you could not re-order society *in toto* then you could not hope to begin to tamper effectively with bits of that social order. The Channel Four User's Group in its publication *What's this Channel Fo(u)r?* concluded, unfairly and certainly prematurely, that it would only provide the same mix as before: 'professionalism, insularity, metropolitanism and the tyranny of established news values'.

Chris Dunkley, in the *Financial Times*, called into question, indeed damned with outrageous historical analogies, a fundamental principle of the thinking behind the channel, the provision of programmes for particular audiences: 'If you suggest to those who promote those ideas that the notion of fundamental differences between groups of people, arbitrarily divided by age, sex or race comes very close to the ideas sustaining Nazism and apartheid, they are outraged. It is fashionable to welcome [minority programming].... Sure enough when you look at such programmes you find that without exception they cater to a stereotype.' (*Financial Times* 17.03.1982)

Against this neo-conservative position was posed the radical critique which contained its own assumptions about the need to differentiate the mass audience into its constituent parts: 'The coming of the fourth channel also raises the question of the attitudes adopted to its likely audiences. A notion of catering as well as possible for a single audience clearly informs all the IBA's musings. This view, infected as it is with the usual paternalism of broadcasting hierarchies, does not recognise that those are multiple audiences which should be served in widely differing ways.' (*Time Out* 26.08.1982) Both positions reflected a dominant characteristic of the whole debate about Channel Four — the resting of political arguments on extremely vague information about public attitudes, tastes and needs.

Within days of the channel starting broadcasting scorn was poured on it: for its lack of audiences; for bad language; for its giving airtime to gays; for pseudish programmes; and, the admittedly ludicrous sounding discussions of how the combination of the monopolistic-capitalist London Rubber Company and the repressive IBA had deprived the right of the public to have raspberry flavoured condoms advertised on television. To the right-wing press the channel was the home of, as Anne Leslie described it 'an Islington co-operative of Guardian reading-feminist-single-parent-social-workers who wear sandals hand-crafted by Guatemalan freedom fighters, and who'd die rather than let a racist South African orange pass their earnest lips.' (*Daily Mail* 10.02.1983)

However grotesque the caricature there was a clear issue of the relationship between the character of programme output, the original intention that the channel be different and the need to build the audience to that 10 per cent level. Jeremy Isaacs was later to admit to, without apologising for, the initial orientation of the channel. The passion and expectation which had been built up in the years of planning had to be allowed to pour forth — however overheated and undirected that might in practice prove to be.

The precise intellectual location of the channel's output in its early weeks and months was uncertain: the *Spectator* was claiming that the channel was run by a bunch of mad radical feminists while the *New Statesman* was simultaneously saying they were a bunch of appalling commercial hacks. Perhaps the most pervasive image was of a kind of 'do-goodism':

> The single candle on Channel 4's birthday cake, you can be sure, was dipped by members of a women's candle-making co-operative. The cake itself is rich in high-fibre ingredients from under-developed countries

but under the brown icing there is a nice layer of marzipan... Thus the popular image of the new channel, insofar as it has a popular image at all: a haunt of improving programmes, of programmes that need a bit of watching; a channel you might seek out once in a while but rarely dip into on spec, and never just leave on. (*Sunday Telegraph* 30.10.1983)

One line of criticism was that while the 'content' of programmes might fulfil the mandate to be different, the 'forms' were not. Albert Hunt, for example, argued in *New Society* that the problem with alternative programmes like *Friday Alternative, Union World, Black on Black, Right to Reply* or in a slightly different vein, *Whatever You Want*, was that they offered radical content in forms that had been borrowed from consensus television; for instance, replacing the establishment expert by a working class expert. (*New Society* 23.12.1982)

One programme about women's rights was used by Richard Ingrams in the *Spectator* as a stick to beat the channel. 'In order to provide an alternative to Miss World contest, which in the eyes of the *Guardian* ladies is a disgraceful male chauvinist orgy of the type which would be banned in a truly egalitarian society, a film called *Rosie the Riveter*, was shown on Channel Four as a sop to feminists. The four earnest women assembled under Miss Stead's lack-lustre chairmanship were supposed to discuss the implications of the film but the conversation soon degenerated into an all purpose moan about the raw deal women get in our society, one speaker even going so far as to suggest that in future women should be paid by the state to stay at home to look after the children...' (*Spectator* 06.11.1982)

By December 1982 the papers and networks were alive with rumours that Jeremy Isaacs was to be sacked because of his controversial programming policies and the low ratings Channel Four had been getting as a result. Some claimed there had been a secret meeting of ITV company bosses to discuss changes and the chief executive's dismissal, a rumour dismissed by the intended victim as 'baloney'. The tabloids were particularly aggressive talking about rock bottom ratings and asking whether 'Emperor Isaacs will fall or bow to the masses?' (*Star* 29.12.1982)

Supporters quickly gathered to defend the besieged executive. The President of the Confederation of Entertainment Unions which covered radio, television and cinema as well as theatre, answered the critics in the *Morning Star* a few days later. Alan Sapper of ACTT defended Channel Four and said: 'We do not believe that it is in the country's or the industry's interest that Channel Four should be destroyed by those barbarians who believe that the new service should never have been created or that it should merely become ITV2... Those of us who have had the opportunity of watching Channel Four schedulings can only congratulate the people responsible for an exciting mix of programmes appealing to a wide variety of interests in our community.'

Nevertheless, a certain fear had entered the collective soul of the Board. Dell dismisses as 'absolute nonsense' the idea that there was even any attempt to get rid of Isaacs. He is quick to add however that: 'During the first few months, my view was that the channel had started badly.'

It had been agreed by the Board that three months or so into the broadcasting life of the channel they would meet with the senior staff to review progress. They had held a residential meeting to discuss policy in the heady days before November 1982, but now met in far more sombre, though not desperate, times in February 1983. The ratings had opened with a curiosity-led 6 per cent, but slipped quickly to 3 per cent, not good even for a channel established quite deliberately not to be besotted by audience ratings. The mood of the meeting was tense and anxious. Brian Tesler, Managing Director of LWT and C4 board member, had been invited to present a paper reviewing the opening month. It was critical, calling for a move towards more popular programming, and away from the apparently unrelenting sobriety and earnestness of the output which was driving away the audience in droves. At the end of the conference Isaacs made what he says 'was one of the most critical speeches in my life. I made a speech for my life, for the channels life." He knew he had to try and balance two potentially conflicting aspirations for the channel: 'One, to be faithful to as adventurous an interpretation of the remit as we could possibly sustain; and secondly, to be popular enough not to have the ITV companies threatening to withdraw their subscription.' Part of the problem of these opening months, as was recognised by the board, was that there simply had not been enough time for many of the more interesting and potentially appealing commissions to see the light of day.

However, by the second birthday, the comments were almost all favourable. There was even praise from the *Daily Star*, and the *Glasgow Herald* declared 'C4 leaves its run of bad luck behind it.' The channel had become a natural part of the broadcasting culture, in danger even of premature venerability. Even the *Daily Mail*, an early and particularly persistent critic, published an article by Mary Kenny in October 1984, which argued: 'In the early months of its existence this paper was very critical of Channel Four's, output; it certainly seemed to be aimed at the oddball and screwball market. But its appeal has greatly broadened... To be sure it still caters for minority tastes and so it should. But it doesn't matter if the interest is a minority one, so long as the programme is well done.' (*Daily Mail* 22.10.1984)

In October 1983, just when Jeremy Isaacs could consider he had weathered the early storms, stories began to circulate of how the Prime Minister wanted to force the channel to justify itself in commercial terms, as it slowly dawned on her that to a considerable extent the channel was in effect being subsidised by the Treasury. The problem was then, as now, that to move in that direction would almost certainly mean the end of the mission implicit within the mandate.

That mandate as we have tried to show had many roots: the years of discussion about the fourth channel among those dissatisfied with the monopoly; the aspirations of a powerful and forward thinking Home Secretary; the neat, institutionally creative footwork of the IBA; the ambitions of the first board; the life, vision and interpretative force of the first Chief Executive. It was also a mandate which, during the creation of the channel and even more so during these first four years of its life, has cohered principally around a number of key themes.

## (3) The Problems with Sex

One of the inevitable consequences of the demands made of Channel Four was its confrontation with issues of morality and sexuality within British life. As with so much else within the intellectual construction of Channel Four there was nothing new in this. When television sets out to explore the nether regions of public and private life, whether that be through factual or fictional programming, it necessarily addresses questions about behaviour, and the relationship between formal and consensual attitudes and aspects of behaviour which fall outside that consensus. In one area Channel Four was markedly different: when it set out to explore and, in effect, assert the position of women and gays within society. This was utterly consistent with the prescription to introduce new voices, raise issues which had been ignored, offer space to those with something to say, particulary if they happened also to be members of a minority group or interest, and generally to add to the sum total of ideas, emotions and understandings circulating within British culture and society. It was also utterly inevitable that it would cause a row.

The major question marks against Channel Four and the ones which at times seemed to be generating such a head of political steam that the future of the channel was raised, were to do with sex and its ever present bedfellow, something called 'bad language'. Traditionally, nothing quite excites sections of British life − public and private − like other people's sex life and other people's language.

The view of Isaacs was that he would to a great extent try to avoid violent content in Channel Four programmes. However, he told *Campaign* that: 'On language I take the view that sticks and stones may break your bones but names will never hurt you. At the proper time at night there is no difficulty whatever transmitting strong language in a decent piece of work ... It upsets the public far less than some people believe it does. The same really with sexuality. The general feeling here is that if you take a film like the latest Godard [*Slow Motion*] and play it in a season and at a proper time of night then there is no difficulty. I am sure that will turn out to be the case. Without touching pornography, of course, British television, if it is to be international and if it is to be conscious of people's tastes and needs in the '80s has to provide from the best range of movies that is available and not insist that there are films that can never be seen on television.' (*Campaign* 31.01.1984)

Under the terms of the Broadcast Act, as with ITV, the channel had to ensure that its output did not offend 'good taste' or 'decency'. The IBA had also issued guidelines in which the channel was asked to avoid the gratuitous use of language likely to 'offend', though such usage could be defended after 9pm on the grounds of 'context' and 'authenticity'.

The argument against 'bad' language was captured by Mary Whitehouse, Honorary President of the National Viewers' and Listeners' Association, who was, from the start of transmission, watching and counting. She was especially concerned with what she insisted on calling, when asked, 'eff dot dot dot': 'Unless something is done and done quickly, we'll have four-letter words littering our programmes in future, just as "bloody" does now. What we're talking about is the crudeness and craziness and innate vulgarity of these words. They tend to destroy the nuance of feeling which language exists to express. They reduce sexual experience to a harsh and crude act. They're destructive to our culture and destructive to relationships. People, ordinary people, are concerned, and frustrated beyond measure.' Language was a problem, particularly when it was seen in the critical mind as but one element in a knot of problems: 'offensive sex scenes, excessive violence, and programmes using foul language during family viewing times'. The early days of the channel were dotted with such accusations without, it has to be said, any particularly clear statement in reply about what it was in the underlying philosophy of the channel which would justify content that could at least be interpreted unfavourably. Indeed there were signs, for example in relation to *Brookside*, that Channel Four agreed with some of the criticism.

No question of morality, however, has come anywhere near in significance illustrating the potential difficulties in fulfilling the channel's mandate as that of the treatment of gays and gay issues. From its early weeks, as for example the announcement that there would be a programme for gays on New Year's Day 1983, the controversy has raged. In that particular instance John Carlisle MP called for the closure of the channel. The *Daily Telegraph* wrote in its editorial columns: 'The broadcasting authorities, no doubt will be inclined to the view that Channel Four is intended to cater for minority needs and that homosexuals constitute a distinct minority with needs which should be catered for. They can also reasonably point out that the law now permits sexual relations between consenting adults of the same sex. Hence, it will be argued, the tastes and interests of such people have as strong a claim on the attentions of television producers as, for example, the tastes of bee-keepers and chess players.' The editorial then suggested that the 1967 legislation had no intention of legitimising homosexuality in any moral sense, merely of decriminalising it in certain circumstances and thereby protecting those poor unfortunates who were victims of their own perverse sexual needs. 'A society, therefore, which chooses to treat homosexual and heterosexual behaviour on exactly the same basis is taking a fundamental decision. It is a decision which the British people have never taken, and one which ought not to be thrust upon them by a media establishment totally out of touch with popular taste and popular moral conviction.' (*Daily Telegraph* 09.12.1982) The overwhelming supposition was that the publicly articulated criticism of the channel about sex and 'bad language' — much less so about violence — was shared by large sections of the population.

The decision to introduce the 'Special Discretion Required' symbol, particularly in the wake of the controversies around the films *Jubilee* and *Sebastiane*, attracted headlines such as 'X marks the slot', 'A ruder triangle'. Jeremy Isaacs commented: 'Tastes differ, but there will continue to be occasion when the channel will — within the Broadcasting Act and with careful scheduling and signposting and the IBA's support — continue to show programmes that will more and more gratify some tastes at the risk of affronting others. Channel Four has a prejudice against violence avoiding most of the kinds of programmes (with the honourable exception of *Hill Street Blues*) which attract such criticism elsewhere. However there are occasions when Channel Four is committed to allowing an individual opportunity to see particular works of individual artistic visions, even though they may prove unattractive to many other viewers.' And on the SDR symbol: 'Viewers are capable of making informed choices themselves about what they watch. This symbol will help them choose and will also serve to warn those who come across one of these films unawares.' (*Evening Standard* 14.08.1986). To the Whitehouse-*Daily Mail* lobby the symbol was a signpost for every voyeur in the land.

Perhaps, however, the most interesting and calm judgments on those types of questions come from the person without whose support the channel probably would not exist, certainly not in of its present form, William Whitelaw. He comments: 'Of course, I had a running encounter with Mrs Whitehouse who said C4 was obscene. Actually, on the whole it hasn't been, anymore than anybody else has from time to time, but it was believed it was going to be a wicked licence for obscenity of one sort or the other. I think she still thinks it has. I suppose it is marginally more permissive, if that's the right word, than the others. That is again the nature of something that is being rather different — given the trends in our society it is almost inevitable... if you do something which is going to cater for minority interests, I don't think it will always be that that minority is on the left, nor do I think that C4 has done that, but I think there will be a tendency for it. For myself I don't think there is anything particulary wrong in that. I think if it had been too left-wing it would have caused me difficulties, but you had to take some risks in this world. I thought it got the name of being left-wing much more than it actually ever was.'

## (4) Journalism, Truth and Channel Four

One of the more obvious themes in the discussion about broadcasting in the 1970s was the question of the inadequacies of television as a source of information on news and current affairs. The criticism came in different shapes and forms but two main strands can be detected. One was that TV news was produced from within a system of power and class relationships which biased it in favour of the powerful, privileged and wealthy within British society, and against those who were weak, under-privileged and without wealth. The best known example of this kind of analysis is that of the Glasgow Media Group. The other criticism was that the problems of TV news were nothing to do with political bias, conscious or otherwise, but with its inability to offer proper explanation, a position captured in the famous phrase about television news and current affairs having a 'bias against understanding'. What in effect this meant was that the emphasis on the visual within television news led to an overemphasis on the 'what' rather than the 'why', on appearance rather than cause, on the 'seeable' rather than the abstract. It was this latter perspective which was to be pursued within Channel Four's news programming: 'We do not want more incident or event, we want more background and perspective.' (2)

In fact the presence of news at all on the new channel, especially if it was to be produced by ITN, was to be one of the most ferocious internal controversies that it had to face. The fear, articulated most fiercely by Tony Smith, was that if ITN were responsible for the news service, then it would simply be more of the same inadequate coverage available through ITN and the BBC. The declared intention was to broaden the traditional agenda of news by tackling subjects previously confined to the inside pages of quality newspapers, eg business and industry, science and technology, the arts and foreign stories. In addition space was to be created for a different angle on the political universe, hence programmes such as the ill-fated *Friday Alternative*. This was described by Liz Forgan, then Commissioning Editor for Actuality: 'I would like to unsettle viewers sufficiently to disturb their notion that they know what is going on because they saw one TV programme. The *Friday Alternative* is designed to make that comfortable certainty quiver. This may prove such an uncomfortable feeling that viewers will turn away in droves to seek security elsewhere. If we can persuade them to stay and understand the process I think we shall have rendered a real service to democracy.' The immediate problem for Channel Four seemed to be that none of this was what the public wanted. Public opinion polls told that what they liked about 'normal' TV news was that is was concise, personal, unbiased, easy to digest and simplified to the degree that the viewer is told enough of what is going on without having to think too much.

The issue is whether the public perception of Channel Four News, in so far as there is one, is of the channel offering the depth, the why, the background, the intelligence and the range of its original conception. There is however another issue which has arisen within the public debate about the channel's current affairs output. This is where the attempt to provide a different perspective on events rubs up against the overriding commitments to a balanced and objective service. The issue raised is a fascinating one since it pinpoints the fundamental question which all journalism faces which is its relationship to the notion of truth and the question of whether the prescription of balance, objectivity and impartiality are the machinery of truth or mechanisms for obfuscation. Here is neatly encapsulated a paradox which looks to be a permanent feature of life with the channel. The more it seeks to pursue its mandate to provide space for different 'voices' – understood both literally and metaphorically – the more it is likely to run into difficulties when those 'voices' are painful to the ears of consensual society. The stark question is how can one be different in terms of the interior values of a programme without potentially getting under the skin of those who do not share those values, do not welcome their [unchallenged] presence on television and who are in a position to apply pressure on the channel?

Channel Four has become caught in a pincer movement of left and right. For example, in 1985 Chris Dunkley, in what was on the whole an admiring piece, argued that all the key figures inside the channel embody 'the ethos of the 1960s new left'. The implication was clear, and was picked up by the *Daily Express* a few days later: 'Such men and women were very formidable propagandists indeed. They scatter a few token pieces of right-wing opinion around the channel, to disarm criticism. But the climate of opinion they live in themselves and encourage their audience to live in is profoundly hostile to the Prime Minister and Thatcherism... [C4] may well be the most effective, dangerous and subversive influence in the country.' It is a view echoed from what at first sight is an unexpected corner.

John Ranelagh, until recently a commissioning editor and formerly special assistant to Isaacs, in a commentary on the work of the channel made a similar observation: 'Today (summer 1987) we can see how conditioned Channel Four was by being conceived in the later 1970s and started in the early 1980s. Then there was a stranglehold of attitudes on the media. It was leftish, liked to think of itself as radical, pessimistic... The 'new class' of media polyocracy looked to the new channel for expression, and were not disappointed... Another assumption of the New Class that Channel Four enshrines is that outspoken reference to topics is the same as thinking about them. That to bring up a topic is somehow to impart structure and reflection to it... The substitution of emotional intensity for hard thought is a New Class characteristic that has also affected our programming to a significant degree... We were, at one stage, almost taboo dependent, finding an important element of our definition in what we would and would not cover. Greenham Common, yes. National Front, no. Homosexuality, yes. Black criminality, no. Aids as a heterosexual / homosexual / bisexual disease, yes. Aids as a homosexual / bisexual disease, no. How organisations work; the inevitability of class in society; the social elements of organisation; the benefits flowing from the domination of the State, are all present taboos. There is a world of difference between hard argument and excitable argument, and all too often we have gone for the latter. We seem to have an emotional attachment to the ideas of the welfare state, but no attachment to the ideas of de-regulation and the market. Hard argument requires time, the eschewing of emotionalism. It requires understanding of the simple point that it is very difficult to get an intelligent person to agree completely with anyone else.'

Not so cry the left, in the shape of people like director Ken Loach, and independent producer John Ellis. Loach railed against the non-showing of his "*Question of Leadership*" as one more example of 'the suppression of left-wing views'. Denis Postle, in the same letters column as Loach, discussed the banning of his programme *Nuclear State* and the arguments of Channel Four's chairman, Edmund Dell about 'the highest standards of journalism' and 'professional television journalism'. Postle commented: 'These phrases mean little more than "the ability to keep within the political consensus on what can be said and shown."' (*Guardian* 22.11.1983) What Postle was arguing was that there had to be a space within 'journalistic' output which allowed for 'emotional commitment' 'as an artistic virtue and not a journalistic error...' It's an honourable, though onerous, tradition. Rather than 'reporting on people, seeing them as resources to be harvested and re-exported, to the home audience, it means making programmes with people, having relationships with them as persons.'

Dell and Isaacs were aware from the early days that the left would inevitably feel betrayed by the channel. Isaacs suggests that the problem is one of heightened expectation; the left, who felt long excluded from British television, thought that the channel was going to be on their side. Isaacs knew that he could never − indeed did not want to − satisfy this particular piece of wishful dreaming. When he took over as Chief Executive, Isaacs claimed that he had two clear ideas: the first to find a way to do opinionated television, and the second to encourage the type of independent film-makers whom he met on the British Film Institute Production Board, 'who were ferocious but able people with excellent minds, and who were talking about a new sort of television, a new sort of media.' He added, however: 'the motive was not to let just the left on at all... I knew that they had to come on. I knew that they wanted to come on, and I knew that they deserved to come on. I knew those voices had to be heard, but I also knew that I had to subsume those voices ... into the total spectrum of opinion that I undertook to put on the air.'

Despite Isaacs' commitment to the workshops and independents, the feeling persists among a certain section of the left that the revolution stalled quite quickly. John Ellis wrote in August 1986 of the way in which in its early years Channel Four had accepted the 'usefully imprecise idea of balance across the whole of the output' or, more accurately, 'balancing what the other channels get up to'. This had in his view been used 'to justify some marvellously opinionated programmes and a general move away from the need to show all the points of view at once'. His explanation for what he believed to be the channel's increasing pursuit of balance was simply that the channel was tired of being hit over the head by the IBA for being unbalanced in its programmes. The pressures to balance programme output in fact came from within the channel. Dell was particularly keen that the channel thought out the idea of balance over time so that they did not have constantly to rush out discussion programmes which filled in the gaps left by polemical programmes or series.

According to Dell, the early years of the channel were plagued by the problem of balance because of inadequate long-term editorial planning rather than a failure of nerve. Dell supported the workshop movement, and tried to persuade some of the doubting members of the board that 'if you are going to get workshops producing material for C4... it would be surprising if those programmes were not left wing and provided that overall the thing did not get out of balance it was all right.' Dell pointed out the importance of the workshops in training people for the future, adding 'you don't say to a man who is showing a great potential .... I'm not going to have your stuff because it's left wing.' Dell added that he thought 'there was an education process going on, partly because I think people have run their own companies, partly the fact that they have understood the atmosphere in which they are working. But there has been a realisation, I think that left wing ideas are not the only one ideas around which are worth exposing on television. And I think that's entirely healthy... I think the experience of Channel Four has had an effect on the outlook of a number of people and I don't say whether the changes are right or wrong, I merely say that I think they have become more interesting television producers because they see more of the arguments.'

*Pace* Ellis, there has always been a feeling at the top in the channel that there is a world of difference between balance across output − a concept established long before Channel Four as a guiding role of TV journalism − and the use of TV simply to render a variety of opinions. Instinctively the channel might have reasonably pursued the latter, except for the simple fact that, unfortunately for it, it had been granted no special exemption from the general prescriptions governing broadcast journalism. What Ellis, and those who thought like him, had touched on was a profound question about the channel: should it aim for better journalism covering more perspectives but from within the canons of balance, objectivity and impartiality, and thus for a more 'truthful' depiction of reality; or should it accept that 'truth' lies within a number of subjective states, with the channel's only purpose being to facilitate their articulation? We will take up this question in more detail in the next chapter.

## (5) New Voices or Minorities?

The clear implication behind the thinking which had gone into the creation of the channel was that historically British television had been too narrow in its range and vision, that it was nothing more than the articulation of the life-style of a mainly white, southern, middle-aged and middle class world, which excluded anyone who was not 'blessed' with such characteristics. A litmus test of the channel was inevitably going to be its ability to offer programmes by and for a whole range of minority groups: minorities of age, race, nationality, culture and taste. The enabling legislation demanded as much, the Authority had called for such and the key figures in shaping the content of the channel had said as much. As early as 1973, in a memo to the Minister for Post and Telecommunications about a possible fourth channel, Isaacs had said that on the new channel 'there should be a heavy emphasis on "service" programmes catering for the interests of minorities'. (3) Paul Bonner, in Brian Wenham's *The Third Age of Broadcasting*, referring to the high cost of making programmes wrote: 'The great mass of people with something to say can't afford to make programmes in which to say it. We need paperback television to go with the hard cover version. We can − and on Channel Four will − agree to lower standards in one or two known slots a week for the purpose of hearing the unheard voices.' (4)

In the summer of 1979 a small group of women media professionals came together to discuss how C4 would be used to improve the position of women in broadcasting. The Women's Fourth Channel Lobby, later renamed the Women's Broadcasting and Film Lobby, campaigned for an increase in the structural location of women within C4 as well as a reassessment of the way in which women were portrayed in television. In an interview with Liz Forgan, then editor of the *Guardian's* woman's page, Isaacs observed: 'One of the things women say is that there are too few opportunities for them to make a complete range of programmes and that if they did get a chance to make certain kinds of programmes − say current affairs − we would get an interestingly different view of the world. I intend to give them the opportunity to demonstrate that. I don't see why my weekly current affairs programme shouldn't be produced by women. I would like to get women to make such a programme which depends for its success on its ability to interest viewers, not to promote a cause, but which had the added bonus that it comes from people who are standing at a different angle to the universe from the male sex. It may therefore come up with a different set of attitudes, a different mix, a different set of priorities.'

Subsequent to this interview, Forgan was appointed the Commissioning Editor for Actuality; one of her first commissions was a current affairs programme made by women − *20/20 Vision*. 'I firmly believe,' she argued in *Cosmopolitan* in late 1982, 'that it matters who journalists are. It doesn't matter how professional you are, you're still influenced by what your personal interests and background are in bringing your professional

31

judgement into play. We're trying to discover whether there's a female way of looking at the world. I think there is.' She added 'I don't believe that women are the same as men or that they see the world in the same way (although they can be quickly trained to do so) but we are missing that female perspective from a whole strand that is called serious journalism.' Isaacs backed her statement in *Broadcast:* 'It is remarkable that although the television is no more than three decades old, most women have been as effectively shut out from any real participation as if the industry had started three centuries ago. With the advent of a new channel the opportunity emerges for redefining women's role in television. The implications of Channel Four's initial brief and its public statements led women who were regarding the industry critically to believe there was a potential for change.' (*Broadcast* 03.07.1982).

Channel Four's commitment to help women did much to shape the negative image of the channel, especially in its early stages. A familiar comment was the following by the TV critic Philip Purser: 'My own bête noire was the honking, humourless cry of the feminists who seemed to be regulating every current affairs show fielded. "I really wonder if this channel likes me" I wrote at the end of the first week... What I would avoid [on C4] at all costs, I'm afraid, would be anything to do with women's lib, sociology or dull, accusing voices...' (*Sunday Telegraph* 30.10.1983) Equally loud was the voice from the other camp; some feminists suggested that little would improve if the structures of the 'antiquated' administration did not change to bring more women into production and commissioning positions.

The most obvious manifestation of this commitment was *20/20 Vision*, a programme which raised much criticism and some interesting questions: were people watching simply to see an all-women show or because of an interest in current affairs? If they did not like what they saw would they blame females and femininity? Could *20/20 Vision* be any different from other, male-run, current affairs programmes? Was the audience even ready for such programmes? And were there enough women who felt concerned by the issues raised?

The policy on minorities ran up against the accusation that amateurism and 'ghetto broadcasting', tied to the inevitable leftish bias of such programmes, threatened to undermine the potential social good which the new channel might achieve. Such early programmes as *The Eleventh Hour, Deep Roots Music, The Irish Angle, Union World, Black on Black, Eastern Eye,* were all criticised for being unwatchable, incompetent and/or utterly marginal. Sean Day Lewis outlined the problem in the *Daily Telegraph:* 'The argument for series like this is that they speak for minorities who do not otherwise have a voice in the white Anglo-Saxon Protestant middle class and male rule of British television. The problem is that such programmes are problem obsessed. Most people of all races have a limited appetite for unrelieved whinge whether it comes from one community or any other.' (*Daily Telegraph* 15.02.1982)

From its birth Channel Four faced the problem which has always faced new cultural forms or efforts to create new forms, with a view to creating television with force, meaning and purpose: how to do it in ways which would appeal not just to the initiates and advocates, but to the wider public. And buried within there was a further paradox which was how to do that without undermining the integrity of the programme-making. For example, Isaacs was criticised over *The Animals Film* for giving too free a voice to the Animal Liberation Front (ALF).

The problem which the critics did not, and in fact could not solve, was how on earth could the channel fulfil its mandate without allowing considerable liberty to such people as the ALF? The only logical alternative was to allow air-time only to those individuals and groups who could broadly be acceptable to some set of consensual values – a position which may have led to a quieter life for the channel but which fundamentally denied its *raison d'être*.

The question of the character of the service now provided for minority groups did not concern only those on the outside looking in. There seemed to be disquiet among ethnic groups in particular that theirs was still too small a space within the channel, particularly after Farrukh Dhondy axed *Black on Black*, produced by Trevor Phillips, and *Eastern Eye*, produced by Samir Shah, in January 1985. Dhondy felt that neither of the two producers were sufficiently committed to the cause of Black consciousness. Shah commented: 'Farrukh is cancelling us irrespective of our quality because he wants to replace us with unbalanced programmes that take a specific view, rather than programmes which attempt to cater for the minority communities in total. It's a very odd kind of reverse racialism and apparently the only black and brown people he will allow to make programmes are those who don't know how to.' Dhondy retorted: 'Anybody watching *Eastern Eye* who is interested in Asian politics has to sit through dancing bears and endless interviews with Indian film stars before they get anything serious ... Samir and Trevor are from the Frankenstein school – creatures of the media who wouldn't know what to do if their company batteries ran down. Me? I'm from the Dracula school. I've got bloodied teeth. I'm not afraid to bite, and there will be plenty more Draculas joining me soon.' (*Sunday Times* 13.01.1985) This image of Channel Four as the Hammer Films of British television was interpreted by one commentator, Patrick Stoddart, as a classic feud between the passionate left and the populist centre.

The impression should not be given that all was criticism of these programmes. Robin Buss in the *Times Educational Supplement* commended *Friday Alternative, Black on Black, 20/20 Vision* and *Voices* for raising subjects not covered elsewhere. He noted that *Black on Black* with its report on workers in the health service and the Pope's problems with the African church were giving a different perspective 'which needs to be shown'. He added: '*Voices* was the first discussion programme I can remember where I found myself looking at my watch and being pleasantly surprised that there was more time for the debate to develop.' Other programmes that were applauded as giving a voice to those who had previously been silent were, for example, a series by the Federation of Bangladesh Youth and seasons of films about the Chinese, Hindi and West Indian communities.

Informed minorities such as doctors, engineers, nurses and trade unionists also hoped Channel Four would adapt the new approach to giving them greater length and more depth to state their views and avoid trivialisation and sensationalism. In a *Sunday Times* article, Elaine Sihera, came out strongly in favour of the channel and in particular of its programming for minorities: 'It must be an anathema to the majority to have the limelight focussed on less fortunate beings, especially in a democracy where the wishes of the former are invariably paramount. Even the label "minority group" implies an out-group, set apart from the mainstream regardless of outlook. To be a member of a minority group is to be without status, non-persons, barely tolerated and often ignored.' (*Sunday Times* 27.03.1983) In *The Times* David Hewson referred to this approach as an 'extension of BBC2's liberal sentiments ... just the sort of thing to inflame that school of opinion so strong in the upper echelons of the Conservative Party which believes that the Left is in control of the nation's television.' (*The Times* 26.10.1982)

It was on the basis of this examination of the background to the channel, on the way in which the general formulation that it be 'different' within the overall framework of British television had become represented through a number of key themes, issues and forms of output, that we conducted the research on public attitudes to the channel and its performance. Running through our minds in conducting the research and in writing this book were a number of questions: Has the channel fulfilled its mandate? What do the special audiences, to whom programmes are addressed, think about them? What do other members of the public think? Do they welcome the channel? Are they offended, disturbed, amused by it? In the final analysis, has it kept faith with the dream?

**References**
1. Lambert S, *Channel Four. Television with a Difference.* BFI, London, 1982.
2. *ibid.*,p. 166.
3. *ibid.*,p. 137.
4. Wenham B (ed), *The Third Age of Broadcasting.* Faber and Faber, London, 1982.

# Chapter Two

# Keeping Faith? Channel Four in Practice

If a faith is to be maintained, its purity must be safeguarded and its essential tenets put into practice. The interpretation of the faith becomes the preserve of the select few, who adopt bureaucratic rules in order to protect the original charismatic statements. All too often, however, a vital faith becomes a sterile dogma when the interpreters take over the role of defining and refining its practice. Has this happened at Channel 4? Have the commissioning editors, who are key interpreters of the mandate, undermined the power and energy of the original vision? Have they kept the faith?

The channel *has* changed in many ways since the heady days of 1981-1982. This is, however, no betrayal of the faith, but rather a consequence of transformations in the social world in which the channel is inevitably embedded. Three aspects of this changing environment stand out. First, three terms of Conservative governments committed to individualism, free enterprise, a materialist ethic and the eradication of socialism or collectivism, have shifted, if not shattered, the intellectual framework of the channel. Secondly, and perhaps ironically given the findings of our study of the public's attitudes to the channel, a large proportion of the electorate — and the channel's public — has endorsed parts of the political package offered by neo-liberals or the new right. Finally, television has changed since 1982. Other channels do a great many of the things which Channel 4 pioneered: for instance, BBC2's *Network East* and *Ebony* are similar to the ethnic magazine programmes developed by Channel 4; *Network* is the BBC's attempt to replicate the spirit, if not the format, of Channel 4's *Right to Reply; Split Screen*, on BBC2, has adopted some of Channel 4's ideas about polemical television; and *Screen Two* is *Film on Four* without the cinema distribution. The price of the channel's success is that it no longer has the field to itself. Furthermore, the structure of broadasting is changing: the idea has been mooted that the channel should sell its own airtime; another four channels will be added when Direct Broadcast by Satellite (DBS) begins in 1989-90; the Luxembourgian quasi-DBS satellite, ASTRA, will offer up to 16 channels in 1988-89; the ITV companies are diversifying and expanding in an attempt to broaden their financial base when these challenges begin, and there is much talk of a potential fifth terrestrial channel.

These changes in the content and structure of broadcasting inevitably affect the ways in which the commissioning editors think about the mandate. For example, if the other channels are producing ethnic magazines, what should C4's ethnic policy be? If other channels produce programmes on business and technology, how can C4 do it differently? Similarly, if the political and moral climate has changed how can the channel address this? These questions are crucial to the understanding of how the mandate operates in the late 1980s. In this chapter we explore the role of editors in developing the mandate, the ways in which polemical television has changed as the eighties have progressed, the difficulties in making television programmes explicitly for minorities and, finally, the reasons why the channel thinks that it is important to make light entertainment, drama and arts programmes.

## (1) The Editorial Imperative

Anthony Smith's publishing analogy, which we discussed in the previous chapter, resonated so powerfully in Britain in the late 1970s because it caught the fragmented and non-consensual mood of the times. Traditional public service broadcasting, with its emphasis on one nation, the mass audience, social integration and education, seemed closer to the mechanical and artificial solidarity of Harold Wilson's social contract than to an organic unity among 'the people'. Ralf Dahrendorf, writing in the year of Channel 4's birth, caught the flavour of the times when he wrote of the growing 'sense of anomie, of lawlessness and isolation' in Britain. Searching for a reason, Dahrendorf suggested: 'Modernity has at last caught up with Britain...The traditional ligatures of family and class, religion and place of origin no longer bind.'(1) Like every British institution in the late 1970s and early 1980s the channel had to deal with the collapse of political and cultural consensus and the pervading sense of doom about the fragmentation of British social life. The combined challenges of Scottish and Welsh nationalism, the 'troubles' in Northern Ireland, the development of a powerful and committed left in the Labour Party and the trade unions, the rise of Thatcherism in the Conservative Party, the emergence of the National Front, and the articulation of Black and Asian ethnic politics (which, in some cases, erupted into riots) left the old order reeling: Britain was undergoing a social drama which might have become a tragedy. Channel 4, at one level at least, represented a cultural response to this social disintegration.

Smith's publishing analogy celebrated this diversity; it assumed that groups had a right to express their views unmediated by television bureaucrats.

However, William Whitelaw's attempt to control as well as encourage diversity by placing the channel under the IBA, transformed the channel and set it on a course where the commissioning editors assumed responsibility for introducing new voices and faces to television. The first questions they asked were: given the myriad voices clamouring for access, who was to receive airtime and which criteria were to be applied to allocate that time? The role of 'gatekeeper' loomed from the start, not as a consequence of the bureaucratisation of the channel, nor of bad faith on the part of the commissioning editors, it was inevitable once the channel was cocooned within the shell of the IBA. After all, no publishing house is ever required to be objective, balanced, impartial, tasteful and decent, whereas the IBA has a statutory responsibility to ensure that Channel Four conforms to these requirements.

The editors had to balance the political and cultural demands of those who placed a great deal of hope in the channel, with the concerns of the government and the IBA that it should not go over the top. It is perhaps apt that the first senior commissioning editors — David Rose in Fiction, Naomi Sargant in Education and Liz Forgan in Actuality — started work on April Fool's Day. As they faced the gargantuan task of commissioning thousands of hours of television in the space of a year they must have wondered who was fooling whom. A programme committee was established comprising these three, Jeremy Isaacs, Paul Bonner and John Ranelagh (who acted as Isaacs' special assistant). This committee set about creating order out of the mountain of proposals before them. Naomi Sargant recalled the early days as being 'pretty pragmatic': 'We had an enormous variety [of programme proposals] and we hadn't determined between us who would do what. David was clear because David was drama, but between Liz and me and Paul Bonner, who [was] the channel controller, it was not at all clear what was going to constitute current affairs and what was going to constitute documentaries.'

Although the channel was beginning to take shape by the time the next group of commissioning editors began work, the challenge remained a daunting one. Mike Bolland, initially Commissioning Editor for Youth and now Head of the Entertainment and Arts Group, started work several months after the first three and he recalled: 'The day I arrived there was a group of refugees who had come from Radio Clyde and BBC and Open University — wherever — and we were all wandering around saying — what's a commissioning editor? We were shell shocked. It was like being dropped on a planet somewhere without any life support system. We were all at the IBA (and) there were three commissioning editors in one room. There was music; youth, which I was doing then; and entertainment and we had to try and make sense of all this. We had tea-chests full of proposals because the thing had been known about for a long time. The first thing, quite apart from all the highfalutin ideas we had before we started, was to get new people making television and going for all those undiscovered audiences. But the overriding horror was: there we

37

were, one year to go and we had nothing. We were all crammed into this office. So there was a feeling of brown trousers really. That was an overriding horror.'

Clearly, the rules which govern the commissioning process were being made up as the editors went along. The mandate or remit may have set the parameters and provided broad guidelines, but the detailed specifications — the channel's circuit-board or blueprint — had to be worked out by trial and error. The channel was trying to change the way television was made in the UK; however, it had few examples on which to draw. Consequently, the commissioning editors set out to test and refine their ideas concerning the imperatives and demands of the Broadcasting Act and the IBA's remit. On occasion, these explorations into the unknown resulted in explosions and controversy which enabled the channel to refine, or as its critics would have it, retreat from its task. The problem was that the channel's remit from the IBA was bound to cause confusion in as much as no one knew which 'tastes and interests not otherwise catered for' should remain so. Clearly child-molesters could not be given a free hand, but what of those who wished to castrate rapists? People claiming that blacks were in a Babylonian captivity were to be welcomed, but what of programmes about black criminality? The depiction of sex was to be extended, but what of rubber fetishists?

In the early days a great deal of discussion centred around the question of whether the channel was a forum for unheard voices or an editorial channel with its own criteria with which to evaluate the truth, legitimacy and quality of the programme-ideas offered. It quickly became evident that a commissioning editor at Channel Four was not simply a broker for minority or special interest groups, nor an open door through which streamed an ideological bestiary of ideas, beliefs and values. That option was denied the moment Wiliam Whitelaw decided that the channel would be subject to the existing Broadcasting Act (with its restrictions of balance, taste and decency). When the fourth channel became Channel Four it closed as many doors as it opened. The OBA — and the notion of free access to television — was shelved and editorial television reaffirmed.

For some commissioning editors the editorial criteria with which they operated were relatively uncomplicated: anything that was not being done on the rest of British television should be done on C4. This meant actively cultivating specialist producers as well as minority audiences. For others, the right-wing or consensualist bias of the rest of broadcasting required Channel Four to seek out the left, and therefore provide a forum for the expression of the only alternative that they could imagine. Some sought to disrupt the smooth images of television with realist or experimental images. Yet others established quasi-access criteria, and encouraged those with strong viewpoints to link up with producers who had the technical skills to enable them to state those views in televisual terms. The implications of the editorial imperative are profound, particularly in the area of balance and minority or specialist television, both of which were key tests of the channel's ability to make breakthroughs in the presentation of issues, viewpoints and cultures. In the next two sections we explore how the decisive move to editorial television affected the ways in which factual television is understood in the channel.

## (2) The Precarious Balance: Journalism and Politics in C4

In the first chapter we demonstrated that one of Channel Four's primary commitments has been to challenge the conventional idea of balance on television. The channel has sought to replace intra-programme balance — where each viewpoint is challenged by its opposite — with balance across the schedule. The question is: is this balance on the never-never? Does the moment ever come when right and left, racist and non-racist, pro and anti have an equal say? Or, are we left simply with the eternal promise that at some point in the future the scales will even up.

The goal of transforming the idea of balance, which is shared by all of the commissioning editors, has caused quite considerable problems in the past five years. In particular, the channel has been held to be politically on the left or, at least, against the right. It is a measure of the power of this image that in 1985, the *Daily Express* proposed, albeit tongue in cheek, that BBC2 should be handed over 'to a similar group of talented people, but of a right of centre persuasion and let them fight it out.' (*Daily Express* 26/6/85) In this section we look at how the editors face up to the charge that the channel is biased to the left but, more importantly we explore the varied approaches to balance which have emerged from within the channel.

Liz Forgan, the channel's first commissioning editor for current affairs, felt that the channel's task was to take risks with debate and polemic, and not be hemmed in by the traditional ideas of TV balance. She argues: 'At a time when there was one television channel, it was a magnificent endeavour to hedge it around with these very tough rules about protecting this extraordinary resource. Somebody had the wit to spot the power of television; to spot its potential for abuse by people who would turn it to nefarious purposes and to protect it by these elaborate rules of balance. It's somebody else's job to say that now we have added another channel it's time to rewrite those rules a little bit. Not to throw them all away, because if we throw them all away it's only too easy to see what happens, but to look at them again. To say, some of these rules are marvellous — a golden protection against the tainting of sources — and some of them are just an unnecessary straight-jacket — the excuse for laziness and the restriction of free thinking. We have this freedom and enough channels to risk a bit more. That was our job.'

David Lloyd, the Commissioning Editor for Current Affairs, outlined the limits of the publishing analogy for the channel's factual output. He insists:

'We are not yet, and never will be analagous to a bookshelf, where one binder says one thing, and another, another, and you don't care whether you published three books in the Autumn which are anti trades union, and none that were pro.' If C4 is analogous to a publishing house then it is a highly regulated one. The editors are still expected by the IBA to achieve a balance, not only in the number of works that they commission, but in the quality of those works. It is clear that the public, and indeed the IBA, will not tolerate one production which is fairly tatty and under-resourced being used to balance a glossy series. Following David Lloyd's metaphor we can say that if one bookshelf contains glossy, full-coloured volumes supporting the trades union movement, the other shelf cannot contain re-cycled, dog-eared paperbacks representing anti trades union views.

Mike Bolland accepted that the channel's heart was on the left in its first years, but he has noticed some important changes since then: 'I think you could put your hand on your heart these days and say the channel is balanced. We did a thing on Nicaragua on Monday Night, but, all is well with the world when we do Threadneedle Street on Sunday night. So, perhaps the thing has evened itself out for the week.

Ultimately, as Bolland indicates, the channel has settled for a rough and ready balance. However, there has been a considerable amount of conflict within the channel about balance. There were long arguments in the beginning between those who believed that the channel should be open to every alternative − a political and cultural Babel reflecting everything from fundamentalist Islam to all shades of militant politics − and those who believed firmly that British television had enshrined right-wing viewpoints and that the channel should provide an alternative on the left.

John Ranelagh recalled that in the early days of the channel 'people wanted to do programmes which simply gave voice to the Ayatollah Khomeni, or something, and I argued very strongly that it was wrong. That we should take our own view and apply it. This does not mean, I hasten to add, that I was advocating censorship; it is simply that it seems to me you should have a view, and if Muslims believe you should cut someone's hand off for stealing a loaf of bread, in my view that is very wicked and we should condemn it.' Liz Forgan recalled that when she commissioned programmes from the right in the early days 'it caused a frightful fuss among some of my colleagues who had assumed that Channel Four's job was to give the left a voice on British television for the first time. This was of course true but, in my opinion, only partly true. Some people screamed and shrieked when we gave the right equal freedom. However, I'm an old fashioned liberal, and it is my professional opinion that the job of people in my position − the gatekeepers of the medium of communication − is to keep the channel clear for the widest possible spectrum of non-violent opinion. This was the freedom which Channel Four gave you.' She continued: 'This meant that if you want to listen to the Communist Party or the people on the far left, or if you want to listen to the Institute for Economic Affairs and people to the further right, as long as they are not advocating sedition and shooting, then you should respect their ideas and listen to them.'

Forgan's pluralist approach is more characteristic of the editors' current views (with Lloyd's caveats) than the Tower of Babel or new left approaches. The key to the successful operation of a balanced channel based on the commissioning principle is a deep-seated *professional* commitment to pluralism on the part of the editors. Judging the political biases in a channel has very little to do with discovering how its producers or editors vote. It is worth restating the commonplace observation that professional values in television, particularly in news and current affairs, involve the rigorous subjugation of personal prejudice. As in all professions, those who put these values into practice do so more or less successfully. However, despite persistent attacks from those who believe that all judgements are inherently biased or ideological, the idea of professional values remains clear and unequivocal. Gwynn Pritchard, Commissioning Editor for Education, certainly subscribes to the clear separation of personal and professional values. While acknowledging that politically most of the editors come from the broad left-liberal consensus, he went on to say: 'I don't think that this is a cause for concern in itself. It would be a cause for concern if it looked as if the interpretation of the remit was such that only certain kinds of views of the world were coming through the channel.' Pritchard felt that the diversity of programme-content was evidence that there was no 'policy of exclusion' operating against ideas and viewpoints with which individual commissioning editors might disagree.

Although the majority of the commissioning editors subscribe to the view that the channel is insulated from the political leanings of its editors, John Ranelagh subscribes to the view that the left-liberal leanings of the majority of the editors has compromised the channel. He believes that the accusation of lack of balance is justified: 'Any national channel in a public service broadcasting system should walk down the middle of the street. It shouldn't have friends on the left, or indeed on the right, or indeed in the middle.' He continued: 'We shouldn't regard ourselves as being beholden to any group or particular collection of views, and I believe we have been, frankly. There is without doubt a left-liberal consensus in the channel and the people representative of that consensus just expand and expand.'

Ranelagh's worry demonstrates that the notion of pluralism has deep roots in the channel, even among those who feel that the standards are not being lived up to. This commitment to pluralism has to extend to every area of life, and not just to politics if the channel is to function successfully. The commissioning system, which invests an enormous amount of power in the hands of one individual, will fail miserably if those individuals have a personal agenda which excludes a range of opinion. After all, there is only one commissioning editor (and his or her assistants) in each area, and if they steadfastly refuse to commission a certain type of programme then it will never appear on the screen. It would, however, be difficult to track down this personal agenda since it would remain largely hidden. The editor may claim never to have exercised the power directly to exclude a programme type or a certain type of independent producer, however the real power lies in the systematic lack of encouragement of such productions or producers. Instead of excluding producers because he or she fundamentally disagree with their worldview, all an editor has to do is claim that the programme-ideas are 'uninspired', 'uninteresting', 'flawed', 'boring'. Controversy may follow when programmes are dropped — which is an expression of visible power — but seldom when programmes are not commissioned. Who could argue with the editor's rights to make aesthetic or journalistic judgments? On the other hand, these judgments are a perfect smokescreen for a personal agenda.

A commissioning editor with his or her own agenda can actually dominate a debate in a way that brooks no argument. And, if an editor excludes viewpoints other than his or her own, then there is very little opportunity to challenge that view. This is particularly important in big projects, as Peter Montagnon, the producer of a major series on China, *The Heart of the Dragon*, points out. Montagnon argues: 'Channel controllers and schedulers deal with programme subjects like seven pounds of bacon or cheese. (They say) "If we did China this year, and we are going to have a repeat of China later this year, then we are not going to put any more money into China. Three or four years on we will look at Africa." Because we did China on Channel Four it meant that broadly no one was going to have a chance to go in there for another four or five years and do another one, so that remains Channel Four's view of China.'

Jad Adams of MEDITEL productions, argues that there is a difference between some commissioning editors who subject everything to their own agenda, and TV journalists who are more concerned with investigation: 'It's a real problem with C4 some think that programmes are there to reflect their view.' He went on to suggest the difference between some commissioning editors and good journalists: 'I happen not to like private medicine but when I was doing a consumer programme for MEDITEL, we found in some cases private medicine was giving a good deal — far better that NHS — and said that. It's not my view — it just happens to be the truth.'

David Graham, of Diverse Productions, put the problem into a wider perspective. He feels strongly that regulated television itself is the problem: 'If you put a group of people in charge of the job of creating space for other people they don't agree with, they will prefer their own views, fortify their position, they will come up with a bureaucracy much quicker than anyone would like to think.' He continued: 'It's such an ambivalent position. The whole idea that a channel is representative is odd when you have got to appoint someone to do the representing and then you have got to put them in gatekeeper position, and then you start screening the input. That's why markets blissfully do not impose the gatekeeping function. They allow any number of people, if they are working freely, to have a go and offer a different product.'

The dangers of imposing personal stances on programming strands is all too clear and therefore it is important to note that the clearest value-commitment within Channel Four is to pluralism: the expression of the widest possible range of opinions, ideas and values. Despite this, however, there have been cases where producers have claimed that their programmes have been dropped by the channel because the Commissioning Editor philosophically, culturally or politically disagreed with them. The gatekeeper function of the editor can lead to a lack of balance in two ways: through the personal interests of the editor or through their collective political leanings. It is a mark of the professional commitments within the channel that such accusations are infrequent.

The pluralist commitment of the editors working in actuality is tempered by the values associated with good journalism: namely, impartiality, investigation, objectivity and, at its broadest, truth. This raises the crucial issue of how opinionated or polemical television should be made. One does not expect fair treatment of the 'enemy' in polemically inspired writing: when reading Luther railing and cursing against the 'whore of Babylon', one does not expect to turn the page and discover him asking the Pope, 'and what do you think your holiness?' The problem which Channel 4 faces is that we as viewers have become accustomed to factual television that claims to be fair, objective and unbiased. If Luther was to reappear and make a documentary for Channel Four called *Rome: The Whole Truth,* by and large the British public would, in fact, expect an appearance from the Pope. Therefore, an important development within the channel has been the shift away from simple pluralism which relied on access-opinioned programmes, to thesis-led television, in which a point of view is only held to be validly expressed if it will accept challenges and arguments against it. This more complex form of pluralism assumes that there are common and accepted rules of debate despite vigorous and fundamental disagreements between (and indeed within) interest groups.

According to Ranelagh, 'the need for balance recedes markedly when what you are actually doing is pursuing a thesis with intellectual rigour: you must, must, must put the points to people who violently disagree. And in that you will find that the crude notion of balance does disappear. So it's only once in a blue moon that you have to manufacture programmes.' The feeling that factual programmes are better when arguing a thesis than simply stating an opinion is shared by Caroline Thompson, Commissioning Editor for Business and Science: 'I like programmes which argue a case rather than presenting a point of view. I have felt that too often opinionated programmes present a point of view and are actually rather unsatisfactory from a viewer's point of view. Although it's good to give other people a voice on the channel – and there is obviously a place for it – there are other commissioning editors who will give the unheard a voice. My job is to present the arguments and to try to provide some analysis and to try and provide some explanation of what is going on.'

Farrukh Dhondy, the Commissioning Editor for Multi-Cultural Affairs, also subscribes to the view that it is extremely important to work within the pre-established codes of British current affairs journalism. He has no desire to present *the* Black interpretation of the news which, in his view, does not exist), rather, he wants Black factual programmes to be judged by the same criteria as would be *Panorama*. He argues: 'The British public are used to sophisticated television, part of which is exposing corruption. It is not a racist act to expose a member of Parliament who looked the other way when Black social workers were beating up old white people in state-owned homes. If Blacks want to hire Saatchi and Saatchi to present a positive image then do it — it would be more honest. But, being part of the fourth estate, one has to accept the best traditions of the function of the press in Britain, namely the exposing of corruption.'

According to Lloyd, the way that a programme is packaged — its code — is important in establishing public confidence. If something looks like a traditional current affairs show, in Lloyd's view the programme should sustain the traditional concept of impartiality of British current affairs. If it does not then it is fraudulent, and more to the point undermines the viewers' beliefs about such programmes. This is not to say that Lloyd wishes to pull the channel back to mainstream television, but he feels that opinionated journalism should signal itself as such. Furthermore, he feels that such journalism is different from simple propaganda: 'Opinionated journalism, and I underline journalism one hundred times, involves taking no easy ellipses in the argument (or) bulldozing through the facts. Now that can be a dishonest piece of journalism. Opinionated journalism has to be able to admit of counter-propositions and the counter-evidence. If you think the evidence from one is less strong than the other, then fine. You cannot and should not stitch the public up, which is what propaganda is — conveniently forgetting facts. I'm very firm about this, I make a clear distinction between what I think is honesty and what I think is dishonesty.'

Editing is a highly selective activity which involves a great deal of judgment. Those on the receiving end of editorial decisions — producers and the public — have to understand and be convinced that the principles underlying the selection of programmes are rational and fair, and that they are being applied fairly. Lloyd outlines succinctly his criteria: 'You need the proper control of editorial. Arguments should be warranted by what is demonstrable, given the facts.' Lloyd has a very journalistic view of the function of the editor, he has no desire to undermine the channel's commitment to a range of contentious voices, but he has a strong sense of boundaries. Such programmes should not appear in a strand dedicated to investigative journalism, for instance, as they would undermine the authority of the rest of the ouput. 'People have got to know the status of the information. If the information is partially presented in itself, people are not going to have any compass bearings on what they should really be believing. If you really start uncovering corruption people have got to know the quality of the information.' In newspaper terms Lloyd is insisting that an opinion piece should not masquerade as hard news.

This challenges the idea, prevalent among the new left, that journalism is essentially subjective and ideological in its reporting of events. Lloyd accepts that journalism is selective, but feels that it is the editor's job, on behalf of the viewers, to ensure that dishonest stories, which suppress information, do not appear.

Apart from these traditional journalistic values, some editors are concerned that individual voices and authors, which do not represent any minority of organisation, will be lost in the desire for 'crude' balance. Nick Hart-Williams, Commissioning Editor for Single Documentaries, is more concerned with what he calls 'the authorial voice', than the obsessive attempt to find people who represent specific viewpoints. 'I suppose the basic definition of this slot', he claims, 'is that it tends to be films that have a stronger authorial voice — the film-maker is making a fairly personal statement, not balanced looks at this or that issue.' Hart-Williams is trying to produce a non-fiction equivalent of *Film on Four* which, although it involves 'seeing that one doesn't go overboard in a particular direction', nevertheless is concerned to let individual authors speak for themselves.

For Ranelagh, the best way to fuse the authorial voice and balance is to insist that the author always deals the best case his or her opponents can muster: 'The best way to do an opinionated piece is to bounce your view off those who disagree with you. In a crude form this is seen as a balanced programme. For instance, Adam Raphael did a very good *Diverse Reports* some years ago, arguing against smoking and he didn't speak to one person who agreed with him, and it was so much stronger in consequence.'

The way that those involved in factual television hope to escape the strictures of traditional current affairs television, without abandoning the positive aspects of that tradition, is through the increasing use of independent producers who are enthusiastic specialists in an area, rather than appointing generalists producers to deal with a range of output. For instance, Ranelagh developed his model for the *Equinox* science and technology strand on the basis that it was better for each programme in the strand to be produced by someone who already knew about an issue in some detail, and then collated by the commissioning editor (or an executive producer). This replaced the established idea of handing the strand over to one independent production company who then had to fill the slots without necessarily having a great deal of knowledge in lots of areas. Lloyd has adapted this model for his current affairs strand. He has replaced his usual supplier with a large number of others, each of whom are bidding for one or two programmes rather than the series. According to Lloyd, this move to specialists means that he will be working with 'producers [who] have an instinct for when something in an area is happening, and can move quickly on it', rather than a team of generalists and researchers who know very little in depth about an issue. (A perhaps worrying by-product of this system is that even more power is concentrated in the hands of the commissioning editor as he or she is the only one with an overview of what is happening.)

Naomi Sargant, despite her tricky role in commissioning 'education' programmes, which touch on thorny issues of health-care, unemployment, sexuality etc, claims never really to have had any problems with political balance. Indeed she states categorically: 'I would have counted it a failure on my part if I had got into those sorts of problems.' Her way of avoiding such problems is to have academics participating in the programmes. 'From my point of view it gives me better and more intelligent programmes. It means I don't have to get in another external adviser to cause regression to the mean of proved mediocrity. If you've got an adviser advising another academic, they argue with each other on a proper basis.'

This level of protection is extremely important because, according to Lloyd: 'I'm not sure that all the audience all the time recognise opinionated journalism — as my in-tray would attest to. I think we haven't cracked it in all people's eyes, but I don't know how you can crack it, except possibly gradually to sophisticate people to the increasing proliferation of channels which will occur and thereby increase the impossiblity really of expecting one channel to fulfil its complete balancing duty.' He continued: 'Now that may be something of a weasel answer because it releases us from our obligations, but all we can do is to continue to signal with something of the subtlety we have done, and not to give up on that because I do think people need certain codes.'

David Graham is an intriguing commentator on the problem of balance. His series, *Diverse Reports*, and, *The New Enlightenment*, represented the few high-profile committed right-wing programmes on the channel. There is very little disagreement, even in the channel, that the views of the right have not been heard on the channel as much as those of the left. Indeed Graham, who is generally supportive of the channel as being the best regulated television has to offer, feels that: 'This is where C4 went wrong, and where history won't be very forgiving. They created a decent bit of space for the extreme left saying very old-fashioned things and they didn't know what to do about the right. I think they are probably social democrats at heart.' The next section will explore the extent to which this charge can be justified.

## (3) The Hidden Right: The Unpalatable Minority?

As we noted earlier in this chapter, the commissioning editors are ranged across a sectrum of more or less pluralistic positions. One would imagine therefore that pluralism would extend to the right. This is certainly the official position. Liz Forgan acknowledges: 'Some of my colleagues would say the rest of British television is fairly much centre-right orientated, and that our job ought to be to look after the left. I don't agree with that. I think our job is to be everywhere where something interesting is happening that other people aren't looking at. At some periods of time this will be on the right, and others it will be on the left. Professionally I am perfectly happy swivelling my periscope, or whatever metaphor you would like to use, from one to the other. What I look for is the moving figure on the flat landscape.' It is clear, though, that people's access to the channel depends on what they are doing on the flat landscape. If they are simply pondering how to privatise the landscape they are perfectly welcome; if, on the other hand, they are skinheads up-rooting the last remaining trees, then they have little chance of appearing.

Liz Forgan, who also recognises that difficult editorial decisions have to be taken about which voices should be allowed onto the channel raises the question of social responsibility: 'If you have to face the serious possibility that putting ideas on a television set can actually end up with a dead body − a threat which is often held over the head of journalists quite wrongly − it is a very difficult judgement. You have to be very sure of yourself, and very strong to tread that line. Sometimes you are too cowardly, usually you are too cowardly I think. In a newspaper it is comparatively easy to report people who say "Well, what if we shot the Prime Minister?" If you say that on television, there is something in the nature of television that it has a completely different impact. So I had somewhat to learn, re-learn some rules and limitations about what you could say and what you could do. Interviewing a terrorist is an obvious example. The newspapers do it every day, but if you do it on television it is a very big deal indeed. People think of an appearance on television as in some way a validation by society of whatever is being said, whereas a newspaper it's a piece of reporting. A bit mysterious, but nevertheless it exists.'

The problem of Northern Ireland is by far the most difficult such issue with which the channel has to deal. The identification of sections of the left with the anti-British feeling in Northern Ireland means that any attempt to block programmes on 'The Troubles' is met with accusations of censorship. As Forgan points out, however, the decisions which they have to take go to the heart of the relationship of television with democracy: can television adopt a Weimar approach, tolerating all arguments, regardless of their practical consequences? Or, must it acknowledge that television might in some ways legitimate terrorism? Does the right of free speech extend to those whose first act would be to abolish it? The emotional essence of images, particularly moving images, means that feelings are given more eloquent expression than rational arguments. Hence, all terrorist movements seek television exposure to strengthen their cause. In the case of the Symbionese Liberation Army −

the captors of Patti Hearst – television exposure was itself the aim of its terrorism. When captured, they turned out to be 24 in number. How the classic liberal dilemma concerning free speech is resolved involves a complex *editorial* trade-off of freedom against responsibility.

There is a very clear difference in the channel's attitude to what one might call the libertarian right on the one hand and the semi-fascist right on the other. The former are reasonably welcome on the channel; indeed, Isaacs claimed at the Edinburgh TV Festival in 1983 that the new right were being sought out. The latter, on the other hand, are unpalatable to every commissioning editor.

Of the former, David Lloyd suggests: 'Some things are more interesting coming from the right: if they say society is in flux, things are changing, it is just more interesting.' However, most of the commissioning editors recount similar tales about right-wing producers; for various reasons the programmes seldom come off. According to Nick Hart-Williams, 'it always seems that there are more film-makers with a leftward political view that get into filmmaking. [But] the channel has often said: "Bring us your right-wing films please".' Gwynn Pritchard claims: 'I have got someone, at my request interestingly... specifically working on right-wing ideas, though it's not working out as a very imaginative project.' Pritchard also sought to challenge the left-liberal consensus in development studies, only to discover that the producers he was working with adopted that point of view: 'I asked someone to do some work on the idea of benign neglect – but, they are moving back to the Third World consensualist view which IBT (International Broadcasting Trust) has been providing for a long time.' Alan Fountain was contacted by the Federation of Conservative Students (FCS) who were thinking of setting up a workshop, only to have the FCS cancel the meetings which had been set up to explore the idea. Like Hart-Williams, Fountain has the problem that almost all of the workshops which produce for his *Eleventh Hour* slot have: left-leaning, experimental or oppositional points of view. Historically, those who use video, television or cinema as expressions of their politics, culture or sexuality do not come from the right. This begs the question, however, of whether Channel Four should have actively sought out and helped develop a right-wing sector as it did with ethnic television; it had the same responsibility to the FCS and the Adam Smith Institute as it did to black or gay workshops.

David Graham's company, Diverse Productions, successfully brought some of the views of the new right into television. Even so, David Graham feels that the channel missed the boat and failed adequately to represent the most important political movement of the late 1970s and early 1980s. This is unfair in some ways; the new right, after all had been developing for ten years before the channel started broadcasting. However, most of the editors felt that there were three reasons why it was difficult to capture the full flavour of neo-liberalism: first, those who developed such ideas had no desire, or need for access to television – their access to real power was virtually guaranteed when the channel started; secondly, historically film- and documentary-makers tend to be on the left, and therefore the right tend not to have access to the technical expertise of putting programmes together; finally, the commissioning editor's themselves are not in sympathy with the ideas of the new right, which might have acted as a filter. These complex reasons are summed up in Gwynn Pritchard's statement: 'No one [on the right] has come up with a television idea which really grabbed me.' In fact, Pritchard feels that the right are not particularly concerned with what appears on Channel Four, they are more interested in the way the channel's structure represents the new entrepreneurship. 'I think that the Thatcherite right are much more interested in the structure of C4 than in the superstructure of stuff that is actually transmitted, and I think that is partly why there hasn't been as much flack as there might have been. Certainly not the same as the BBC.'

Even when the new right do come up with exciting television ideas, there are still some in the channel who find absurd the idea that neo-liberalism balances up the overall left-liberal consensus in the Channel Four. According to Ranelagh, 'Diverse Reports is not what we are on about; the whole point of the thing is greyness. The new right, to be absolutely frank − the voices in those sorts of programmes − are on the margins of conservative thinking. They are the equivalent of Militant.'

On the other hand, Forgan found the new right to be the acceptable face of Conservative thinking: 'I don't mean lunatics, I mean the really exciting thinking, which as we now know, was the engine that was turning into the great political revolution of the seventies and eighties, and if you look at Diverse Reports you will see it all there, at the time when everybody still thought they were a bunch of nutters. It is the only place where it's all there.'

David Graham, whose company produced the type of right-wing television which found favour with some commissioning editors, initially followed the approach to current affairs which seemed to fit the mood of Britain in the late 1970s. He developed a kind of adversarial television, which recognised the limitations of television argument and made a virtue of lack of balance. Graham argued: 'I think in a sense Diverse Reports has achieved a pattern of television which is more modest than Panorama and World in Action. It doesn't think it knows best. It doesn't think it knows the answer to every question — it accepts the fact of partiality. It does its best to sum up what the other side thinks about a topic but it doesn't pretend to be comprehensive.' Graham was interested initially in producing current affairs television which was 'a sort of gutsy committed pamphleteering in the tradition of Paine and Addison.' He went on to say: 'We didn't believe in balance. Our job was to do the opposite of what the other people do. To systematically drive in the opposite direction.'

Graham now argues that perhaps the codes and formats he and C4 developed for polemical television were wrong: 'Maybe the format for opinionated television we developed was the wrong one. Maybe opinion-led television should be in short series.' This is an extremely important statement: if the most successful opinionated programme-maker in the channel's short history is now acknowledging that the experiment is over, and that opinionated journalism is not the same as current affairs, and should be signalled differently, then the channel and its producers are clearly undergoing a sea-change. A change brought about perhaps, as we argue in the next chapter, by a recognition that the nature of debate has changed in Britain under the impact of Margaret Thatcher's third term.

Although the new right was perfectly acceptable, indeed exciting, as an option for several commissioning editors, there was no doubt that the 'populist' right of racism, hanging and flogging, was simply rejected out of hand. John Ranelagh who, as an ex-speech writer for Mrs Thatcher, was considered the channel's most Conservative voice, was adamant that the fascist right was unacceptable. 'I don't think anybody here would actually lend themselves to NF programmes. I certainly would never commission it myself. Somebody else is welcome to − I wouldn't stop it going on but I don't want to do it. I think in that respect I am part of the consensus.' Alan Fountain, who is politically very different from Ranelagh, expresses a similar point of view: 'If I am being completely honest, I am opposed to putting on right-wing or racist programmes. If somebody made me make such a programme, I wouldn't do it.' Like Ranelagh, he would no longer try to prevent the appearance of the programme on the channel, but he would certainly resist the idea that he personally should commission such a programme.

Even Liz Forgan who, despite her role as the channel's gatekeeper, is a committed pluralist, wavers over allowing racist voices:

> I think I had a bit of a wobble about racism.....I think socialists can insult conservatives and conservatives socialists without doing anyone any damage. I think the old can yell at the young and visa versa. I even think you can insult women despite their somewhat precarious hold on certain aspects of society. But, for racial minorities, many of whom have recent memories of atrocious physical cruelty and worse, to hear the words of Nazism either shouted through their own front windows with Front marches or actually in their own sitting rooms. I really am very uneasy about that all together. So, it's perfectly right, we never went searching for it. We have never lifted the phone to the National Front. Fortunately they never really caught on. The only time I did actually have them on was in the 1983 election, when we had a great internal argument about whether we should accept their party election broadcast. Most of my colleagues were very much against it on simple grounds that they were racist. I said we should have them because it was an election, they were a legal political party standing for election in a democratic system. I didn't think under those circumstances − so

long as the text of their broadcast didn't conflict with the law – that we could possibly exclude them. So we did transmit them, and it caused a terrible row, and I had to put myself on *Right to Reply* to explain why we had done it. It was a very uncomfortable experience indeed.

Mike Bolland, who had responsibility for youth in the channel's early days, attempted to ensure that the section of white youth most identified with racism had some kind of voice, but even he ultimately rejected the idea that it was his responsibility to allow racist views to appear. 'We did have skinhead views on *Whatever you Want* but, did we commission right-wing programmes per se? No. Partly because they never seemed to arise.' Bolland recognised the dilemma though. If a significant section of the population has a viewpoint which is held with great conviction, but which does not appear on television because the people who hold it lack the technical expertise or money to do so, should the channel actively encourage the expression of this unvoiced group? He notes: 'The dilemma for the commissioning editor is – are you a reactive beast? Or do you go out and take initiative? There isn't an easy answer to that either – it's a bit of both. Ultimately you have got to be quite reactive I think. If you say, the door is open, there has got to be an element of truth in that and it can only be an element of truth when you have got 50 proposals a week coming in and you have got two or three slots a week.' In a sense, this is the dilemma of access rather than editorial television. Only if the commissioning editors subscribe to the idea that they are pursuing an open-door rather than an editorial policy, do they have to worry about allowing the Front or its offshoots to appear.

Whatever the attitudes to the far-right, one thing is certain; there is a strong feeling among the commissioning editors that the channel has changed its approach toward opinionated television. The certainties and imperatives which guided the channel in its early attempts to develop polemical television have given way under the impact of the cultural shifts and transformations which have occurred in the 1980s. As Alan Fountain pointed out, 'there was a simpler world a few years ago', and therefore the 'struggle to put on images which question things' now involves a much more complex understanding of pluralism. The tentative responses to the the social and cultural shifts in Britain in the late 1980s, and the review of the channel's approach to polemical television, mirrors the confusion which reigns among those opposed to the lurch in values toward individualism. If there has been a major sea-change in culture in the UK – and as we are in the middle of it we cannot be certain – television has to respond. However, no one is certain what television should respond to. We might be witnessing another middle-class revolution to match that of the Corn Law repeal movement and the middle-class religious and political successes of the 1840s. Then again, the values of collective endeavour, civic culture and conservativism (with a small 'c') which have long characterised British culture may reassert themselves. In the meantime, the channel's commissioning editors are trying to respond to barely-understood cultural changes.

This uncertainty is breeding a certain amount of confusion about the future of polemical and minority-oriented television. It would seem, however, that two responses are emerging. First, there is a feeling that as the rules of debate have settled down again and that as politics are gravitating toward complex discussion among and between all shades of political opinion, as opposed to polemic, the channel must reflect this. This group advocates thesis-led opinionated television. Secondly, there is a residual fear that by pursuing this approach the channel might loose any contact with its access beginnings. One commissioning editor, whilst agreeing that 'better programmes do include arguments within them', bemoaned the fact that he was fighting a losing battle to save even a couple of hours for access-type programmes. What is at stake here is the definition of television pluralism. For some, pluralism implies commonality. Those engaged in debate assume that those opposed to them agree that discussion is important: minds, attitudes, values, opinions might be changed in the process. On the other hand, the idea of polemical pluralism is one where someone's mind is already made up and he or she simply states his or her viewpoint in a proselytising fashion. Television provides another means so to do – an electronic equivalent of *Militant, Bulldog, Socialist Worker,* the *Watchtower* etc. If this latter approach ever characterised the channel, it has been apparently comprehensively defeated if someone is having to fight for two hours a week for such programmes.

One area of the channel's factual output that we have not mentioned is *Channel Four News.* Since the disasterous early days, when the programme lost its editor and several presenters amidst much bitterness and acrimony (a minor storm in the television teacup of the early 1980s), *Channel Four News* has become something of a flagship for C4. However, we have deliberately excluded it from this analysis of the ways in that C4's mandate has been interpreted. Although Channel Four's brief to ITN about *Channel Four News* allows the programme to explore issues in depth by allocating an hour every weeknight, and to experiment with authored, indeed biased, items as part of the news, it remains an ITN production. The values which inform the programme are inextricably linked with the news values and principles which have been built up in ITN since the late 1950s. An overall appreciation of how news operates would take us well beyond the scope of this chapter.

Thus far we have been talking about factual television, but one of the great complaints about the channel (indeed about most British television drama) has been the leftward leaning of its fiction, and in particular the serial *Brookside.* It is important to draw a distinction between the overt politics of news and current affairs and the implicit politics in fictional and entertainment programmes. Politicians may want to see a script in order to check what they will be asked but until the past decade they were relatively unconcerned about whether they were in mid-shot or close-up. The image was less important than the word. This is clearly not the case in drama, the powerful fusion of image and word, sound and light, gesture and costume, music and light combine to structure political statements which can be profoundly moving, irritating or infuriating.

It is probably a fair assertion to make that British television drama is left of centre. The reason for this is relatively simple: playwrights tend to be on the side of those who make the best characters and can elicit the most response. This tends to be the poor rather than the rich; the unhappy rather than the satisfied; the radicals rather than the conservatives; the committed rather than the comfortable. Secondly, unlike France, Britain has no substantial tradition of right-wing playwright. The right in the UK has seldom operated politically in the cultural domain. The commissioning editors for fiction recognise the problem of bringing a right-wing perspective to bear on fiction though, like their colleagues in actuality, they feel that the problem is that the proposals which they receive from the right are simply not up to scratch as drama. Furthermore, they feel that drama should not be cast in simple political terms; indeed, they argue that drama dies if it is politicised to that extent.

According to David Rose: 'If you're looking for a real balance to represent the world at large, somehow, because of the nature of most of the writers, they are not there. I would welcome some more really persuasive right-wing views. But, really we are chooosing what we believe to be the best talent.' This is echoed by Peter Ansorge, Commissioning Editor for Drama Serials, who claims: 'I don't think we should make a right-wing soap opera. You see it is a misreading of drama to think that because someone is saying something in a drama, that is necessarily the point of view of the channel or the writer.' He went on to say that 'It is probably true that the writers have not been fair to their more right-wing characters. I think that is legitimate to say: yes,there is that tension in *Brookside*. I don't think you then say that the problem will be solved by putting in a very right-wing character, I don't think that would persuade anybody.'

Both drama and factual programmes face similar problems when attempting to commission programmes or films from the right but, much more important in some ways than the artificial balancing act of left and right political perspectives has been the emergence of a new strand of programming directed at businessmen and, particularly, the participants in what has come to be called popular capitalism. If the channel is to face down the charges of bias, and of being essentially the creature of 1960s left-liberalism, one of the key tests is the way that it treats science, technology and industry. It is to this that we now turn.

## (4) Taking Care of Business

Industry is not the preserve of the right. The organised left was, after all, conceived within and by industrial culture. However, there is a distinct tendency among sections of the intellectual left to treat science and industry as necessary evils at best. The celebration of industry and business, which united the middle and working classes in their struggle against the old agrarian elite, as well as dividing them in their battle for industrial society, was abandoned by the intellectual left after what they considered to be the manifold failures of Wilson's technology-fixated governments in the 1960s. This suspicion of capitalism and of industry itself seemed to be present in the early days of the channel. John Ranelagh, for one, feels that this has yet to be rectified: 'We only do twenty hours on science, technology and wealth creation.' Although Ranelagh's statement does not take into account the many hours devoted to business, computing, marketing etc. as part of the channel's educational output, if his condemnation of the rest of the non-educational factual output is correct then the channel has problems. It cannot be counted as fully contributing to the debate about the future of British culture, let alone British industry. The question of whether the channel is industry-affirming or denying is important: it is a key to understanding the perception it has of itself as responding to 1980s Britain.

The channel *is* trying to come to terms with the implications of Thatcherism. Caroline Thomson, Commissioning Editor for Business and Science, points out that she wants 'business programmes which are brash and lively.' However, she has no desire to see the channel's critical edge blunted by fear that it is out of step with the national mood: 'I don't want the channel to be taken over by the *Stocks and Shares Show* and the *Business Exchange* for one minute. On the other hand, it's easy to decry these things when what they are about is some sort of popular capitalism. What you are talking about is ordinary people that earn quite significantly less than all commissioning editors and television producers, who are making a bit of money by buying BT shares or their council house or whatever. It's no good sitting here and saying it's a greedy society or whatever, when what you are talking about is someone who would never have contemplated leaving anything, leaving a house worth £10,000.' However, she feels that it is important that 'I don't get myself into a psychological position where I think that making money is the only thing that matters. I think you have to have a range — you have programmes which cause problems with big businessmen, because they are critical about their take-over tactics. I think as long as I keep that, people within the channel rather appreciate what I do.'

Thomson disagrees with Ranelagh's main point. She argues: 'Most people recognise that developing a strand across the business/work/technology area is something that C4 is recognised as having done rather well.' She agrees with him, however, that the channel and its critics should no longer think in simple left/right terms. She says: 'I think it is a bit of a mistake to see business programmes as being right-wing and *Union World*-type programmes as being left-wing. I think that is rather seeing things in pre-Thatcherite terms; the truth is that now there are a lot of nice liberal people who make lots of money in the city, and equally there are lots of pretty hard-nosed right-wingers in the old left.' Interestingly, in the light of the previous discussion of thesis-led television, she argues that she has commissioned a programme to replace *Union World* because the latter seemed a creature of the 1970s. 'In *Union World*,' she said, 'we had a rule — which I think was mistaken in the long run, which is one of the reasons we are changing it — that we never have management on. That was because it was a programme from within the union movement about the affairs of the union. I took the view that having run it for three years, its purpose, which had been designed in the late 1970s, had run its course, and that there was actually a wider programme about work issues which would encompass union affairs and would be aimed at the workers. It would be about the affairs which trade unionists have to deal with every day of their lives — like health and safety, equal opportunity and redundancies — it would be about those issues, but not specifically about unions. Because I felt as you got more into the '80s — or post-79: post-winter of discontent — the unions were getting increasingly negative, and I just think that the audience finds that offputting.'

John Cummins, the former Commissioning Editor for Youth, echoes Thomson when he says that the programmes that he commissions reflect the fact that 'young people, while being emotionally socialist, are frightfully capitalist. They don't want the overthrow of capitalism.' He went on to say: 'They want things — it's the Barratt new home phenomenon. Those from young working-class backgrounds want out, they want a different sort of life, and that we do reflect.' Cummins feels in general that 'we don't look at how power has shifted over a five year period. A few years ago it would have been unthinkable to talk about a privatised British Telecom with two thousand million profits.' He concluded: 'That's the sort of thing I hope we look at more.'

This is not to say that the channel is responding to the renewal of capitalist values by buying the ethics of materialism. Gwynn Pritchard claims that *'Equinox* isn't the first series that is glorifying science and technology.' He went on to say that 'the BBC is full of series that are trying to popularise and glamourise and celebrate a certain ideological view of science, and given the channel's remit there was no need to continue with that.'

In practical terms, Thomson addressed the problem of business by commissioning programmes 'with a much more distinct identity than the [BBC's] *Money Programme.* The Money Programme catered for two audiences: the business audience, who tended to watch it because it was the only thing on television which catered for them, and then it had this curious section which was for the amateur small investor. Usually there were two separate audiences, and although it's got a good popular format, and attracts good audiences, and does its job rather well, there was nonetheless room for more specialist programmes which split those two subjects up. So, the idea I had was to do *The Business Programme* which would be the current affairs, businessman's end of it, and do serious analysis, and unashamedly go for small audiences.' (As part of this overall approach, Thomson and Sargant developed *Moneyspinner*, a consumer programme about personal and family finance). When asked by someone in the channel about the size of audience which would have satisfied her for *The Business Programme*, Thomson replied: 'I think you would be doing well if you got 500,000.' (In fact it achieved considerably higher figures). Thomson's thinking reflects the problems of being a commissioning editor. She had to respond to what the BBC were doing; she had to work with a minority or specialist audience in mind; and, finally, she had to accept that her audiences might be well below the legendary zero rating. This brings us on to the question of minority audiences.

## (5) The Courage to be Boring: The Editors and Minorities

The press stereotype of the Channel Four viewer as a one-armed, black, lesbian undoubtedly raises hackles in the channel. Indeed there is a strong feeling that one should not use the term minority at all. Almost every single editor rejected the notion that the channel has a mission to cater for downtrodden or excluded minorities. They pointed out, very forcibly is some cases, that the Broadcasting Act did not mention the word minority. Most preferred the act's terminology: 'tastes and interests not otherwise catered for'. (It should be pointed out that the IBA's terms of reference for the channel contains explicit references to minorities, as did the note on programme policy prepared by Colin Shaw for the Board of Directors.)

Naomi Sargant pugnaciously claimed: 'I think the word minority is a snare and a delusion, and shouldn't be used. It was never written down, it's not in the act. Catering for tastes not otherwise catered for is in the act, and being experimental in form and content is in the act.' Seamus Cassidy, Commissioning Editor for Entertainment, when asked about the mandate also pointed out that 'the act did not say minority'. Liz Forgan was prepared to accept the description of the channel as minority-oriented, however she redefined the notion: 'Only in so far as you ruthlessly define a minority as anyone who, at the moment you transmit a programme, does not belong to the biggest group in the audience — but it's a semantic game in a way.' She also points out that the Broadcasting Act 'doesn't say we must always cater for the underdogs, which is another connotation of minority. It gives us licence to cater for merchant bankers or very rich people in exactly the same way as we cater for Greeks or lesbians.'

This is very different from the early expectations of the channel, when it was assumed that Channel Four was precisely the channel for the downtrodden. It was, after all, supposed to bring us those voices that had been systematically excluded from television. Furthermore, in the wider scheme of things, it was part of a conception of democracy based on the idea that Britain was composed of interacting minorities, each with its own collective voice, linked by a channel which, nevertheless, remained a passive intermediary. If this was ever true of the channel in the beginning, then it appears to be no longer the case.

We have already noticed that the commissioning editors are profoundly worried about simply becoming brokers and putting the views of their clients – the minorites – on screen. There are several threads to this, not least a fear that once the hounds of minority programming have been unleashed they will pursue any commissioning editor in sight. Furthermore, it turns out that the minorities are a bit like the 101 dalmations, superficially very friendly, but there are just so damned many of them. It is not just that there are what one might call the demographic minorities of ethnicity, age, and sexuality – but there are myriads of taste and interests each clamouring for its fifteen minutes of fame. The persistent demands of these interests and minorities means that the commissioning editors seem like Gulliver in a Swiftian world of giants and little people, half men and half beasts, those who eat fat and those who eat lean. It is simply impossible to service every minority of taste and interest.

The second difficulty with the idea of minorities is that most of the commissioning editors appear unhappy with the form that these programmes take. Some types of programmes are relatively unproblematic. For instance, magazine programmes aimed at the elderly or the disabled, such as *Years Ahead, Same Difference* or *Listening Eye,* work because they have an informative content aimed at uncontentious minorities. On the other hand, programmes aimed at or made by potentially controversial social, cultural, taste or sexual minorities which feel oppressed or excluded from mainstream British culture often fall into the trap of being either confessional or evangelical. At its worst the minority either speaks to itself in whispers and jargon, so that no one else can either hear or understand, or in a proselytising rant demanding attention. Many such programmes end up with an unhappy compromises between the confessional and the evangelical. Just as the style of polemical television has yet to be set successfully, so minority television has yet to overcome this very real difficulty in tone.

One can see the difference in the views of the commissioning editors from those espoused by those who thought the channel was simply going to service minorities. Gwynn Pritchard pointed out that 'one of the interesting things is that C4 does not have a commissioning editor for women's programmes – the understanding of the changes and the emergence of a kind of feminism into the culture in the last twenty years is such that it would be an inappropriate response to have a commissioning editor for women and a particular strand of programming that was exclusive to women.' John Ranelagh feels similarly about the ethnic output. He argues: 'I think that one of the things that we should get rid of is the multicultural commissioning editor. I would have thought that we were a small enough channel to be sure that there is a black voice in a whole range of programmes instead of creating a commissioning editor with a limited budget and limited slots to ghettoise it. You put it into the *Bandung File* and one or two other places and it's away. We should have far more Blacks at C4.' Farrukh Dhondy, the Commissioning Editor for Multicultural Programmes, claims: 'As a commissioning editor you have to ask: is this interesting, or is it simply somebody trying to get something off their chest? – which I don't want.'

Not only are there too many minorities, there is not enough time or money to go around to allow the real cultural and political complexity of the minority in question to emerge. Naomi Sargant points out: 'Nobody else on this channel is going to do the over-sixties, who are a much larger minority than any of the other minorities which people talk about.' The over-sixties may share the same number of years on this earth, but they might not have anything else in common. This creates a lot of pressure on commissioning editors, who inevitably alienate somone when developing minority program- mes. Alan Fountain points out, for instance, that a film about gays, which does not show them in a particularly favourable light, will be strongly objected to because there will only be one or two such films commissioned in that year. Fountain argues: 'One film exists as a rare object and has completely unrealistic expectations focused on it.' Similar stories could be told about other minorities. A programme about, for instance, Asian wife- beating, would be seen as a betrayal by the Asian community. An anti-Indian programme made by a Pakistani would produce uproar, as would an anti- trades union piece in *Union World*. Minorities might well be delighted by the idea that they have a programme aimed directly at them, but that delight can turn into possessiveness. If 'our programme' changes, is moved, or confronts some difficult issues the feeling that the minority in question has been let down is inescapable. The very idea of minority programmes raises expecta- tions which television, with its limited resources, cannot fulfil.

These contradictory demands emerge, according to Dhondy, because the public overestimates the power of television, and therefore expects too much from programmes for their own minority. He argues: 'The population believes that television can change other people's lives on their behalf. Gays feel great when a gay programme comes on because they think that other people are watching it. Similarly with blacks: they don't want to watch their own programmes.' Dhondy's response to the complex demands on multicultural programmes is to make an editorial decision about what he thinks is important about black issues in Britain. He points out: 'By and large what television should do – and that is why you require an editorial mind to do it – is to make a very humble judgment of what the country needs and do that.' This is a far cry from the idea that an editor is an extension of a minority community.

In particular, one can see the pressures associated with making programmes for minorities in the channel's ethnic strand. Farrukh Dhondy is a self- confessed realist when it comes to ethnic television. He is firm that it cannot transform the world and feels that it is important to demonstrate to ethnic communities that 'television is an industry not wish-fulfillment'. Puncturing the inflated image of television is important because it frees the commissioning editor from the overwhelming sense that he or she has total responsibility for a minority. Dhondy's task, as he sees it, is to ensure that blacks are visible at all levels in television, rather than in ghetto programmes. When he took over the position from Sue Woodford, who commissioned *Black on Black* and *Eastern Eye* from LWT, he decided to construct a black independent sector which would gain the skills to apply for commissions outside of the multi-cultural area. In that respect Dhondy saw himself 'answering a much smaller challenge, but a similar challenge to Jeremy when he started up the channel.'

Dropping *Black on Black* and *Eastern Eye* was an extremely controversial decision among the Asians and Afro-Caribbeans – one that is still deeply felt – and yet, as Dhondy pointed out: 'If one added up the material of *Bandung, Club Mix* and *Sunday East,* it amounts to three times the volume of the same kind only better.' According to Dhondy, the reason for the apparent rejection of his policy is that in some ways blacks and Asians have what he calls a nationalistic consciousness; they want to retain an image of separate culture from that of the rest of the UK. Dhondy's strategy, on the other hand, is to recognise that 'Once you get used to the idea that blacks are a permanent part of the British population you will have to get used to the fact that we are going to be doing mainstream programming.' He suggests that '*Bandung* is the type of programme that the people who watch *Newsnight* might watch.' In other words it is not a programme aimed at ethnic minorities, although it is made by such minorities. Dhondy is adamant that 'If blacks were offered *EastEnders*, the *Paul Daniels Magic Show, The Price is Right* or *Black on Black*, I guarantee that 90 per cent of blacks will watch these other shows..... By and large the black audience is pretty similar to the white audience.' He added: 'I know what the Asian population wants, it wants more movie stars and auction shows.' The reason why *Bandung* does not go down so well with his constituency, he argues, is that it 'lacks a black nationalistic identity and that identity is strong in Britain, but I think that it is a lost cause and it is going to die.'

Curiously, for the writer of the only successful multiracial situation comedy, *No Problem,* Dhondy's programming strategy has confused the black working class, as we shall see in the next chapter. Although he has commissioned black popular cultural programmes, such as *Club Mix* or *Movie Mahal*, his programmes are regarded as highbrow and middle class. Dhondy is trying to rectify the serious image of multicultural programmes, and is looking for a new comedy series to replace *No Problem;* is expanding the music and light entertainment side of his remit; and, overall, attempting to put together 'a kind of *Network 8*'. He has, however, a major problem: he knows that Asians want Asian movie-programmes, soap operas and game shows, but on the other hand they want factual programmes that present their community in a favourable light.

One important problem identified by Dhondy is that his realist view of ethnic minorities and television is not shared by many whites, who prefer the romantic nationalistic image which Dhondy abhors: 'white liberals have not yet resolved which side, which faction of blacks to support: the nationalists or the realists. I place myself very firmly in the realist camp.' The over-compensation by white liberals was also picked up by another commissioning editor, who was worried that the channel was becoming overly identified with minorities. 'It is one of the things that annoys me when arguing with the IBA. There are one or two people there who are black first, and everything has to reflect that. They do not understand that in Inverness or Cardiff or Swansea or Bangor or Colwyn Bay — yes — there are some black people but when you are watching your mainstream network TV you really get pissed off at constantly having the problems of England's inner cities thrust down your throat. I don't think the remit should be interpreted as being small groups talking to small groups.' Alan Fountain echoes this; he does not 'particularly like the idea of people talking to themselves.' However, he went on to say that 'if there are important views around which aren't on television, it might alienate people — but it has to be on.'

The fiction editors do not want to fall into the trap of commissioning with specific minorities in mind. Ansorge argues that 'rather than do a programme on racial tensions we would rather do one that had strong themes, and which are strong and unusual fictions.' He went on to echo Dhondy's sentiments: 'If you do a drama for black people my feeling is that the black audience would prefer it to work for a white audience as well.'

Just as most editors feel that the ethnic minorities are better handled as part of society as a whole, rather than in a separate pigeon-hole, so gays are 'normalised'. According to David Rose, 'I think it is best handled as part of society as a whole without someone pointing a finger, putting a spotlight on it.' David Lloyd points out the impossibility of presenting a representative programme on gays. He argues 'The politics of the gay movement are such that it would be impossible to hold together non-proselytising gays and proselytising gays and make an intelligent programme. It would not work, it would not happen.'

Each commissioning editor clearly feels that he or she has a diffuse set of responsibilities to specific minorities, although these are not turned into specific policies. 'Yes, I do feel responsibility in the broad sense', said Thomson, 'I put a lot of pressures on *The Business Exchange* to make sure that within their examples of successful business people they have women and they have blacks. I have never commissioned a programme specifically about or made by these groups. I see my commissioning very much in the traditions of journalism: you stand outside subjects and report them and analyse them and look into them.' This is echoed by Hart-Williams, who said: 'I don't feel that I've got a concrete agenda to do that in a sense, but I think on a personal level in the way that one has to make judgements about one's projects. I think I'm probably likely to move a little more in the direction of a film that comes from a woman or a black director or a gay director. I just feel that there aren't enough black directors in the sense that one is looking for a wider range.'

In the arts, Michael Kustow refuses to sanction the idea that he should commission on the basis of social need rather than aesthetic pleasure; indeed he questions this distinction. He believes that putting on a top black ballet company, like the Dance Theatre of Harlem, is both aesthetic and social. Nevertheless, at a very basic level he argues forcibly that if a production is no good, 'it's just not good. Period. No amount of social rightness will justify my scheduling in that slot'.

Kustow feels that he has a scarce number of spots for the arts, and he cannot sacrifice them to community arts, or anything that is not of the highest artistic ability. At its most basic his philosophy is: 'I want people to see work that will be accomplished.' If, therefore, the rest of his arts output is of an extremely high standard then community art would look ridiculous. 'It is cruel,' Kustow argues, 'to have community ballet following Ballet Rambert.' And just as Kustow judges productions by their artistic quality rather than their social value, so Naomi Sargant argues: 'I have a fairly strong ethical code about only commissioning things that are good enough, and there have not been very many good proposals [in the area of ethnic minority programmes] that are actually shrieking to be commissioned.'

Apart from minority audiences, the channel has always considered itself to be searching out audiences with special interests. When Caroline Thomson started work at the channel she was worried that one of her specialist programmes was, to put it simply, boring. When she expressed this view, however, Jeremy Isaacs explained: 'No, no Caroline you have got to realise that you must have the courage to be boring. I thought that was a wonderful remark. Nowhere else in television would anyone else say to you: "Have the courage to be boring". It is a wonderful thing about working in C4, because no one ever says to you − "you can't do that programme, no one will watch it". No one has ever said that to me since I arrived, and that is staggering.' Isaacs' comment goes to the heart of the matter in some ways. Television has a tendency to be terrified that the viewer might not be interested in a subject for its own sake. Directors and producers, if they have the money, fill every possible gap with music or images in case the audience's attention wavers for an instant. One sees this terror, for instance, in programmes about art. As viewers we are seldom allowed the space simply to look at a picture; there is always some kind a baroque music bumbling away in the background. Isaacs' remark suggests that audiences, particularly specialist audiences, do not necessarily need the trappings of powerful images — the subject matter is sufficient.

The problem with this appeal to specialist interests and the courage to be boring is that if you consistently bore the majority of the population they might turn against you. Peter Ansorge pointed out the channel's dilemma: 'I don't think anyone should embark on a drama thinking that it is only going to appeal to three people in the population – even if it ends up doing so. But, there's a great difference between thinking that and thinking that a success is marked by 10 or 13 million.'

The Channel Four commissioning process takes account of ethnic and sexual minorities, but as this section has shown, it is by no means dominated by them. The one area of special interest we have not yet covered is that of sport, which has been one of the channel's success stories.

## (6) This Sporting Life

Adrian Metcalfe, Commissioning Editor for Sport, moved to Channel Four rather than TVAM 'because it was obviously more interesting (and better for your sleep). The fascination – I mean, that blank sheet of paper.' Metcalfe's filling in of the blank piece of paper has been one of the more interesting developments in British television over the past five years. Although he had to contend with the simple fact that the BBC had most of the big sporting occasions sewn up, his own vision for television sport was more important than the limitations imposed on him by what he could not buy. Sport helped the channel to survive in the tough first six months. Metcalfe suggests that the reason for this was: 'It is difficult to put people off sport. So I feel that in the early days, people felt at least there's something on C4 which feels safe.'

Metcalfe holds to the old-fashioned public service broadcasting ethic that: 'People don't know what they are interested in until you tell them that they are interested'. The way to achieve public interest in a new sport was 'not just to put it on the air, but, to put it on the air in such a way that the public saw it in different ways, come up with different techniques so that they didn't have to work hard to understand it.'

The infectious and insightful nature of Metcalfe's approach can be seen from his description of how to present cricket. Given that many people in the country do not in fact understand the rules of cricket you say to the production company: 'look, sorry to bore you again but nobody's ever told me the rules of cricket. Nobody's ever told me what a leg-break is, what an off-break is. Most people watching do not see the off-side or the leg-side. The commentators say: "Oh, coming in on an off-break here". Why? And what does it mean. Which way is it spinning? How did it get the spin? How is he using the temperature in the air to get that little bit of moisture on it? I don't know, but it you are sitting next to someone who does you suddenly see the incredible tactical plan. When you see that kind of strategy it becomes absorbing. But I don't think that British television comes close to doing it.'

Metcalfe's new approach to special interest sports involved technical breakthroughs ('We started to ask for things that the Saatchi and Saatchi television department would be asking for automatically') and, perhaps more importantly, a re-evaluation of how to present sport to audiences. In particular, it involved not patronising the audience. Metcalfe noted that American football, for instance, which is now virtually synonymous with the channel, was tried by both main channels, but it did not take off because they approached it as if they were 'slumming, in a slightly patronising way'. Metcalfe insists that his companies do not treat the audience as experts nor as fools, but as intelligent adults, capable of understanding and following quite complex rules. 'We do 50 or 60 sports a year. I'd rather have someone who knows about it, who's a reasonable communicator than have Mr Smoothychops in a blazer who gets you on and off the air, but on the other hand his knowledge is a millimetre thick – he doesn't know anymore than you do.'

Metcalfe has another reason for insisting that his producers do not treat sport as a minority interest. 'Sport loses its vitality when run by a patronising, elderly white male club. It is dangerous in some ways because sport is about important values: it is fundametally about being fair, honest, courageous, decent, good and in some ways selfless. It is quite an interesting way for human beings to discover things about themselves. And, I don't like to see it manipulated and packaged.'

Thus far we have dealt with the key issues concerning the mandate – namely, the introduction of new political and cultural voices onto television, the problems of polemical programmes, and the difficulties of dealing with minorities. The channel, of course, is more than an experiment in social democracy, it contains its fair share of feature films, sit coms, drama serials, comedy shows, ballets, opera etc. The problem is: how can such programmes fit in with the channel's commitments to be different?

## (7) That's Entertainment

On November 2nd, 1982, those of us who knew how to had tuned into the new channel and waited with bated breath for the first rush of new, challenging, inventive, innovative programmes: what did we get? A quiz show. This very British approach to opening a TV station (let's not become too excited chaps) is intriguing. It signalled the channel's continuities with the rest of British television before we were allowed to see how it was to be different.

Entertainment was thus embedded in the channel from the first day, but has never seemed to be the channel's primary commitment. Indeed, only around 10 per cent of the channel's budget is spent on entertainment programmes as opposed to nearer 70 per cent at LWT. A question mark could be entered against the very idea of entertainment on an 'alternative' channel. Why produce sit coms when the BBC does them better? Is there room for a soap opera when every channel already has one? The very simple answer to these criticisms is that there is every reason. Popular culture is vitally important to any society and therefore a serious television station has to address this culture in a multitude of ways. It has to do it all, but differently.

Mike Bolland caught the flavour of this when he began as Commissioning Editor for Youth. Bolland built up a group of advisors — everyone from the bass player in the Sex Pistols through to people he met in pubs — and his conclusion was: 'There was no humour that addressed them. Now it's really hard to believe when you think of all four channels — whether it's *Spitting Image*, *The Young Ones*, *Filthy, Rich and Catflap* or *Saturday Live* — but then there was nothing. Humour was one of those things very very high up on the list. The last thing anyone wanted to talk about was unemployment. Most felt that it's bad enough being unemployed without seeing it on TV.'

He realised that to fulfil his commitment to be different he had to discover what made this new generation laugh. The BBC somewhat undermined his ability to do this in that as soon as he signed up *The Comic Strip*, the BBC exercised its option on its various members and *The Young Ones* was born. Being an alternative is difficult when the thing you are alternative to keeps changing.

Bolland and his successor as Commissioning Editor for Entertainment, Seamus Cassidy, are aware that they must constantly stay one step ahead of the competition. Not simply because of the IBA's remit that they cater to different tastes and interests, but also because they feel that their audience is much more demanding. Bolland insists: 'Our audiences are younger and less tolerant than those for ITV and BBC. We operate outside of peak-time so we tailor our entertainment to meet that hour, to meet that audience.' Cassidy notes that he finds it helpful sometimes to think of his audience as 'the Rock and Roll audience, in that it's over thirty years since the birth of Rock and Roll. By and large they are people who have those values rather than the values of the *Paul Daniels Show* or *Terry and June* or *Bob's Full House* or *Bruce's Big Night*. These satisfy a very large number of people and who am I to knock it? But, I don't watch it; a lot of people I know of a very wide range of age and class don't watch it, they want something different and those are the people we are aiming at.' Consequently, Cassidy has lists of things that would be inappropriate for the channel: 'Disco dancing championships, beauty contests, game shows with women with big tits; sit coms that are about antique dealers who live next door to each other called Chip and Dale. Variety specials with dancing girls and staircases.' Summing up his approach, he claims: 'We're not showbiz.'

Although they are not showbiz the channel commissions programmes in every light entertainment genre. The situation comedies have yet to come into their own, and there has yet to be an enormous success like *Monty Python* (or even *The Young Ones*), however, Cassidy argues that there are one or two areas where the channel has made some breakthroughs: its chat shows and revue programmes. According to Cassidy: 'We have taken on the chat show and we've won.' *The Last Resort* and *After Dark* have been innovative and interesting, garnering popular success and critical approval. Another area in which Cassidy claims success is the comic short: '*The Comic Strip* are alone taking on the short comic film for the first time in 20 years.' He went on to say: 'We've made two types of game show our own — *Countdown* and *Treasure Hunt*.' This strategy of taking on genres and trying to present *the* Channel Four version is the result of the demands of a young and discerning audience and the sense that the channel must be different in order to survive. According to Cassidy, 'The sit com is the next one — we will be having a go at that.' He notes that the present thirty minute style of the ITV comedy is 'not really quite right for us or our audience. So I think we have to look outside the established form.'

Cassidy believes that entertainment has an important role to play in the channel. 'I think there have been changes,' he noted, 'I think in some ways we have become smoother and slicker.' He went on to say: 'At the start we were all very taken up with the notion that to be dangerous you had to challenge political consensus alone. It is necessary to challenge political consensus, it's necessary to challenge the idea of balance, and that is something everybody from John Ranelagh to Alan Fountain do, and our current affairs output does that. I think in entertainment we have not shied away from that. Programmes like *the Cornerhouse* takes up issues, *Who Dares Wins* takes up issues, and in its own funny way *The Comic Strip* takes on issues. It is doing it in a different way and is not quite as up-front.'

Bolland is aware that much of the channel's comedy and entertainment comes out of the group of comedians and performers that emerged out of London pubs and clubs in the late seventies and early eighties. And that the audience for those performers is growing older and might well turn into viewers of *Terry and June*. Television consumes ideas to such an extent that yesterday's frightfully daring comedy is tomorrow's crashing bore. Bolland argues: 'The next trick really is to find a new generation of audience and a new generation of performer as well. We are not in the business of going out with a cheque book and buying star names. In a way that financial constraint is a luxury because it means that we have to work even harder at finding the Jules Hollands and the Jonathan Rosses of this world.'

The other main area of entertainment with which the channel is involved is that of drama. *Film on Four* has given the channel an international profile, and the serial *Brookside* has topped the channel's ratings since the first week. Again, the question could be posed why should Channel Four have a soap opera? David Rose, who commissioned it, outlined his and the channel's reasons. 'Clearly with all the minority programmes we were going to be producing, commissioning and transmitting, we also needed to try to build an audience.' The reason he chose *Brookside* reflects the constant need to be different. Phil Redmond, whose production company made the proposal, had a reputation for making no-holds-barred drama serials, which were very contemporary in tone and approach. Secondly, because the channel was required to be innovative in form as well as content, Rose was impressed by the plans to make the programme on location with lightweight cameras, and edited on site. Peter Ansorge, who now has responsibility for drama series, feels that *Brookside* has made an important contribution to changing British television: 'Undoubtedly you wouldn't have had *EastEnders* without *Brookside,* in the way that it tackles certain issues. I would have thought that from the beginning *Brookside* has helped to bring people's awareness to the channel and an audience to the channel that might not otherwise have come to it.'

Rose accepts that the channel's drama output leans toward conventional narratives, conventionally told. However, he argues: 'You cannot shift the monolith of television drama or television fiction overnight and the same applies almost anywhere in television. You can take away old building blocks but you've got to find something to put in their place. Drama is about ideas and writing and performance through direction.' Good one-off narrative dramas, then, is what Rose is primarily aiming for, and the channel has been extremely successful in this area.

Given the channel's commitment to be different, it is important to note that its coverage of the arts has been consistently challenging. Michael Kustow, the Commissioning Editor for the Arts, has written a detailed account of his understanding of how Channel Four's arts policy differs from that of the other channels in his book *One in Four*(2). In summation he argues: 'I start from the position that what I am trying to do is not arts coverage, nor the arts documentary in the regularly-signalled series like *The South Bank Show, Omnibus* or *Arena.* What I'm seeking is art television, not simply the arts on television: television that is shaped and altered by the insights and practice of art and artists.' In order to do this he is encouraging collaboration between different types of artist: for instance choreographers and editors, painters and directors. He is aware of the channel's responsibility in acting as a kind of second Arts Council and directly funds productions which would not otherwise have taken place. This makes 'playwrights, choreographers and composers think seriously about television, as more than a means of displaying a pre-existent work.'

## (8) A Question of Sex

One of the problems which haunts the channel's fiction output has been that of sex and censorship. Somehow, as we will see in the next chapter, it has been embroiled in debate about the depiction of sex on television since day one. And yet, according to John Ellis, the producer of a programme about Brazilian cinema which fell victim to one of these debates, the depiction of sexual activity is never a problem on Channel Four. Ellis claims that Jeremy Isaacs is essentially happier fighting liberal battles with the censors than in struggling to allow the channel to give voice to difficult political issues. When discussing Isaacs' support for the banned *Visions* programme about Brazilian cinema, he argued: 'Sex is a pre-eminently Isaacs-supportable thing. Had we as a production company been doing a programme about the structure of the Conservative Party it would have been very different. I think that's the problem: Jeremy is very hot on issues of morality. Had we been doing a programme on the structure of the Conservative Party, I think that we would have found our support from C4 rather less.'

Reflecting in the *New Statesman* about his experience as an independent producer Ellis wrote: 'There is a wider battle for censorship that should be fought now, and Channel Four and its independent suppliers are in the best position to fight it. The IBA conceives its role as a censor entirely in terms of vetting individual programmes, and where it deems necessary, banning or altering some of them. This is not its job. As a regulatory body, the IBA should be putting its primary emphasis on overseeing the whole of television output, rather than interfering with this or that detail.'

Ellis, however, also stressed the difficulties Channel Four faced in taking up a case like the censorship of his programme with the IBA: 'Independent suppliers to Channel Four are more able to create a press furore by virtue of being independent rather than salaried employees. Channel Four actively encourages independent producers to publicise 'their' cause but the necessary back-up from Channel Four was not forthcoming. No press release was produced on either occasion that the *Visions* programme was withdrawn from the schedules. It seems that the channel as an institution is abandoning individual issues of censorship to its independent suppliers, reserving its own position for the confrontation with the IBA that many see as inevitable.

'There are two flaws with this strategy. First, even the best-equipped independent does not have the press contacts and information systems that Channel Four has, and journalists do get the impression, from the channel's official silence, that perhaps the producers are spinning a yarn. So the coverage that independents do manage to get is less than it could be.' He concluded that as a result of this death by a thousand cuts Channel Four's ability to fight the IBA was declining: 'The IBA is gaining ground, producing an ever narrowing definition of what is possible on Channel Four. They want to subject it to the same rules as are applied to ITV, despite the different audiences of the two channels. So as the IBA is fighting the war of attrition, when the day dawns that Channel Four does decide to stand and fight, it will find it has less room to manoeuvre than it might imagine.'(3)

Although Ellis has his own axe to grind, we cannot discount this view of the channel. Indeed, John Ranelagh, who has been with the channel since it began broadcasting, argues forcibly: 'When we did cause a stir, it was with programmes that were accused of offending against good taste and decency: *One in Five; Scum; Jubilee; Sebastiane*. It is not that programmes that offend against good taste or public feeling should not be shown. What is wrong is that our budgets, energies and talents have been concentrated, as the result of a founding interpretation of our remit, on programmes that deal with subjects of little importance to the future of people's lives. Instead of applying ourselves, as we have, to seeing how many "fucks" we can get away with or how many explicit homosexual films we can present, we could have interpreted the requirements to validate hard-hitting investigations of matters that will vitally effect our future as a nation.'

There is certainly a difference in the channel's attitude to sexual and political controversy. The former provokes one long collective sigh of exasperation in the channel as it has to deal with yet another complaint from the IBA; the latter, on the other hand, greatly worries the channel, and provokes it on occasion, as we see in the next section, to withdraw programmes which Isaacs or the board consider unacceptable.

It is important, though, to understand the depths of Isaacs' feelings about censorship. He is not a member of the dirty mac brigade, and his struggle to show films and programmes which depict explicit sex is precisely about the struggle to open television to politically challenging programmes. It is perhaps a little cliched to say so but there is a generation gap between Isaacs and Ellis. For liberals of Isaacs' generation, battle was enjoined against the Lord Chamberlain's office, which censored the theatre, in order to allow the exploration of controversial issues, whether political or moral. Just as the overall gains in freedom of expression began with the loosening of the sexual stays, so any attempt to re-impose restrictions is seen by Isaacs as a reduction in the total freedom in British culture. To put it crudely (in both senses), in Isaacs' eyes there is no difference between defending the right to say 'fuck' and the right to criticise the government.

He is worried that these gains are being eroded as the Government's censorship juggernaut rolls on.

It happens to be a paradox of our time, that a government which is practising, in some regards an economic liberalism – even if part of it is simply turning public monopolies into private monopolies – but nevertheless which does preach, and try to practise some degree of economic competition, should also apparently be yearning for a sort of centralised control in broadcasting. I say apparently because I would like to believe that any British government would think long and hard before imposing any statutory control, or indeed repression. Of course, all Prime Ministers in their dark moments, or their angry moments, or their panicky moments think they'll cut these blighters down a peg or two, but I would hate to think that opinion has so shifted in this country, that it is necessary now to say — we've had enough of the ideas of the sixties and therefore let's do without them. Let's go back to the Lord Chamberlain, let's have censorship of books, let's, put something back in place of the British Board of Film Censors, let's tell broadcasting that its gone too far. I heard Hanif Kureish (author of *My Beautiful Launderette*) the other day on a Channel Four programme, *UK Late*, moaning and groaning about repression and censorship, and how wonderful it would be if we could do and say the things that were done in the 60s. He doesn't know what he is talking about. In the sixties I couldn't put a homosexual on a respectable current affairs programme without blacking out their face, and the idea that *My Beautiful Launderette* could have been made either by the British film industry, such as it was then not, or by the British television industry is absolute balls. We've got to hang on to these gains. I think that the fundamental argument is what liberalism delivers, not that its destroying us, its making us a better place.

The difference between Isaacs and Ellis (as a representative of the new left) is that like the blind men and the elephant, they approach freedom from different angles. Neither are de-regulators (unlike neo-liberals such as David Graham of Diverse Productions) however, as a result of his struggles in the 1960s, Isaacs feels that the freedom to broadcast sexually explicit material in context is the basis for more general freedoms in television. Ellis, on the other hand, who inherited the freedoms of the late 1960s is more concerned about television being opened up to voices from the margins of British politics and culture.

Isaacs' stand on sex on television has to be seen in this wider debate about the nature of freedom and responsibility. Further evidence for this can be adduced from the fact that Isaacs, unlike many people in the current censorious climate, uncouples sex and violence. In his announcement of the Special Discretion Required symbol, he explicitly attacked the connection between the sex and violence, indeed he claimed that 'Channel Four has a prejudice against violence' (*The London Standard* 14.08.86). Although Isaacs argued the liberal position with such fervour, he is not averse to self-censorship when he deems it necessary. The Channel Four series, *Sex with Paula*, which was due to be screened early in 1987 was postponed at Isaacs' request because, in the words of one of the commissioning editors, 'the whole country had gone AIDS crazy'. The series had been heavily trailed in a book of the same name which had been serialised in the *Sun*, and Issacs was worried that the programmes would not receive a sensible reception in such a highly charged atmosphere (at the time of writing, the series has yet to be shown).

The issue of sexual censorship is important then as part of the liberal viewpoint which C4 represents. However, the commissioning editors in the channel will not sanction controversy for the sake of it. David Rose, Senior Commissioning Editor for Fiction, and the man responsible in large part for the success of *Film on Four*, acknowledged that he encourages self-censorship, but insisted that films need not be watered down as a result: 'Having been in broadcasting as long as one has, I know the BBC guidelines, I know the IBA guidelines and I know the audience's responses to certain kinds of language. And I certainly on occasions encourage writers of productions not to use certain words. I don't call that censorship. I believe that it can be an equally good and effective piece of drama without that language..... But, I certainly don't want to go so far that it's all watered down and you know completely unconvincing, unbelievable. I think one's got to strike a balance.'

The current difficulty, according to Rose, is that he is not called upon very often to defend the rights of his writers and directors. He feels that writers are responding to the current censorious climate by cutting things themselves: self-censorship begins at home. Rose feels that the censorship lobby 'creates a climate which means that from a blank piece of paper that people perhaps are being a little more reticent in what they are doing, what they are saying. In the writing and in the direction maybe people are saying "Oh I won't write that scene because I don't think it'll get through" and that doesn't make for the greatest free expression that the audience deserves.'

The fuss over the Derek Jarman films, *Sebastiane* and *Jubilee*, demonstrates that in order to fufil the mandate to be different, while respecting the viewer's right not to be shocked, the channel would have to be inventive. What it came up with was the Special Discretion Required symbol, the red triangle, which is universally praised by the public as a major extension of the viewer's rights. Liz Forgan, Deputy Director of Programmes, points out the importance of SDR to the channel.

> I really think that the restrictions on television about swearing and moral judgments are absurd, but I have every sympathy with people who don't want to see bad language on television and we should do everything in our power to enable them to avoid it if they want to. That's why I am actually in favour of the red triangle. Although it does deface the screen, I see no other way of keeping your pledge to those people so that the minute they turn it on they can see that it contains language or material of the sort that may offend, and they can exercise their rights to turn it off. I think that is a perfectly reasonable obligation to ask us to have.

In this section we have shown that the channel's struggles with the IBA over sex and swearing are more important, at least in Isaacs' mind, than they are given credit for. These struggles represent the channel's battle for freedom of expression for all groups. Although, in reality, there is no more sex on C4 than on ITV, the feeling lingers that the channel has pushed back the boundaries of what is acceptable, and has fulfilled its mandatory responsibility to be different. However, the important question raised at the beginning of the commentary concerning the extension of freedom of expression to political groups is an important one. Does sex now stand for freedom? Or, is the attempt to extend the limits of what is permissible in the depiction of sex a case of wasted and misdirected energy? Is there any point in struggling with the IBA, the Government or the National Viewers and Listeners Association, in order to show a film about homosexuality, while at the same time withdrawing films about plastic bullets and trade union conservativism.

## (9) Style Wars

In its remit, Channel Four is required to innovate in form as well as content. This problem of making a breakthrough in the way in which to present the arts is reflected throughout the channel. Formal breakthroughs have been few and far between. Mike Bolland recalled: 'The thing that really frustrated me when I first came here was things like *Whatever You Want* and *The Tube* were actually quite easy and a lot of content was quite new, but there was very little of the innovative style everyone was talking about. And then, I went out and knocked on doors which is how we came up with *Alter Image*'

In the early days on Channel Four some programmes seemed to make a virtue out of a chaotic visual style. In some ways, as Peter Montagnon notes, this was quite endearing compared to the predictability of the rest of television. 'I thought it had an engagingly amateurish look, hugely interesting but enormously unpolished. I think the nice thing was that the BBC had become polished to the point of mannerism, really rather uninteresting in a sense that one could predict by reading the *Radio Times* what a programme would be like. I defy anyone to predict from the *TV Times* what Channel Four's programmes will be like.' Caroline Thomson, who was at the BBC when C4 began, felt something similar: 'I did feel the emphasis in the BBC was far too heavily on reporting conventional views of what was interesting. If you tried to get them to do a programme about pension fund investment everyone would look at you and say — that sounds really boring, where do you get the pictures?'

David Graham feels, though, that amateurism can work against the channel. 'I just don't like the idea that C4 is the experimental channel because it seems to marginalise C4 and I don't think it's good for you constantly to make marginal television. It leads to bad attitudes and self-consciousness.' There is a similar feeling among those commissioning editors with responsibility for introducing new forms of television. Alan Fountain notes that 'People who offer material often appear either to have not thought about it at all or they have thought about it so much that it is just like the rest of television. The difficult thing is to make something that worked on television which is sufficiently different, which is often quite minimal, to actually attract your attention as being different and interesting, engaging, but not 'experimental'. That is the area in a way that I have got most interested in in some ways, which I think is the most difficult, it demands a lot of skill to do it.'

The style of early programmes, in particular *Whatever You Want*, turned out to represent the end of the 1970s rather than a new approach for the 1980s. That kind of anarchy was represented by Keith Allen who was, in Mike Bolland's words, 'Mr. Angry himself — Mr. Extremely Angry, Mr. Very Funny and Mr. Very Almost Impossible To Work With.' Most of the people involved in *Whatever You Want* felt that, as Bolland says, 'in retrospect it was just ill thought out. It wasn't that anyone was saying, look Keith, you can't say this but they were saying, look Keith, you have got to think about how you say it. I don't know that Keith and I would ever agree on it now. He may look back on it as a big joke.'

Seamus Cassidy was a researcher on *Whatever You Want*. He felt that it had had its day by the early 1980s. He suggests, 'I think that something quite as rough and ready as *Whatever You Want* has had its day and it actually came out of the seventies. Now we are in the eighties and a number of editors and television professionals have looked at the impact of pop promos and commercials. You have people saying we should be learning from the visual literacy of those commercials — how to tell a story very fast and really use images — and I think there is a lot to be said for that.' John Cummins, the Commisioning Editor for Youth, places it even earlier: '*Whatever You Want* was muddled sixties sloppy thinking; it thought it was furiously novel but access television only serves dozens of people — those who appear on it or make it — it doesn't serve millions of people. It's about the programme-maker rather than the audience. One isn't saying let's go number crunching, but one is saying that television is about mass audiences being served either by interest or by intellect or by entertainment or by recreation or whatever.'

Bolland, it should be noted, agrees with this estimation in some ways: 'It would have to be different — yes — it would be great to have something like that again but obviously the times are changing — here we are, we have been with the same administration the whole time we have been on air, the whole political consensus has shifted and people are now into buying British Gas shares and Telecom. There is a shift. I think the danger is that because *Network 7* is so London-based the shift there epitomises the North/South divide. I know that's an over-sold over-simplification but I fear that's one of the things that may be happening.' '*Network 7*', Bolland adds, 'is Yuppie-anarchism. It is very neatly controlled — it's filofax anarchy.'

Marc Lucas of *Alter Image* summed up his frustration at those who refused to accept that television should attempt to break visual conventions: 'It's like the "Bricks in the Tate" argument, you know, — what is this fucking rubbish, we are not having it here. You can't get it right the first time, yes some of it was deeply boring, and it continues to be deeply boring! Channel Four has made a lot of mistakes. In a way, they've a tendency to make their mistakes sometimes known, whereas other stations you wouldn't notice it. Channel Four ought to be a lot more adventurous but there again that is in comparison to what exists on the other channels.' Despite his desire to be adventurous, he also feels a 'responsibility to be accessible − I think we want to make programmes that people want to watch.' This echoes Fountain who wants his strand to 'make something which works on television, which is different and engaging but which is not experimental (for its own sake).' He wants those who produce for his strand to push the boat out while keeping sight of the shore.

## Conclusion

We have tried to show in this chapter something of how the commissioning editors responded to the challenges of the mandate by re-interpreting their role. The decisive shift to editorial as opposed to access television, which took place in the early years of the channel, is now working its way through in perhaps unexpected ways. The development of the idea of thesis-led as opposed to opinionated factual programming and the shift away from being dominated by the need to service minorities and be experimental for the sake of it, will be interpreted by those who respect the traditions of British broadcasting as an extension and development of that tradition, and by those on both the left and right, who perhaps expected more, as a failure.

**References**
1. Dahrendorf R., *On Britain*. University of Chicago Press, 1982.
2. Kustow M., *One in Four*. Faber and Faber, 1987.
3. Ellis J., *It's Not What You See, It's How Often You See It*. New Statesman, 4 October, 1987.

# Chapter 3

# The Right to Choose:
# Channel Four and the Public

## (1) Introduction

In some ways it is difficult to characterise the relationship between Channel Four and the public. The channel stands for something more than the sum of its parts: not so much a television station; more a social experiment. In a fascinating and curious way the public appears to believe in Channel Four the way that it believes in some abstract concept like 'truth'. People continue to tell lies despite holding 'truth' to be an ultimate value, and they want Channel Four to be committed to the culturally and politically disenfranchised even though the majority will never watch such programmes. Furthermore, the public's perception of the cultural and political responsibilities of television frames its analysis of the role of Channel Four. In a very profound way, the public believes in the channel as an expression of the need for television to challenge, renovate and, occasionally, disturb. In his capacity of viewer someone may never watch experimental or challenging television, but as a citizen the viewer is committed to the existence of such programmes.

Our research, which is based on forty-four discussion groups and a national survey (see Technical Appendix), demonstrates that Channel Four provokes insightful and wide-ranging debates about the moral and cultural obligations of television. The quality of the audience's arguments should disabuse ideologues of Right and Left of their elitist beliefs about the passivity of the public. Indeed, above all, this research shows that there is a very considerable desire on the part of the population to be treated as active contributors to the process of regulating television; and, in particular, to be regarded as adults, capable of making rational choices for both themselves and their children.

The most important plumbline against which to measure the success of Channel Four is what we call its mandate: namely, the responsibility of the channel to experiment with programmes exposing the public to new tastes, new cultures and new interests. Fundamentally, we have established that the majority of the population understands and approves of this mandate. This is exemplified by the support given to minority programmes. When asked to evaluate the channel's policy in this area, around one-quarter of the population 'strongly approved' and a further two-fifths were generally supportive. Most importantly, only one person in twenty strongly disapproved of the channel's mandatory commitments (see Table 1). What are the roots of this support?

Three basic themes emerged in our research to shed light on attitudes to Channel Four. Most importantly, there is a profound ambiguity within British society about ethnic and sexual minorities. Although most people want to be regarded as fair and just – our second theme – their fears about alien cultures and sexuality affect their judgement about the rights of free speech. Finally, worry about the dilution of Britain's cultural integrity vies with a realistic (if not embracing) acceptance of the idea that Britain is a multi-ethnic society. These themes may sound somewhat grandiose for a discussion of television, particularly in the light of the recent attempts by some Conservative backbenchers to reduce broadcasting to the status of soap powder, but the British public, as we have shown in our previous study, *Invisible Citizens,** evaluates television according to criteria drawn from its attitudes to the Common Weal. It is committed to what we loosely call the values of public service broadcasting – in particular, that television should serve the public interest and not simply deliver audiences to advertisers or any other interest group.

This new research confirms the findings of *Invisible Citizens:* nine out of ten people believe that television should inform and educate people, as well as entertain. But, more importantly perhaps, a large section of the population believes that information is the most important service that television provides (see Tables 2 and 3).

Although they tell us that the public has general commitments to public service television, these questions are a bit like asking people if they are against sin. In order to gain a deeper understanding of what people mean when they say that television should inform and educate, we gave them the chance to build their own television system. They were offered four channels and asked to produce a two-channel system from which they would gain most benefit, and one which would contribute most to the country (see Figure 1).

*David Morrison, *Invisible Citizens: British Public Opinion on the Future of Broadcasting.* John Libbey & Co. London, 1987.

## TABLE 1

As you may know Channel 4 has a policy of allowing minority groups and people not normally seen on television to state their case. How much do you approve or disapprove of this policy?

BASE: ALL

| | Total | SEX | | AGE | | | | | CLASS | | | | ETHNIC ORIGIN | | | TV TOLERANCE | |
| | | Male | Fe-male | 16-20 | 21-24 | 25-34 | 35-54 | 55+ | AB | C1 | C2 | DE | White | Afro-Carib | Asian | Toler-rant | In-Toler-rant |
|---|---|---|---|---|---|---|---|---|---|---|---|---|---|---|---|---|---|
| TOTAL | 974 | 431 | 543 | 109 | 57 | 149 | 334 | 325 | 199 | 235 | 256 | 284 | 948 | 117 | 119 | 376 | 588 |
| Approve a lot | 27% | 29% | 25% | 29% | 26% | 30% | 29% | 23% | 39% | 27% | 24% | 21% | 26% | 59% | 52% | 38% | 21% |
| Approve a little | 41% | 40% | 42% | 42% | 40% | 38% | 43% | 41% | 37% | 45% | 38% | 44% | 42% | 25% | 29% | 42% | 41% |
| Neither | 16% | 15% | 16% | 16% | 19% | 20% | 13% | 16% | 12% | 11% | 20% | 18% | 15% | 5% | 9% | 13% | 17% |
| Disapprove a little | 8% | 9% | 8% | 11% | 7% | 9% | 7% | 9% | 7% | 9% | 9% | 8% | 8% | 3% | 3% | 2% | 12% |
| Disapprove a lot | 5% | 4% | 5% | 1% | 4% | 3% | 5% | 6% | 3% | 3% | 7% | 5% | 5% | 1% | — | 0% | 7% |
| Don't know | 3% | 3% | 4% | 1% | 4% | 1% | 4% | 6% | 4% | 4% | 3% | 4% | 4% | 7% | 6% | 5% | 3% |

77

## TABLE 2

How much, if at all, do you think television should aim to inform people about news and current affairs?

BASE: ALL

| | Total | TV VIEWING Light 1-14 | Med 15-27 | Heavy 28+ | C4 VIEWING Light 1-7 | Med 8-14 | Heavy 15+ | CHANNEL FOR SELF W | X | Y | Z | SOCIAL TOLERANCE Tolerant | In-toler-ant | TV ACTIVE Crime | Moral-ity | Swear-ing | PSB | TV TOLERANCE Toler-ant | In-toler-ant |
|---|---|---|---|---|---|---|---|---|---|---|---|---|---|---|---|---|---|---|---|
| TOTAL | 974 | 337 | 267 | 348 | 407 | 297 | 207 | 816 | 569 | 257 | 240 | 432 | 542 | 93 | 124 | 312 | 269 | 376 | 588 |
| A great deal | 45% | 50% | 46% | 39% | 46% | 42% | 47% | 46% | 46% | 31% | 53% | 43% | 46% | 45% | 48% | 46% | 50% | 44% | 45% |
| A fair amount | 47% | 43% | 45% | 53% | 44% | 52% | 47% | 46% | 47% | 57% | 41% | 48% | 46% | 47% | 44% | 46% | 44% | 49% | 46% |
| A little | 7% | 6% | 8% | 8% | 9% | 6% | 6% | 7% | 6% | 11% | 6% | 8% | 7% | 8% | 7% | 7% | 6% | 6% | 8% |
| Not at all | 0% | – | 1% | – | – | 0% | – | 0% | 0% | 0% | – | 0% | 0% | – | 1% | 0% | 0% | – | 0% |
| Don't know | 1% | 1% | 0% | 0% | 1% | 0% | – | 0% | 1% | 1% | 0% | 1% | 1% | – | 1% | – | – | 1% | 0% |

## TABLE 3

Which do you think is the most important thing for television to do: to inform, to entertain, or to educate?

BASE: ALL

| | Total | TV VIEWING Light 1-14 | Med 15-27 | Heavy 28+ | C4 VIEWING Light 1-7 | Med 8-14 | Heavy 15+ | CHANNEL FOR SELF W | X | Y | Z | SOCIAL TOLERANCE Tolerant | In-toler-ant | TV ACTIVE Crime | Moral-ity | Swear-ing | PSB | TV TOLERANCE Toler-ant | In-toler-ant |
|---|---|---|---|---|---|---|---|---|---|---|---|---|---|---|---|---|---|---|---|
| TOTAL | 974 | 337 | 267 | 348 | 407 | 297 | 207 | 816 | 569 | 257 | 240 | 432 | 542 | 93 | 124 | 312 | 269 | 376 | 588 |
| Inform | 28% | 33% | 29% | 22% | 29% | 25% | 29% | 29% | 28% | 19% | 35% | 29% | 27% | 30% | 37% | 29% | 33% | 27% | 28% |
| Entertain | 46% | 37% | 50% | 52% | 45% | 50% | 42% | 45% | 48% | 60% | 32% | 45% | 46% | 42% | 39% | 42% | 40% | 46% | 46% |
| Educate | 14% | 14% | 12% | 16% | 15% | 12% | 14% | 14% | 14% | 11% | 20% | 12% | 17% | 18% | 18% | 15% | 14% | 13% | 15% |
| Can't pick one | 12% | 16% | 9% | 10% | 11% | 13% | 14% | 12% | 11% | 10% | 13% | 14% | 10% | 10% | 6% | 13% | 13% | 14% | 11% |

## Figure 1

| (1) Channel W (Mixed) | (2) Channel X (Specialist) | (3) Channel Y (Entertainment) | (4) Channel Z (Minority) |
|---|---|---|---|
| News | Sports only or | Situation | Ethnic |
| Soap | News only or |   Comedies | Trade Unions |
|   Operas | Films only or | Soap Operas | Business |
| Chat Shows | Music only or | Game Shows | Hobbies |
| Religious | Children's only | Chat Shows | Specialist |
|   Programmes | Current Affairs | | Women's |
| Sports | | |   Programmes |
| Plays | | | Crafts |
| Feature Films | | | |
| Nature Programmes | | | |
| Travel Shows | | | |
| Documentaries | | | |

The majority of the population opts for a system with a mass appeal channel – which has programmes in which everyone might be interested – and a minority channel – which appeals to those elements in each of us which differentiate us from our neighbours. Although a large proportion of the public wants champagne, in the form of feature films, sports and drama, and will presumably pay the premium price for such programmes, it prefers the staple diet of more solid fare offered by the mainstream channel. Channel W, which is similar to BBC1 or ITV, is nominated as the most important by the vast majority of people (84 per cent), followed by Channel X, the specialist channel (58 per cent), Channel Y, which is populist entertainment (26 per cent), and, finally, Channel Z, aimed at minority and special interests (25 per cent).

People are very aware of the difference between their personal pleasure and the public interest, as can be seen from the rise in the proportion of people nominating Channel Z as best for the population as a whole rather than for themselves: 'Z' increases from 25 per cent to 35 per cent, whereas Channel X drops from 58 to 42 per cent. The proportion of the population which chooses Channel Y for the country as a whole, as well as for themselves, does not vary.

Fewer than three in ten television viewers do not value public service television. Indications as to the social composition of the anti public service broadcasting viewers can be gleaned from the social structure of those who chose Channel Y. These people are mainly older, working class women, who spend a great deal of time watching mass entertainment television: 73 per cent of those who chose 'Y' were heavy television users, 40 per cent were over fifty-five, 44 per cent were working class, and, finally, 68 per cent were women. These viewers, it would seem, are inclined to regard television mainly as a mass entertainment medium, and are disinclined to accept its role in differentiating tastes or interests. It should be noted though that Channel Z also attracts cross-class support — around one quarter of those who nominated the minorities channel were working class — therefore one should be wary of any simplistic explanation of taste which assumes that the working class would be happy with a reduced television service, presided over by 'Wizard of Oz' Rupert Murdoch (see Table 4).

Although the British public grasps the political and cultural importance of television one should not romanticise or idealise the television audience (any more than one should imagine that every TV executive or politician is motivated by public, rather than self, interest). There are many harsh social realities underlying the surface commitments. In particular, our research shows that the British are deeply ambivalent in their attitudes to minorities. Most wish to see themselves as fair-minded people and, at a surface level, they are. However, when asked to translate general statements which approve of Channel Four and public service television into concrete behaviour, many tensions and ambiguities emerge. General approval of minority and experimental programming breaks down when people think that these programmes might invade 'their' television time.

Our discussion groups demonstrate that public debate about television is concerned with two main questions: what is television for? and what effects does it have on behaviour and attitudes? Those who believe that television should mainly be used to entertain are deeply antagonistic toward the idea that it should be used as a means of giving disenfranchised or specialist groups a voice. On the other hand, those who evaluate television according to its contribution to the wider public good are deeply committed to the extension of television's concern with developing and extending the public's knowledge of the world. Similarly, those who think that television undermines the social and moral fabric of British culture are extremely unhappy about the idea of specialist or non-entertainment television. They want television contained and constrained in order to prevent it effecting change in people's lives.

Our survey examined the intensity and generality of these attitudes among the population as a whole. Its most important finding concerns the level of the public's tolerance of what appears on television. This is particularly important in the light of television's panic over the Hungerford killings in 1987 — when many programmes were not shown due to 'public' sensibilities. Above all, this reaction demonstrated that despite the many studies that consistently undermine any simple causal connection between violent behaviour and TV, judgements about TV violence, sex, censorship and political bias continue to be made on the basis of scant knowledge of the public's views, often drawn from the telephone calls from 'Outraged of Tunbridge Wells' and tabloid journalism.

## TABLE 4

If you could only have 2 of the 4 stations, which two would you choose....?

BASE: ALL

| | Total | SEX | | AGE | | | | | CLASS | | | | CHILDREN | | | ETHNIC ORGIN | | | |
|---|---|---|---|---|---|---|---|---|---|---|---|---|---|---|---|---|---|---|---|
| | | Male | Fe-male | 16-20 | 21-24 | 25-34 | 35-54 | 55+ | AB | C1 | C2 | DE | U5 | 5-15 | None | White | Afro-carib | Asian | Miss C4 a lot |
| TOTAL | 974 | 431 | 543 | 109 | 57 | 149 | 334 | 325 | 199 | 235 | 256 | 284 | 124 | 209 | 693 | 948 | 117 | 119 | 158 |
| **To give you the best service** | | | | | | | | | | | | | | | | | | | |
| Channel W | 84% | 80% | 87% | 79% | 86% | 89% | 86% | 80% | 91% | 85% | 84% | 77% | 89% | 87% | 82% | 84% | 76% | 85% | 85% |
| Channel X | 58% | 63% | 55% | 63% | 63% | 50% | 60% | 58% | 67% | 61% | 57% | 51% | 53% | 57% | 59% | 59% | 38% | 39% | 57% |
| Channel Y | 26% | 19% | 32% | 28% | 25% | 36% | 17% | 31% | 10% | 21% | 30% | 40% | 31% | 26% | 26% | 26% | 25% | 23% | 25% |
| Channel Z | 25% | 29% | 21% | 22% | 26% | 19% | 30% | 22% | 26% | 26% | 23% | 24% | 22% | 24% | 25% | 24% | 56% | 50% | 26% |
| Don't know | 2% | 3% | 1% | 3% | — | 1% | 3% | 1% | 2% | 2% | 1% | 2% | 2% | 1% | 2% | 2% | 2% | 1% | 1% |
| **To give the best service for the population as a whole** | | | | | | | | | | | | | | | | | | | |
| Channel W | 86% | 84% | 88% | 88% | 91% | 93% | 87% | 81% | 86% | 88% | 88% | 83% | 93% | 88% | 85% | 86% | 81% | 85% | 85% |
| Channel X | 42% | 46% | 38% | 31% | 44% | 39% | 42% | 46% | 44% | 42% | 42% | 40% | 36% | 38% | 43% | 42% | 33% | 37% | 41% |
| Channel Y | 28% | 26% | 30% | 28% | 14% | 32% | 25% | 33% | 25% | 28% | 28% | 32% | 30% | 28% | 29% | 29% | 27% | 28% | 30% |
| Channel Z | 35% | 36% | 35% | 47% | 51% | 33% | 36% | 29% | 36% | 32% | 36% | 37% | 35% | 39% | 34% | 34% | 54% | 49% | 40% |
| Don't know | 2% | 2% | 2% | 1% | — | 1% | 3% | 3% | 3% | 3% | 2% | 2% | 2% | 2% | 2% | 2% | 1% | 1% | — |

The difficulty with the TV sex and violence debate is that it takes place on the wrong intellectual terrain. Instead of arguing about the effects of violence on television, we should be exploring the level of people's tolerance towards experiences which may disquiet them, but which nonetheless they feel should be explored. Until the connection between television and violence or prejudice can be conclusively demonstrated, we must take seriously the public's attitudes to the limits of tolerance. Most people want to be responsible for the choices that they make about what to watch, and most want to be responsible in their choice. But they do want choice.

The new debate about television must take place around an understanding of what the public means by responsibility and tolerance. We must appreciate what shapes and moulds social and television tolerance. The two are not identical: the former may feed television tolerance but the latter has a very distinctive and separate existence. Television tolerance is not simply a liberal virtue. For instance, those who support anti-racism, and who we would consider socially tolerant on every index are, as we show below, deeply worried by the appearance of avowedly racist programmes on television. They will not tolerate those expressing views diametrically opposed to values which they hold dear. On the other hand, even those who hold racist views have no wish to see those views forcibly expressed by political groups on television: they are consistent in their television intolerance.

We constructed an index of social tolerance by examining four aspects of social life where the public is called upon to be tolerant. Firstly, the acceptance of public demonstrations by various controversial groups; secondly, attitudes to the presentation of religion in schools; thirdly, attitudes to Britain as a muti-racial society; and, finally, acceptance of the contravention of social mores and cultural propriety. Out of these various components we gained a strong sense of what the British public regarded as the legitimate expression of public debate. We also developed an index of television tolerance by asking the public which morally or politically contentious groups it would accept on television.

Television tolerance is the thread running through this study. It enables us to understand how people's general attitudes to political and sexual balance, social and cultural minorities and censorship relate to their views of Channel Four. At its simplest, the higher people come on the index of television and social tolerance, the more likely they are to appreciate Channel Four. However, while there is a measure of unanimity in positive attitudes to Channel Four, there remains much ambiguity when one picks away at those attitudes. It is to these ambiguities that we now turn.

## (2) Channel Four: An Image Problem?

There are two sets of attitudes to Channel Four; the first based on it's distinctiveness within British television and the second on the question of political and social balance within the channel's output (see Technical Appendix). These attitudes emerged out of the statistical work which we did with our discussion groups, where we asked respondents to indicate their level of agreement with a set of twenty-six statements, representing a range of issues about censorship, political balance, programme-variety, sex, and so on: for example, 'I like programme makers to make their political position clear' (see Technical Appendix).

The answers to the various statements were combined in such a way that four types of viewer emerged:

1: The Committed
1 – Like the way C4 is run
2 – C4 should show programmes made by homosexual groups
3 – Documentaries need not show both sides of a story
4 – Without C4 black people would not have a voice on British television

2: The Middle Britons
1 – Like the way C4 is run
2 – Neutral about programmes made by and/or for homosexuals
3 – Producers and presenters should not make their political positions clear
4 – Documentaries need not show both sides of an argument

3: The Unconvinced
1 – C4 is badly run
2 – C4 should not show programmes about homosexuality
3 – Documentaries should always show both sides of the argument
4 – Programme makers should not make their political positions clear

4: The Unreconstructed
1 – C4 caters for trendy lefties
2 – C4 should not show programmes made by homosexual groups
3 – Black people already have enough access on British television
4 – Programme makers should not make their political positions clear

(See Appendix 2 for cluster and factor analysis)

Around one-third of respondents had strong feelings about the channel: half of these – The Committed – loved it, the other half – The Unreconstructed – hated it. The basis for these strong opinions appears to be the channel's commitment to minorities and to assertive, opinionated television. It is intriguing to note that it is possible to approve of the channel without being at all committed to what the channel stands for. The Middle Britons, so called because of their desire to occupy the middle ground, appreciate the channel without accepting the idea that television should be radical or assertive.

assertive. Although they are prepared to go some way with the idea that documentaries can present a one-sided story, they continue to hold that programme-makers should be politically neutral. Furthermore, their attitude to homosexuals which, as we shall see, is the touchstone of tolerance, remains guarded.

The Unreconstructed are not quite as intractably wedded to their views as the statistical analysis makes them appear. Perhaps the most useful function of research with discussion groups is that through structured conversation qualifications are introduced into people's statements. In the Channel Four groups, positions which were stated forcibly in questionnaires were often moderated in discussion. When people have to explain why they hold an opinion the paradoxes, inconsistencies and qualifications in their arguments emerge; furthermore, often respondents will modify their judgement in the light of further thought. For this reason, the group discussions about C4 reveal a greater leaning towards the middle ground and a small rump which hates the channel and everything for which it stands.

The discussion groups reveal four images of Channel Four, the axis of which bisects the viewing population according to its attitudes to the channel's programming strategies. Broadly the groups consist of: (1) those who like C4 because it is different from the rest of British television;(2) those who dislike C4 because it is different from the rest of British television; (3) those who like C4 because it is the same as the rest of British television; and (4) those who dislike C4 because it is the same as the rest of British television. Each image is composed of many elements and it is to these that we now turn (see Table 5).

### (1) 'A Wee Trendy Channel'?

Most people agree that C4 is 'different', but this is either pejorative or praiseworthy depending on the overall evaluation of the channel. The Committed and The Unreconstructed agree on one thing, namely that Channel Four offers a range of programmes unavailable on the rest of British television. The latter, however, regard this as a form of betrayal of their rights as consumers who pay for the channel: 'different' is a double-edged appellation. According to those with the most positive image: C4 is bold, imaginative, necessarily controversial and provides a much needed challenge to the rest of British television. These attitudes are not confined to one class or age group: the archetypal media image of a C4 viewer as a left wing, gay, disabled, black community worker is a gross caricature; but, as the following quotations from the discussion groups demonstrate, the less scandlemongering stereotype of C4 as a channel for the young left is also wide of the mark.

> The four channels should get together and try to have something different on each*.

**TABLE 5**

These days, would you say that....?

BASE: ALL

| | Total | SEX | | AGE | | | | | CLASS | | | | CHILDREN | | | ETHNIC ORGIN | | | |
|---|---|---|---|---|---|---|---|---|---|---|---|---|---|---|---|---|---|---|---|
| | | Male | Fe-male | 16-20 | 21-24 | 25-34 | 35-54 | 55+ | AB | C1 | C2 | DE | U5 | 5-15 | None | White | Afro-carib | Asian | Miss C4 a lot |
| TOTAL | 974 | 431 | 543 | 109 | 57 | 149 | 334 | 325 | 199 | 235 | 256 | 284 | 124 | 209 | 693 | 948 | 117 | 119 | 158 |
| Channel 4 is very similar to ITV | 5% | 6% | 5% | 1% | 2% | 4% | 4% | 9% | 2% | 3% | 8% | 7% | 6% | 5% | 5% | 5% | 5% | 8% | 4% |
| Channel 4 is fairly similar to ITV | 30% | 28% | 32% | 28% | 19% | 31% | 27% | 36% | 19% | 31% | 31% | 37% | 30% | 30% | 31% | 31% | 35% | 24% | 20% |
| Channel 4 is fairly different from ITV | 35% | 37% | 34% | 39% | 42% | 41% | 37% | 28% | 41% | 34% | 36% | 31% | 40% | 35% | 34% | 36% | 38% | 34% | 46% |
| Channel 4 is very different from ITV | 19% | 19% | 20% | 27% | 30% | 21% | 20% | 13% | 26% | 20% | 16% | 16% | 19% | 19% | 19% | 19% | 19% | 21% | 28% |
| Don't know | 10% | 10% | 10% | 6% | 7% | 3% | 12% | 14% | 12% | 11% | 9% | 9% | 5% | 10% | 11% | 10% | 3% | 12% | 1% |

C4 are very young ... they seem more outrageous. They seem to go for it a little bit more.

They are much more daring which is good.
Group 19                                    [Female Under 35 C2D Woking]

Usually C4 has something that is eye catching and interesting and worth a debate the next day at work. I think that the three main channels which existed before C4, I think that they do tend to mollycoddle us as viewers ... I think that it is very refreshing to be able to watch a channel that leaves it up to you to decide what you want to see.
Group 17                                    [Male Under 35 BC1 Esher]

Channel Four doesn't mind, they like experimenting a bit. I get the impression it is more of an overspill from ITV, things that they haven't got time for in the whole day's viewing, they put them on, not so much the obscure, but selective programmes that would appeal to a small minority on C4.
Group 9                                    [Male Under 35 BC1 Nottingham]

Channel Four seems a wee trendy channel.
Group 35                                    [Female Catholic Belfast]

Not everybody wants to sit and watch soaps, as you know there are people who want to watch something else. And if there's another channel where you can put it on then its great.
Group 24                                    [Female Asian]

C4's objective − give everybody a say.

Generally it appears that they have a certain sense of being avant-garde.
Group 31                                    [Male C4 Heavy User]

(Channel Four) shows sort of old programmes, shows like sex films, it shows music, shows gardening and all that, whatever you want to watch sort of thing, it's on Channel Four.

Yes − it's better that way, because you know if you don't want to watch that programme for the skinheads you can turn over and there is going to be something on the other side; and they, by the time that programme

(* When sentences are given in a block then only one speaker is making a contribution; when the quotations are separated by a gap, then several individuals are having a dialogue.)

(C2D = Manual Workers.
BC1 = Middle Class and White Collar Workers.)

is finished, the programme that you might want to see is going to be on Channel Four. So, it's like a station for everybody.
Group 34                                      [Male 16-20 C2D London]

There isn't much for kids on C4 (it's all French films).

It's different styles, the way people live. You get sick of watching the same thing over again so they try to be different.

It's for all types of religion isn't it.

I like studying about different communities, that thing tonight on Afghanistan, it's very good that.
Group 25                                      [Male 12-16]

I don't think you can, that's the problem with Channel Four to me, I don't think you can actually say there's such a thing as a typical Channel Four viewer because they cover so much.

I just consider it as a side channel, where it's got different kinds of programmes you might want to watch.

With Channel Four there is always something new.

And you can't really relate to it unless you start watching it regularly.

And it's good that they're giving people who you know can't express themselves like on BBC1 and BBC2, they're giving them the chance to say what they feel, and they must be the only channel that does that and I think that is really good.
Group 39                                      [Female Asian Nottingham]

C4 is unpredictable, could have anything, I think it's good.
Group 7                                       [Male Under 35 C2D Newcastle]

You can guarantee that Channel Four is trying to be different.

Yes, but we've got used to it and see it as not being as original as when it first started.

It still spans a wide range of subjects.

Yes, it appeals to a different range of people.

It's not afraid to approach a subject.
Group 38                                      [Lesbians Nottingham]

There are two strands to the idea of an alternative channel. Channel Four is applauded for being a narrow alternative to the rest of British television, precisely because it allows experimental programmes which would otherwise not have been shown. Against this, however, one has to place the fact that many people appreciate it because it presents broad alternatives within existing television genres. Situation comedies such as *Cheers*, the varied diet of sports (with American football mentioned in every single discussion group), the *Film on Four* series, *Brookside* and *Channel Four News* constitute many viewers' total exposure to C4, and they welcome the channel for programming which is alternative within mainstream television rather than as a narrow alternative to that mainstream.

> I can see a fair difference in 4 now, it has improved steadily, I do like the sports they show which are minority sports... basketball, like fishing, the most common sport in the country, there are more people who fish than do anything else, any other sport.
> Group 7                                                    [Male C2D Under 35 Newcastle]

> I watch C4 if there's baseball or American football and basketball.
> Group 23                                                                    [Male Asian]

> I don't usually watch C4 unless it is sport or a money programme or documentary.
> Group 31                                                          [Male C4 Heavy User]

> Sport: it's certainly more adventurous Channel 4. They show cycle racing – Intercity. Sumo wrestling. Well I shall certainly watch that! It shows you how other cultures live.
> Group 4                                                      [Male Over 35 C2D Edinburgh]

> You know, perhaps it's a little bit cruel, because the only things I really like off C4 is the sports... I think that's the only thing going for it.
> Group 20                                                        [Male Over 35 C2D Esher]

*(2) 'Oh Well, that's Four, I'll Go and Finish the Painting'*
The negative image of C4 is based on a concern about the amount of variation in the channel's programmes. It is considered to be too different. Many in the groups were deeply unhappy when they could not establish a rhythm with the channel. The rhythms of TV watching are important because families are time-centred; people have to be fed, children played with and put to bed, financial and personal matters discussed. All of this frames television viewing. Therefore, for many people, the time that they want to watch television is important to them, and they do not want to worry constantly about what is coming on television next, or whether their family will like it. People may convert to a more individualistic viewing pattern late in the evening when family life is perhaps not so structured, which might account for the feeling that the appropriate time to put on specialist programmes is

Furthermore, apart from the structure of television, taste being shaped, in part at least, by the rhythms of family or collective life, many people simply like order and pattern – the unexpected in anything disturbs them.

We have to be careful here not to stereotype these attitudes as the preserve of the older working class, as the following quotes show.

> The programmes on C4 are too varied. I mean there is too many different things that keep coming on all the time, and you can't sort of like stick to ... and you can't stick to that channel all the time, because the things that come on are so different it's unbelievable. I mean, straight after *Brookside* I mean if they've got something it's completely different.
> Group 21                                          [Afro-Caribbean Male]

> The trouble is that programmes on C4 are so random.
> Group 17                                     [Male BC1 Under 35 Esher]

> When you turn it on you don't know what you are going to see, so therefore, I think really there is too much swearing, too much sex, we don't want all that, we don't want anything too explicit. We don't want to be shocked, yes we don't want to be shocked.
> Group 16                              [Female Over 35 C2D Southampton]

> The other night I turned to something, it was between stations or something, and it suddenly came on, and they'd got blue hair, and I looked at it, and: 'oh what the hell is that?', and I think I'll go and finish the painting, and just left it, you know, and there was just nothing, there was not encouragement at all to watch it. Oh well, that's 4, I'll go and finish the painting.
> Group 20                                      [Male Over 35 C2D Esher]

> First thing I saw, must be C4, black one-legged lesbian, must be C4. It is different. Wondered whose cup of tea it was when I watched it when it first came on.
> Group 7                                    [Male Under 35 C2D Newcastle]

> C4 is really different. I don't think it has really got going yet, it is not established. They don't have enough soap operas like that on to make you want to turn over, to have it on your brain so you think at 7:30, it's time to turn over to C4 for so and so, and therefore we don't really bother with it.

> It always looks boring. They should have called it something like Central 2.

> There is a lot of weird things on C4.

89

I like a routine (of soaps). I watch routine things every week.

C4, they are all blacks.

That is the worst of C4 I think because there are better programmes than that. They have the best comedies and films. Yes, I thing it's great. If you look at ITV at 10:30 and then at C4, there is something more interesting on C4 than ITV.

Maybe they should have more things like *Brookside* to get you to turn over and then slip the nuclear bomb in.

I'd rather watch nothing on ITV than nothing on C4.
Group 12                                     [Female Under 35 C2D Birmingham]

The so-called comedy (on C4) it is childish.

You get some weirdos though, some extreme ones. They call them the Eleventh Hour. If you have ever seen some of them, some of them are way out to me. I can't stand any of them.
Group 11                                        [Male C2D Over 35 Nottingham]

[C4] should be entertaining instead of hard work − lighter.
Group 12                                     [Female Under 35 C2D Birmingham]

Curiously, those who show most hostility toward Channel Four, namely older working class people, are most likely to say that the channel is similar to ITV, which they watch and enjoy. This demonstrates perhaps that they do not watch Channel Four's minority and specialist programmes with any degree of frequency, and that when they do watch they tend to tune into *Brookside*, feature films or sport − the stuff of 'normal' television. In fact, they still do not like Channel Four's 'normal' programmes; they feel that there is something not quite right about them: the soap opera is all social conscience, the feature films are in a foreign language and the sport is played by large black men in shoulder pads. Although these people dislike the channel, their hostility is based on hearsay and general prejudice against changing their viewing habits, rather than any first-hand acquaintance with innovative or specialist programmes.

When pressed to explain why C4 had a wide range of programmes most respondents assumed it was caused by the channel's youthful radicalism, and the attempt to create an distinct identity by distancing itself from other channels. Rather more world-weary people put all thought of altruism aside and claimed that 'television with a difference' was a strategy with distinct commercial advantages.

I think that they're trying to battle for an audience, they are putting out anything, so to that extent they don't care what they're putting out.

C4: Oh, they seem to be searching for a market at the moment, they've tried a lot of things haven't they, but they're very experimental with new programmes and they run them for a while, and if they don't work they'll try another thing. I think their more, their biggest success has got to be American football.

I think it's sort of bringing a different audience, different sorts of groups of people watching different sorts of things all the time. I mean like they've got the Irish ... and all that stuff. Things for knitting, I mean it's all sorts of minority.
Group 21                                          [Afro-Caribbean Male]

It is acceptable to me that 90% of C4 output will not appeal to me, but is it acceptable to C4?
Group 9                                        [Male Under 35 BC1 Nottingham]

Just to create the programme.

Or to capture an audience really. It's trying to find itself.
Group 20                                          [Male Over 35 C2D Esher]

I get the feeling that C4 is now doing what BBC2 tried to do when it was first launched, and BBC2 has now become part of the establishment, and has settled into their own niche, whereas C4 is still spreading around and trying to find where it wants to be.

BBC2 is supplying what is being demanded, [Channel] Four has gone out to find something to supply for a demand that possibly wasn't even there in the first place.
Group 17                                          [Male Under 35 BC1 Esher]

Not all the comparisons with BBC2 are flattering. One middle class woman said: 'I don't think there's enough entertainment programmes on C4. [BBC2 programmes] seem more sophisticated somehow. I think. I can't explain it. More polished I think.' One man thought that 'C4's business programme, on a Sunday evening, doesn't come up to the shoulders of *The Money Programme* on BBC2.' This was countered by another member of this group who claimed: 'I used to enjoy the travel programme on C4. I think because they cater more to the average man, as opposed to people gassing off about the Seychelles and Jamaica.' Even more illuminating than these quotes was the answer to a question concerning an imaginary programme called 'Our World' (based on *7 Days*); one group identified it as a BBC2 programme, giving the reason: 'Morals, that's the word that makes it sound BBC2 rather than C4.'

Some interesting comparisons between the images of Channel Four and of the other three British channels can be made. Compared to BBC1 and ITV, Channel Four is seen as being experimental, daring, aimed at minorities,

91

unusual and anti-establishment. But, on the other hand it is seen by more people as having a high sexual content, a great deal of swearing, not professionally produced, having a narrow range of programmes and not being entertaining (see Table 6).

Interestingly, there are as many differences as similarities between BBC2 and Channel Four, despite their overall identification as specialist channels. In particular, BBC2 is thought to be high-brow and a bit more right wing and pro-establishment, but it is not considered to be as experimental, daring or unusual. Indeed, people consider it to be the most boring channel by far. Furthermore, Channel Four is thought to contain a great deal more sex, violence and bad language than BBC2 but, as we shall see later, there is evidence to suggest that Channel Four is still suffering from a hangover from the early days of the tabloid attacks. Although people feel that Channel Four has more programmes which contain sex and violence, one has to be careful in interpreting this; many approve of the channel's ability to allow controversial issues to be explored, and therefore approve of the amount of sex and violence. Looking at the range of people's attitudes to the channel it would appear that Channel Four is not being condemned for the level of controversial programmes that it shows.

The channel retains a clearly distinctive voice: half the population think that it has maintained a separate identity from that of ITV, and a further 14 per cent think that it has increased the level of difference. In *Invisible Citizens* there was evidence that almost half of the population thinks that Channel Four has improved over the past few years. Of particular importance is the fact that two-fifths of ITV and BBC viewers think that Channel Four has improved. There are several possible reasons for this: it is of course possible that C4 has introduced the British to a new range of television programmes, and that they approve of the differences between C4 and the rest of British television. Our survey shows, however, that one quarter of the population thinks that C4 has become more like ITV over the past five years, and, presumably it approves of this change, as the increase in the channel's popularity demonstrates.

> I don't think that C4 tries to compete with BBC or ITV.
> Group 4                                    [Male C2D Over 35 Edinburgh]

> BBC is not controversial enough, I know they had this big thing over the news, but generally speaking I don't think that they are controversial enough – I mean you are less likely to find something that you really like or you hate, whereas on C4 you can.
> Group 17                                    [Male Under 35 BC1 Esher]

> And C4's relatively new isn't it? If you think about it so obviously you do not know what to expect of it.... But STV is so humdrum.
> Group 3                                    [Female Under 35 C2D Glasgow

**TABLE 6**

Which of these descriptions do you think apply to this television channel?

BASE: ALL

| | Total | TV VIEWING | | | C4 VIEWING | | | CHANNEL FOR SELF | | | | SOCIAL TOLERANCE | | TV ACTIVE | | | PSB | TV TOLERANCE | |
|---|---|---|---|---|---|---|---|---|---|---|---|---|---|---|---|---|---|---|---|
| | | Light 1-14 | Med 15-27 | Heavy 28+ | Light 1-7 | Med 8-14 | Heavy 15+ | W | X | Y | Z | Tolerant | Intolerant | Crime | Morality | Swearing | | Tolerant | Intolerant |
| TOTAL | 974 | 337 | 267 | 348 | 407 | 297 | 207 | 816 | 569 | 257 | 240 | 432 | 542 | 93 | 124 | 312 | 269 | 376 | 588 |
| Experimental | 60% | 60% | 67% | 55% | 57% | 61% | 69% | 62% | 61% | 51% | 63% | 64% | 56% | 53% | 60% | 63% | 68% | 67% | 55% |
| Cheaply produced | 36% | 39% | 39% | 33% | 39% | 39% | 30% | 36% | 38% | 36% | 35% | 36% | 37% | 33% | 39% | 38% | 32% | 38% | 36% |
| Wide range of programmes | 14% | 17% | 10% | 14% | 12% | 11% | 26% | 15% | 15% | 14% | 11% | 18% | 11% | 12% | 10% | 16% | 15% | 18% | 12% |
| Daring | 58% | 59% | 61% | 57% | 57% | 60% | 68% | 60% | 61% | 53% | 61% | 62% | 55% | 54% | 57% | 60% | 61% | 64% | 55% |
| Entertaining | 14% | 13% | 12% | 17% | 11% | 16% | 22% | 14% | 15% | 11% | 17% | 17% | 12% | 12% | 10% | 13% | 18% | 16% | 13% |
| High brow | 11% | 11% | 13% | 11% | 10% | 13% | 12% | 12% | 11% | 11% | 11% | 13% | 10% | 11% | 12% | 14% | 11% | 13% | 10% |
| Aimed at minorities | 51% | 50% | 59% | 48% | 54% | 49% | 56% | 54% | 52% | 41% | 56% | 56% | 47% | 38% | 52% | 48% | 58% | 57% | 48% |
| Unusual | 63% | 66% | 65% | 61% | 60% | 65% | 72% | 65% | 63% | 61% | 65% | 69% | 58% | 60% | 64% | 64% | 71% | 69% | 59% |
| Professionally produced | 14% | 15% | 12% | 15% | 13% | 13% | 20% | 15% | 14% | 12% | 17% | 18% | 11% | 6% | 6% | 15% | 19% | 17% | 12% |
| Middle of the road | 12% | 11% | 10% | 14% | 10% | 16% | 10% | 12% | 11% | 14% | 12% | 12% | 12% | 11% | 10% | 11% | 12% | 13% | 11% |
| Responsive to viewers' attitudes | 15% | 18% | 15% | 14% | 13% | 16% | 21% | 16% | 15% | 11% | 20% | 21% | 11% | 10% | 10% | 17% | 20% | 18% | 14% |
| Left wing | 20% | 22% | 24% | 16% | 22% | 17% | 21% | 20% | 22% | 13% | 25% | 24% | 17% | 22% | 27% | 21% | 18% | 23% | 18% |
| Right wing | 3% | 3% | 3% | 4% | 3% | 5% | 3% | 4% | 4% | 4% | 3% | 2% | 4% | 5% | 5% | 3% | 4% | 4% | 3% |
| A lot of sex | 58% | 53% | 59% | 65% | 57% | 59% | 64% | 59% | 57% | 60% | 59% | 55% | 61% | 58% | 62% | 61% | 54% | 59% | 58% |
| Violent | 38% | 34% | 38% | 44% | 39% | 37% | 42% | 40% | 37% | 39% | 39% | 37% | 40% | 35% | 42% | 45% | 37% | 36% | 40% |
| A lot of swearing | 52% | 46% | 57% | 56% | 48% | 55% | 59% | 53% | 53% | 53% | 50% | 51% | 53% | 52% | 51% | 56% | 53% | 55% | 51% |
| Aimed at the family | 5% | 4% | 4% | 7% | 4% | 7% | 5% | 5% | 5% | 4% | 5% | 5% | 5% | 6% | 5% | 5% | 4% | 5% | 5% |
| Anti establishment | 31% | 33% | 33% | 29% | 32% | 28% | 36% | 33% | 34% | 21% | 34% | 35% | 28% | 25% | 32% | 30% | 33% | 35% | 29% |
| Social conscience | 18% | 20% | 20% | 14% | 16% | 17% | 26% | 19% | 20% | 11% | 22% | 24% | 13% | 18% | 20% | 19% | 22% | 19% | 17% |
| Boring | 23% | 25% | 23% | 22% | 26% | 23% | 14% | 23% | 24% | 19% | 26% | 25% | 22% | 28% | 23% | 25% | 21% | 18% | 26% |
| Don't know | 4% | 4% | 3% | 3% | 4% | 4% | 0% | 3% | 4% | 4% | 5% | 4% | 5% | 8% | 3% | 5% | 4% | 5% | 4% |

*(3) 'As Good a Variety As the Rest of Them'*
Those who think that similarity is a positive trait believe that Channel Four should advertise itself more, pointing to programmes like *Hill Street Blues, St. Elsewhere, Cheers* etc as evidence for C4's 'good' aspects. They acclaim the channel because of its presentation of conventional television, and are clearly baffled by their friends' and neighbours' apparent hostility toward the channel.

Just advertise, let the people know and see what is on because there are good programmes that people don't know about.

C4 should advertise itself more — because I watched *St. Elsewhere* last night and [my friends] go... Oh, is that on — and when you say it was on C4 they say that they never watch that, I only happened to find the programme out by looking down the paper. I watched it and I really liked it.

And in fact you don't think of them as an alternative, I... watch more probably than, I think their situation comedies now, although they've quoted a, I mean every British situation comedy I've ever seen, they're terrible now on television, but they've got... a good one on just about very night.
Group 1                                    [Male Under 35 BC1 Edinburgh]

There are a lot of late night programmes that are very, very good, and you think, 'well, why the heck didn't they put it on at eight o'clock because it would have got very good ratings'.
Group 6                                    [Male Over 35 BC1 Newcastle]

And C4's relatively new isn't it? If you think about it. Well I must admit I've not found a lot on C4 that I like.

You know I would hate to have a young teenager. I think that there is too much sex on television.

The VD clinic ... was really funny.

Well I wonder if I've harmed my children, I turn it over immediately and I still do it.

*The Cosby Show*, that's a real family show.

I always think that's on too late because that's something the whole family could watch.
Group 2                                    [Female Over 35 BC1 Glasgow]

When I've turned Channel Four on, all it has been is comedy or soaps..

I've never actually turned it on to a political thing, or a documentary. I've only ever seen the funny things, like *Saturday Live*.

When I watch it its something like *The Cosby Show*.

It's all comedy when I think of, you know, Channel Four — I'll just think of comedy.
Group 36                                                          [Female Protestant Belfast]

C4 is supposed to be extreme left wing.

No. it's a mixture.

There's as good a variety as the rest of them.
Group 28                                                                         [OAP Female]

### (4) 'Just Another Channel'
On the other hand, there are those who think that Channel Four is too similar to the rest of British television and, consequently, is not fulfilling the mandate. In the words of one disillusioned respondent — 'it is just another channel.' In fact, those who dislike the similarity between C4 and the rest of British television seem to be more anti-television than anti-C4: C4 is tarred with the collective brush.

Channel Four isn't really all that different from the others. I don't think you get much of a choice with four channels because they are pretty much the same.
Group 28                                                                         [OAP Female]

C4 is a bit too Americanised for my liking.

There is not one channel that has a succession of good programmes so you've got to look around.

C4 is (just) there, it's another channel.
Group 17                                                              [Male under 35 BC1 Esher]

The worry that Channel Four might not continue with its innovative programmes was expressed by one of the respondents from Northern Ireland:

I think ultimately to survive they have had to chase advertising and to chase advertising, they've got to put on programmes that are going to be acceptable and attractive to the mainstream, but at the outset what they said they were trying to do, was not to follow the mainstream but to set up a new direction and alliance to people, people who may have been previously ignored, to break new ground in terms of television. I think that the commercial instinct has possibly dragged them back to a more central position — such as the American football. The American football is a classic, quite successful, I mean I watched that, I rarely missed it , and sat up to watch the *Superbowl*. I mean at the end of the day the reasons why that is on; I don't think it's any longer through a desire on the part of the controllers of Channel Four to bring new sports into the home, it's because they know that it is going to hit the ratings, that it is going to get them up, and they are going to be able to sell drinks advertising on either side of it.

Group 37                                                                      [Male Catholic Belfast]

In summation, most people have a positive image of C4. The complicating factor is that many of those who approved of the difference between C4 and the other channels watched few specialist programmes, whereas those who approve of C4's similarity to the rest of British television watch a great deal of the channel's output — indeed they were among the few to mention specific programmes that they had liked. Those who hold the negative image of C4 do so because they either dislike radical approaches to television, or fear that the channel has succumbed to the temptations of the flesh and declined into complacency and greed like the rest of British television.

As we have seen, the general images of Channel Four are based on perceptions of the channel's success or failure in presenting challenging and interesting programmes. The price which the channel pays for fulfilling the public's mandate is that it is perceived to be more risqué than the other channels and, in particular, to be more sexually oriented than the rest of British television. It is to this question of the moral location of the channel and the implications of this for the thorny question of who should be responsible for taste and standards in programmes that we now turn.

## (3) All Bottoms and Bosoms?

'Well, I ought to start watching C4,
I'm missing a lot if it's all bottoms and bosoms.'
Glasgow Woman (BC1 Over 35)

'Censorship should be a matter of parental responsibility and viewers' rights.' This view — expressed by an Afro-Caribbean respondent — sums up the feeling of the majority of the British population; most people feel that they are quite capable of making sensible choices over whether to watch programmes which are thought by some critics to be morally and socially corrupting. Consequently, as we shall see below, there was widespread resentment in the discussion groups about individuals who sought to impose their morality on others. One name figured quite spontaneously in all the discussion groups as embodying the spirit of negative moralistic censorship - Mary Whitehouse. Regardless of class, age, sex, creed or colour most people in all groups registered an overwhelming objection to Whitehouse and the National Viewers and Listeners Association (NVLA), on the basis that such groups usurped the viewer's right to choose. For this reason there was an equally overwhelming approval of Channel Four's policy of indicating that a feature film contains potentially difficult scenes by screening a Special Discretion Required (SDR) symbol. In the main the public felt that the use of the symbol took their moral judgement seriously; by allowing them to choose whether to watch a film knowing that it may contain controversial and difficult scenes the symbol acknowledges the public's ability to make responsible choices.

Four clear themes emerged from the public's debate about television censorship and Channel Four. First, although willing to allow television a great deal of latitude there is widespread recognition of the need for some form of censorship; secondly, the most important criteria for rationally censoring programmes are temporal, textual and social context – what is shown is secondary to how and when it is shown; thirdly, given the flexibility of people's thinking about televised sex and violence, they are unhappy that the debate is dominated by people who have no such flexibility, namely the NVLA and its supporters in government; finally, the underlying reason for people's tolerance is that they do not have a television-centred view of the world. In essence, people are unafraid of television because they are aware the world is an infinitely complex place and that their families, work, education, and personality are where their attitudes are formed and actions generated. We will explore each of these themes in turn.

*(1) 'Drawing the Line'*
One respondent sympathised with the task of programme controllers, arguing: 'I think it must be very hard for them to suit all tastes and draw the line: people vary so much I'm sure. In this room there are eight of us. I bet we don't agree on more than 40 per cent of subjects.' As this man recognised, 'drawing the line' is an immensely complicated business. For most people, the 'line' involved barring hard-core pornography and protecting children. After these two conditions are fulfilled most people seem willing to accept that there are no hard and fast rules for censoring programmes.

Most people felt:

> I don't think you should have blokes molesting little girls on television, or you should have snuff movies on television.
> Group 9                                  [Male Under 35 BC1 Nottingham]

> When it deals with kids, I think that is the line.
> Group 3                                  [Female Under 35 C2D Glasgow]

> I am broad-minded; much censorship should be left to individuals, but there would have to be some guidance.
> Group 7                                  [Male Under 35 C2D Newcastle]

> It's up to the individual — if the station in question, you know, warns you in advance, in the paper, that this programme is of an explicit nature, whatever, then you would've had the warning and then you watch it after that, and it's disgusting, then it's your own fault isn't it, you shouldn't have watched it.

> It's alright for people that are responsible [but] what if you get some prude who watches it.

> What about the kids?
> Group 17                                                [Male Under 35 BC1 Esher]

The problem most people had when trying to draw the line was which criteria and standards to apply. For instance, should they use the moral structure which they themselves were brought up with or, on the other hand, should they recognise the complexity of the social world in the 1980s and try to find criteria for censorship which faced up to these realities? The second option was expressed the most forcibly in the groups.

Most adults acknowledged that the public standards which they were brought up with were no longer valid. They felt that children in the late twentieth Century had to cope with an increasingly bewildering world of sexual morality and mores, but felt that this was one reason why children should not be closed off from one potentially vital source of discussion of these issues — namely, television. Lying behind this view was clearly a strong feeling that to attempt to protect children was not only dysfunctional and inappropriate, but also futile. An Afro-Caribbean respondent summed up this view when he said: 'Kids nowadays, right, are very clever, you can't hide something like that from kids.'

> C4 don't mess around, do they? They say exactly what they want to say and that's it.

> Most children know more than we do anyway. [They] have sex education in the playground.

> I mean it happens, and you've got to talk about it, you can't keep it bottled up and there are things like lesbians and homosexuals, and it's all got to come out into the open. It happens, and you've got to face up to it really.
> Group 13                                         [Female Under 35 BC1 Southampton]

> C4 is more realistic [about] what is really going on, don't cut out swearing like the BBC.
>                                                  [Male Under 35 C2D Newcastle]

> I don't say I enjoy it. I can put up with it when we're on our own, but

when the elderly person's there I'm very conscious of it. I think the age gap ... think ... oh gosh. But, between ourselves, you think 'he knows the words, and I do really'.
Group 10                                        [Female Over 35 BC1 Birmingham]

They might as well show you it − it's real, that's what is happening.

It's no good curling up and thinking everything's all nice because it isn't.
Group 25                                                    [Male 16-20 Leeds]

Not a bad thing, socially aware. It gets me when people say language is too bad, you don't tell me that 11 and 12 year olds don't swear.
Group 7                                            [Male Under 35 C2D Newcastle]

Obviously it's a matter of personal taste. And there's an off-button for all of them you know.

If you bring your kids up blind to all the bad parts of life, I think you've blown it. You're better letting them learn it in the house than find out outside when it's too late.

I couldn't control what they were watching, and I don't think it's affected them anyway.
Group 4                                            [Male Over 35 C2D Edinburgh]

Have you ever seen a programme about homosexuality?

I've never seen one, I think that's bad.

I think people should know .....children don't know about this and they should know.

They should know what people decide to do.
Group 26                                                    [Female 12-16]

That's what I find about C4. I think that [if] anything is going to be discussed that they certainly wouldn't put on BBC1, because I find that more strict than C4. Southern isn't so bad, but C4, anything goes, anything at all, which doesn't mean I disagree or agree, it depends on what's on. But I think it's like anything, you can turn it off if you don't want to watch it, nobody's forcing you to have it on, but it's nice to know it's there. If there's something that you know damned well that wouldn't be put on another channel, that's what C4 means to me certainly. If you read in the paper, if something is going to come up and the critics hit it, you can bet your sweet life nine times out of ten it's on C4.
Group 13                                      [Female Under 35 BC1 Southampton]

The key to 'drawing the line' is the context in which potentially embarrassing or difficult scenes appear. Even those people who are most committed to censorship are willing to tolerate nudity or violence if they add meaning to a play or film.

> I think that someone's got to draw the line as regards to what you see on television personally. When it comes to what I call high sex things. I don't particularly — sometimes when it's relevant to the theme of the play — like last night when you had the old people's home\*, it was very well done, tastefully done, but I think that the limit, and you go over the limit when you start to draw the line somewhere.
> Group 15                                                    [Male Over 35 BC1 Bristol]

*(2) The Context of Sex*
As the above quote demonstrates, most people recognise that the context of nudity is extremely important when drawing the line between acceptable and unacceptable programmes. The public appears to have a rule of thumb censorship equation: acceptablity = scheduling time plus programme genre. The later a programme is shown, and the more serious it is, the likelier it is that the public will tolerate nudity, sex and violence. For example, only 17 per cent of the public objected to a scene with a topless woman; but, when this is broken down by genre we can see that acceptablity varies according to the seriousness of the programme: 31 per cent accepted it in a situation comedy, 40 per cent in a feature film, 38 per cent in a serious play, 51 per cent on a holiday programme and 62 per cent in a documentary about strip clubs.

Similarly, full frontal nudity is more agreeable in some programmes than in others. In order of acceptability we have: documentaries, serious plays, feature films, holiday programmes and situation comedies. The public feels that when televised nudity approaches the limits of tolerance (namely the full frontal male nude) it requires a context in which it can be properly understood. Serious nudity requires serious programmes.

The public distinguishes between fact and fiction when deciding what is considered acceptable. Documentaries and educational programmes are allowed freedom not extended to fictional programmes and, in particular, situation comedies. We have something of a paradox here: presumably the most sexually explicit form of nudity would appear in a documentary about strip clubs (strippers after all intend to titillate), but the public is much more willing to tolerate nudity if it is presented in documentary form. People will accept fairly explicit sex-shows rather than see a topless woman in *Duty Free* or *Three Up, Two Down.* This is an extremely complex and sophisticated judgement; they are saying that a woman caught topless in an embarrassing

---

\*This was a BBC play which had a sex scene involving a patient (Denholm Elliot) and his nurse (Connie Booth).

**TABLE 7**

On which of these types of television programmes, if any, do you think it would be acceptable to show a topless woman?

BASE: ALL

| | Total | SEX | | AGE | | | | | | CLASS | | | | CHILDREN | | | ETHNIC ORIGIN | | | Miss C4 a lot |
| --- | --- | --- | --- | --- | --- | --- | --- | --- | --- | --- | --- | --- | --- | --- | --- | --- | --- | --- | --- |
| | | Male | Female | 16-20 | 21-24 | 25-34 | 35-54 | 55+ | AB | C1 | C2 | DE | U5 | 5-15 | None | White | Afro-carib | Asian | |
| TOTAL | 974 | 431 | 543 | 109 | 57 | 149 | 334 | 325 | 199 | 235 | 256 | 284 | 124 | 209 | 693 | 948 | 117 | 119 | 158 |
| Situation comedy | 31% | 40% | 25% | 45% | 21% | 34% | 34% | 24% | 34% | 35% | 31% | 26% | 36% | 41% | 29% | 32% | 21% | 21% | 35% |
| Feature films | 40% | 53% | 29% | 50% | 46% | 55% | 46% | 21% | 48% | 44% | 36% | 33% | 55% | 51% | 35% | 40% | 32% | 31% | 47% |
| Serious plays | 38% | 50% | 28% | 44% | 46% | 52% | 41% | 24% | 53% | 48% | 31% | 25% | 44% | 46% | 34% | 38% | 30% | 26% | 48% |
| Holiday programme | 51% | 60% | 44% | 57% | 56% | 57% | 58% | 38% | 58% | 57% | 49% | 43% | 62% | 61% | 47% | 51% | 35% | 36% | 56% |
| Documentary about strip club | 63% | 67% | 59% | 77% | 70% | 70% | 70% | 45% | 75% | 69% | 62% | 49% | 65% | 68% | 60% | 63% | 59% | 54% | 73% |
| None | 17% | 13% | 21% | 7% | 9% | 8% | 12% | 32% | 14% | 13% | 17% | 24% | 9% | 11% | 20% | 18% | 16% | 19% | 14% |

**TABLE 8**

And how about a full frontal male nude?

| | Total | SEX | | AGE | | | | | | CLASS | | | | CHILDREN | | | ETHNIC ORIGIN | | | Miss C4 a lot |
| --- | --- | --- | --- | --- | --- | --- | --- | --- | --- | --- | --- | --- | --- | --- | --- | --- | --- | --- | --- |
| | | Male | Female | 16-20 | 21-24 | 25-34 | 35-54 | 55+ | AB | C1 | C2 | DE | U5 | 5-15 | None | White | Afro-carib | Asian | |
| TOTAL | 974 | 431 | 543 | 109 | 57 | 149 | 334 | 325 | 199 | 235 | 256 | 284 | 124 | 209 | 693 | 948 | 117 | 119 | 158 |
| Situation comedy | 11% | 14% | 8% | 16% | 5% | 11% | 13% | 8% | 9% | 11% | 12% | 11% | 16% | 13% | 10% | 11% | 13% | 6% | 15% |
| Feature films | 21% | 28% | 15% | 29% | 28% | 29% | 27% | 6% | 23% | 22% | 23% | 16% | 33% | 27% | 17% | 20% | 23% | 19% | 29% |
| Serious plays | 24% | 34% | 16% | 25% | 26% | 32% | 33% | 11% | 37% | 26% | 22% | 15% | 35% | 32% | 20% | 24% | 28% | 19% | 30% |
| Holiday programme | 12% | 16% | 9% | 17% | 11% | 13% | 17% | 6% | 13% | 13% | 14% | 10% | 19% | 15% | 11% | 12% | 12% | 7% | 19% |
| Documentary about strip club | 40% | 46% | 36% | 59% | 47% | 53% | 45% | 22% | 43% | 41% | 46% | 32% | 56% | 52% | 35% | 40% | 34% | 29% | 51% |
| None | 41% | 31% | 50% | 27% | 32% | 25% | 33% | 65% | 39% | 44% | 34% | 48% | 23% | 29% | 47% | 41% | 37% | 49% | 33% |

101

moment in a fictional comedy is less acceptable than a woman deliberately taking her clothes off to cause sexual excitement in a factual documentary. Like McGill postcards, in a sit-com, sex should be implied rather than shown.

What people do when they are naked is not as important as the programme genre in which they are naked. Situation comedies, which by their nature have a frivolous attitude to sex, are not considered suitable for intimate depictions of human sexuality (see Table 9). If people are going to watch something which might involve some embarrassment if someone else is in the room, they have to feel that there is a reason for the scene. They need to have an answer to anyone who questions why they are watching that scene, and the best answer appears to involve a feeling that the scene is true to life. If 'life is like that', then the public are happy watching that particular slice of life; on the other hand, if they are watching fiction they appear to feel that the sex scene need not have been there and therefore requires justification.

We can see this even more clearly from responses to the question of whether a television programme should show a scene in which a couple make love in explicit detail. In fact, around one quarter of the population would be willing for such a scene to appear, which adds further weight to the evidence that 'drawing the line' is by no means a simple matter. If such a large proportion of the population accepts such scenes, why not show them? Or, more to the point, programmes should not necessarily be banned because they contain scenes of explicit sex. Nearly one in four older teenagers would be happy with such scenes on a sex education programme, which suggests that they have quite fine judgements about context. The story itself is insufficient to justify explicit sex: even if the context of the scenes explains the intensity of the sexual activity, most people are still unhappy. But if sex scenes have a wider purpose, namely education, they become more acceptable.

As one would expect from the literature on sexuality, women are less willing than men to accept nudity as such on television. Although voyeurism is clearly one part of the explanation for this it is not sufficient. Women are less likely to tolerate male nudity than men: half the female population do not want to see the male nude as opposed to less than one third of men. Furthermore, women are less likely to tolerate male nudity than female nudity.

Further evidence for the complexity of the censorship equation can be adduced from people's attitudes to the depiction of rape. For instance, whereas 40 per cent of the population is willing to have a rape described in great detail in a documentary after 9 o'clock, it is unwilling to have it so described on the *9 o'clock News* or *Newsnight*. Although the 9 o'clock watershed is important for people, as we will see later when discussing Channel Four's Special Discretion Required symbol, textual context is as important as time. They appear to feel that the description of rape cannot be done properly on the news, because it is not set in any context in which it can

## TABLE 9

Would there be any circumstances in which you think it would be acceptable for a television programme to show a scene of a couple making love in explicit detail?

| | Total | SEX | | AGE | | | | | CLASS | | | | CHILDREN | | | ETHNIC ORGIN | | | |
| --- | --- | --- | --- | --- | --- | --- | --- | --- | --- | --- | --- | --- | --- | --- | --- | --- | --- | --- | --- |
| | | Male | Fe-male | 16-20 | 21-24 | 25-34 | 35-54 | 55+ | AB | C1 | C2 | DE | U5 | 5-15 | None | White | Afro-carib | Asian | Miss C4 a lot |
| TOTAL | 974 | 431 | 543 | 109 | 57 | 149 | 334 | 325 | 199 | 235 | 256 | 284 | 124 | 209 | 693 | 948 | 117 | 119 | 158 |
| **Yes** | | | | | | | | | | | | | | | | | | | |
| Films | 6% | 8% | 5% | 10% | 12% | 9% | 7% | 2% | 6% | 5% | 6% | 8% | 11% | 8% | 5% | 6% | 18% | 13% | 11% |
| Documentaries | 5% | 7% | 3% | 6% | 9% | 10% | 6% | 1% | 7% | 5% | 5% | 4% | 9% | 9% | 4% | 5% | 12% | 10% | 7% |
| Plays | 5% | 8% | 3% | 8% | 7% | 7% | 5% | 3% | 8% | 3% | 5% | 5% | 6% | 6% | 5% | 5% | 7% | 5% | 8% |
| Comedy | 0% | 1% | 0% | 4% | – | – | | – | 1% | 1% | | 0% | – | – | 1% | 0% | 4% | – | 1% |
| Sex education | 10% | 12% | 8% | 21% | 5% | 15% | 12% | 3% | 10% | 12% | 10% | 10% | 13% | 14% | 9% | 10% | 19% | 23% | 11% |
| Only after 9pm | 2% | 1% | 2% | – | 4% | 5% | 2% | 0% | 1% | 1% | 2% | 3% | 4% | 3% | 1% | 1% | 2% | 5% | 3% |
| Only after 10pm | 6% | 7% | 6% | 9% | 4% | 11% | 7% | 3% | 5% | 6% | 7% | 7% | 14% | 9% | 4% | 6% | 11% | 19% | 7% |
| Only if it is crucial to the story | 6% | 8% | 5% | 12% | 5% | 11% | 6% | 3% | 8% | 5% | 7% | 5% | 8% | 8% | 5% | 6% | 3% | 11% | 6% |
| Any circumstances/ no restrictions | 1% | 1% | 0% | 1% | 2% | – | 0% | 1% | 1% | 1% | – | 1% | 1% | 0% | 1% | 1% | – | 3% | – |
| Other | 2% | 3% | 1% | 3% | 4% | 2% | 2% | 1% | 2% | 2% | 2% | 2% | 1% | 0% | 2% | 2% | 3% | 2% | 3% |
| No | 64% | 60% | 67% | 48% | 58% | 50% | 63% | 78% | 64% | 65% | 65% | 62% | 56% | 56% | 67% | 65% | 44% | 46% | 62% |

103

be fully understood. It is almost as if information without explanation does not justify such potentially difficult and embarrassing material. On the other hand, a documentary, which by definition is explanatory, provides sufficient context to help the viewer understand the rape and sympathise with the victim. The public seem to be saying that information on its own is potentially seedy if the human dimension to the story is not sufficiently established.

Despite the fact that one in four of the population thought giving a full description of a rape was unjustifiable, television has established itself as a more trustworthy, appropriate and sympathetic place for the description of rape than newspapers. It seems that newspapers have forfeited the trust, and in some ways the admiration, of the public. Undoubtedly the public wants the full description of rapes, but does not think that newspapers will deal with it in a reasonable, non-titillating fashion (Table 10).

Those who are most committed to Channel Four are also more willing to tolerate all forms of nudity and explicit sexuality. It would be easy to suggets that they actually watch the channel because of the sex but more probably the explanation is that they are generally more socially tolerant, and less likely to be shocked by any depiction of sex. Furthermore, they seem to see sex as an issue of freedom and will defend it as such.

Those who are socially tolerant are much more willing to accept topless nudity in fiction that those socially intolerant (although this distinction disappears in factual programmes). Full frontal nudity again is related to tolerance: over half of those in our tv tolerance category were willing to accept a full frontal male nude compared to only one third of those who were tv intolerant. Those who say that they would miss Channel Four if it stopped broadcasting tomorrow are also the most tolerant of what should appear on television: 50 per cent are tv tolerant. Similarly, almost half of those who are socially tolerant would miss Channel Four compared to around one third of those intolerant. This suggests then that committed Channel Four viewers are more likely to accept the depiction of nudity and sexuality because of their general social disposition, rather than because of any prurient interest.

This can be seen from examining a small but very pertinent example: the Special Discretion Required symbol − the famous red triangle. The red triangle is not a voyeur's charter as Mary Whitehouse would have it. The fact is, fully nine out of ten people agree that it is a good idea to warn viewers if they are about to see something which might contravene their social rules. Furthermore, when asked when they would like these films to appear, 97 per cent were happy that they were shown between nine o'clock and midnight. It is of course always possible that people object not only to the red triangle, but to the type of film that Channel Four considers in need of such notification. Furthermore, it is possible to approve of the SDR symbol, but massively disapprove of the actual films which are shown. Our respondents were in fact willing to allow television, and Channel Four in particular, to

**TABLE 10**

For which of these do you think it would be appropriate to describe a rape in detail?

| | Total | SEX | | AGE | | | | | CLASS | | | | CHILDREN | | | ETHNIC ORIGIN | | | |
|---|---|---|---|---|---|---|---|---|---|---|---|---|---|---|---|---|---|---|---|
| | | Male | Fe-male | 16-20 | 21-24 | 25-34 | 35-54 | 55+ | AB | C1 | C2 | DE | U5 | 5-15 | None | White | Afro-carib | Asian | Miss C4 a lot |
| TOTAL | 974 | 431 | 543 | 109 | 57 | 149 | 334 | 325 | 199 | 235 | 256 | 284 | 124 | 209 | 693 | 948 | 117 | 119 | 158 |
| Legal Journal | 23% | 28% | 19% | 17% | 30% | 28% | 27% | 17% | 35% | 29% | 20% | 12% | 24% | 22% | 23% | 23% | 17% | 27% | 22% |
| Daily newspaper | 11% | 13% | 10% | 12% | 12% | 11% | 12% | 9% | 15% | 7% | 11% | 11% | 12% | 11% | 11% | 11% | 14% | 24% | 13% |
| Daytime radio news | 2% | 3% | 2% | 2% | 4% | 4% | 2% | 2% | 3% | 2% | 2% | 2% | 3% | 2% | 2% | 2% | 5% | 4% | 2% |
| Radio after 9pm | 13% | 13% | 12% | 19% | 12% | 15% | 14% | 8% | 22% | 12% | 10% | 9% | 17% | 16% | 11% | 13% | 9% | 23% | 12% |
| Six o'clock television news | 3% | 4% | 3% | 2% | 2% | 3% | 3% | 5% | 1% | 1% | 4% | 6% | 3% | 4% | 3% | 3% | 5% | 8% | 2% |
| Seven o'clock news on Channel 4 | 2% | 3% | 1% | 3% | 2% | 4% | 1% | 2% | 1% | 2% | 2% | 2% | 3% | 3% | 2% | 2% | 7% | 8% | 3% |
| Nine o'clock news | 9% | 9% | 9% | 14% | 4% | 17% | 7% | 6% | 11% | 9% | 6% | 10% | 15% | 10% | 8% | 9% | 10% | 22% | 9% |
| News at ten | 20% | 19% | 20% | 22% | 25% | 35% | 17% | 14% | 19% | 22% | 18% | 19% | 31% | 27% | 17% | 20% | 16% | 36% | 21% |
| TV documentary after 9 p·n | 40% | 36% | 42% | 60% | 42% | 48% | 39% | 30% | 34% | 37% | 45% | 42% | 48% | 41% | 38% | 40% | 56% | 49% | 41% |
| Newsnight | 19% | 23% | 16% | 25% | 16% | 27% | 22% | 12% | 21% | 19% | 20% | 18% | 27% | 23% | 17% | 19% | 14% | 31% | 23% |
| None of these/ never justified | 26% | 26% | 26% | 16% | 26% | 17% | 26% | 32% | 29% | 27% | 20% | 26% | 20% | 24% | 27% | 25% | 20% | 18% | 28% |

**TABLE 11**

When do you think films which require the symbol should be shown?

BASE: ALL

| | Total | SEX | | AGE | | | | | CLASS | | | | CHILDREN | | | ETHNIC ORIGIN | | | |
|---|---|---|---|---|---|---|---|---|---|---|---|---|---|---|---|---|---|---|---|
| | | Male | Fe-male | 16-20 | 21-24 | 25-34 | 35-54 | 55+ | AB | C1 | C2 | DE | U5 | 5-15 | None | White | Afro-carib | Asian | Miss C4 a lot |
| TOTAL | 974 | 431 | 543 | 109 | 57 | 149 | 334 | 325 | 199 | 235 | 256 | 284 | 124 | 209 | 693 | 948 | 117 | 119 | 158 |
| Before 9pm | 2% | 3% | 2% | 3% | 2% | 3% | 3% | 2% | 3% | 2% | 4% | 2% | 2% | 3% | 2% | 2% | – | 8% | 3% |
| After 9pm | 16% | 13% | 18% | 20% | 21% | 20% | 14% | 14% | 18% | 17% | 14% | 15% | 21% | 17% | 15% | 16% | 14% | 16% | 18% |
| After 10pm | 34% | 34% | 34% | 30% | 37% | 40% | 36% | 30% | 44% | 37% | 31% | 28% | 36% | 37% | 33% | 34% | 32% | 38% | 43% |
| After 11pm | 25% | 27% | 24% | 28% | 28% | 26% | 18% | 24% | 20% | 28% | 21% | 25% | 27% | 24% | 25% | 25% | 23% | 18% | 21% |
| After 12pm | 18% | 18% | 17% | 17% | 12% | 10% | 18% | 22% | 13% | 11% | 21% | 24% | 11% | 14% | 20% | 18% | 28% | 19% | 13% |
| None | 3% | 3% | 3% | 1% | – | 1% | 3% | 6% | 1% | 4% | 2% | 5% | – | 2% | 4% | 3% | 2% | 1% | 2% |
| Don't know | 2% | 2% | 1% | 1% | – | 1% | 2% | 2% | 2% | 1% | 2% | 1% | 2% | 2% | 2% | 1% | 2% | – | – |

show films which might require prior notification. Only 3 per cent say that films which require the symbol should not be shown (Table 11).

The great benefit of SDR for most people was that it allowed greater scope for realism and the presentation of a broad range of difficult social and sexual issues. Most felt C4 was to be commended for this, although some felt that C4's SDR films (as apposed to the SDR symbol) had gone beyond the pale, whereas others openly acknowledged the prurient nature of their interest in the SDR symbol − it saves having to look for sexually explicit films. But in the main people understood and appreciated the point of the symbol.

There is universal praise for the idea that the SDR symbol gives back to individuals at home the right to decide for themselves what to watch. According to our respondents, at heart, the SDR symbol restores a sense of personal responsibility to the process of watching controversial television programmes.

> The red triangle is useful for putting the onus on viewers.
> Group 27                                          [Male OAP Sutton]

> It's not a good thing if you've got to switch the programme off is it? I would say it is bad planning.

> Do you not see what's going on first and choose what you want to watch, rather than putting it on and then switching it off.
> Group 2                                   [Female Over 35 BC1 Glasgow]

> To me they should tell you if there is going to be sex scenes ... because it does offend some people.
> Group 3                                  [Female Under 35 C2D Glasgow]

> With C4 I don't think that their programmes are a cross-section of programmes compared with ITV and BBC because ITV and BBC are sort of staid middle class types of programmes that would suit every youngster and adult. It's only lately that BBC and ITV have started this after nine o'clock whereas C4 would show it anyway.

> I think that the red triangle is a good idea, because at least you know it could be disturbing to someone who is nervous or young children, you don't want them to watch from a violence or sex point of view, and if you actually watch and you find you don't like it you don't have to watch it.
> Group 4                                  [Male Over 35 C2D Edinburgh]

> If you don't want to watch it, if a film is going to be on C4 and it says it is going to be rude then it's going to be rude, and if you don't want to

watch it, then you had better go and switch it off.
Group 13                                    [Female Under 35 BC1 Southampton]

Although most people were keen on the SDR symbol there was a continuing concern with the effect of the film on children and people who might be susceptible to deviation (needlessly to say, always other people, or people who did not live in the respondent's district). This concern is actually quite sophisticated; the respondents acknowledged that they had to make complex moral choices about what they watch, and what they allow their dependents to watch.

One Edinburgh man spoke of how his wife had walked in on a C4 programme and immediately said: 'That's disgusting,' a feeling which she extended to the whole channel. When the respondent was pressed on why she thought C4 was so disgusting he said, 'Well that's the only place she's really seen anything that bad. She's watched the channel once, I think for about five minutes, and that's it.'

As we saw earlier most of our respondents are deeply suspicious of this type of five-minute moralising, and another respondent in the group gave an example of more complex decision making. When one night he was watching C4 with his family, a sex scene appeared on the programme. He was faced with a choice: leave it on or switch it off. 'But, we didn't switch the television off, I didn't see the point, since they'd wonder even more what is going on, so we left it on. I don't think that it affected them. I mean, she has grown up into a perfectly normal person.' [Edinburgh, Over 35 C2DE Male Group 4]. Others said:

> The only trouble with having them on a Friday night very often parents go − maybe not in this area − but a lot of parents go out and leave the kids and the kids think oh, a red triangle film, go up to the bedroom and watch it.
> Group 21                                    [Afro-Caribbean Male]

> It depends if there are kids watching it. It's not nice is it? They should put those kinds of films on after a certain time. Not to ban them, but put them on at a certain time.
> Group 20                                    [Male C2D Over 35 Esher]

*(3) A Matter of Choice*
It was perhaps inevitable that Mary Whitehouse would figure prominently within the groups' discussions. The focus of such discussions however went far beyond opposition to the activities and views of the lady from Ardleigh, though it has to be said even those who agree with censorship are reluctant to accept the values of Whitehouse and the NVLA. The more significant and revealing criticism of the censorship lobby depended on feeling that it represented an elite view, which neither took 'ordinary people' seriously nor extended to them the right to choose for themselves what they did or did not

watch. Our suspicion is that the real issue was not the particular right to watch a television programme, but the more general democratic right to make an individual decision. As with other aspects of the position and condition of broadcasting in Britain, it is on firmest ground when it recognises that its central principles rest upon the foundation of democratic rights and procedures.

Whitehouse represents the censorship lobby in the minds of many viewers; indeed, many feel that she epitomises the 'nanny state'. One respondent committed a glorious malapropism, calling Mary Whitehouse 'Barbara Woodhouse', unconsciously suggesting perhaps that, like Woodhouse, Whitehouse was more concerned with obedience than rights, treating ordinary people as if they had no free will or ability to decide for themselves the difference between acceptable and unacceptable programmes. This was the nub of the argument against Whitehouse-like attitudes to television programmes. If the Government is genuinely concerned with the public's fears about television in the aftermath of Hungerford, it must pay close attention to the deep and intense desire on the part of most adults to be treated as responsible citizens.

Quite simply, the public wants to retain its right, within reason, to decide what to watch on television. As we shall see from the discussion groups, this feeling persists in the face of the possibility that one mad individual might be triggered by watching *Tom and Jerry* or *Rambo*. (Let us not forget that *Rambo* has never appeared on broadcast television in the UK, nor is there any evidence that Michael Ryan had seen the film. In fact, one of the intriguing things about Hungerford is the way that the newpapers took up the description of Ryan as *Rambo*. This had some basis in that one of the witnesses mistakenly thought they saw a sweat-band around Ryan's head of the sort that Rambo used. What the witness was doing was describing something for which he had no real-life experience, namely a gunman shooting people in his High Street, and he resorted to one of the pre-set descriptive categories available to him: namely, it was like Rambo − a term the newspapers had been using to describe everyone from Ronald Reagan to football players. The film itself had little to do with Hungerford and yet, because the newspapers described the events using a category which they practically invented, or certainly added meaning to, television was blamed. This confuses the power of images to frame and give voice to reality − which no-one would deny − with the ability of images to create reality.

In asking for freedom from excessive censorship, the public is making judgements about the Whitehousian elements in the Conservative Government, as much as commenting on the lady herself. However, there were also more specific complaints: that the values of the censorship lobby were simply out of date; that this lobby is not representative of the public; that it goes over the heads of the public to exert power over their lives, without having the elected authority to do so; and, finally, that the television companies deal adequately with controversial material, scheduling it so that those who might be offended or affected by it should anyhow be in bed.

> The bureaucracy has got Victorian ideas ... it is run by people that are sixty. If you have someone like Mary Whitehouse, as soon as something comes on − woof − she has seen it before anyone else.

> It annoys me that some people hamstring viewing. Someone up there says the average general public cannot watch this. They can go and pay to watch it, but cannot watch it [on television].
> Group 31                                    [Male Heavy C4 user]

> They have all these big-wigs who haven't a clue as to how ordinary people live and what their ideas are.
> Group 16                        [Female Over 35 C2D Southampton]

> It gets me annoyed when people like Mary Whitehouse voice their opinion, and it's in the paper and you think: 'God, what must she do all day...' What gives her the right to say what we can or can't watch?
> Group 13                          [Female Under 35 BC1 Southampton]

> People like Mary Whitehouse do a certain amount of good, but, you have to admit they also do a lot of bad.

> They should not stop good programmes on TV. There should be a more modern or younger Mary Whitehouse on the job, up to date.

> Who is she? Just a housewife.

> She is out of date.
> Group 14                            [Male Over 35 C2D Bristol]

Most people felt that Mary Whitehouse herself was hopelessly dated but, more to the point, they objected that her whole organisation is unrepresentative of the public's view on major issues. Furthermore, many cannot understand why she insists on personally auditing the output of the four channels: the feeling persists that she does not trust people to look after themselves. It is a feeling which causes great resentment: people do not like things being done in their name when they themselves are politically deprived of any appropriate counter-response. There was also general suspicion about complaints to broadcasting companies:

> Thirty letters and it's a deluge, isn't it? I mean ... I'm very suspicious about those. I mean you talk about complaints and criticisms − a lot of them come from a few influential individuals and a lot of them get hyped up by the media, certainly in some daily newspapers, and if you ever look into it in one or two cases as you're able to, you find actually

the basis of the complaints is very slender indeed. I mean, for example, and I think it is relevant, the Viewers and Listeners Association that Mary Whitehouse fronts, there was a very good *Sunday Times* article about two years ago on that ... I mean I'm sorry if anyone here actually − no offence − if you actually agree with its precepts, but the fact is that she claims to represent lots of people, the article proves she didn't, the paid up membership is about ... people in a population of 52 million.
Group 15                                    [Female Over 35 BC1 Bristol]

Well our Mary Whitehouse watches all the way through and then complains about it.

Mary Whitehouse don't watch C4.

I've always said that she's got a warped mind, and nobody else has. Because she sees things in things that are not there. I'm sure she does.
Group 20                                    [Male Over 35 C2D Esher]

I think that we're grown up enough.

If we don't like what we're watching we'll switch it off, but don't let's treat us like children. I don't like the idea where someone says, 'You're not big enough.'

That's exactly what I thought about that Sebastiane film, because I watched it and I never saw anything.

Perhaps Mary Whitehouse errs on the side of safety. Who the hell needs three parachutes.

She would censor some religious programmes.
Group 4                                    [Male Over 35 C2D Edinburgh]

Mary Whitehouse.

She is a stupid bat.

No, I don't agree with that, she is trying... No I think somebody has got to be on their back.

I would agree with you, to an extent.

She goes overboard.

I mentioned it earlier on and I believe in it firmly − there is an agenda that is set by minds that we don't even know. People who are faceless, people who are unknown to us, set an agenda, they decide what we are going to see, they decide what's fit for viewing.

Now and again they become visible, but it is unusual − now the extremes that all reach can be offensive to us − similarly the extremes that are reached in censorship I personally find totally repulsive to me. I find that Mary Whitehouse is naive, uninformed and overpublicised. I think that we should've the power over which should be good censorship. What should be sensible censorship, and a censorship of a nature that we can conduct within our own homes − she'll push people to the other extremes. My nature would be to say − 'that silly old fart says: this shouldn't be seen.' I'll stand up and say − 'I want to see it' − because I don't like the power or her − and I'm being totally subjective in that that, because I find her, she is abhorrent to me.
Group 37                                            [Male Catholic Belfast]

Most people were frustrated that the censorship lobby would not accept the distinction between adult time and general time on television and, furthermore, why those who advocate censorship cannot exercise their basic right to turn the television set off.

If anything is shown pretty late on in the evening, then you should not be offending anybody.

All kids should be in bed and the old dears should be in bed.

Mary Whitehouse has got the button [to change the channel] but she won't use it.
Group 15                                            [Male Over 35 C2DE Esher]

Extremists like [Mary Whitehouse] I mean if she had her own way *EastEnders* would be off the air.
Group 17                                            [Male Under 35 BC1 Esher]

The final point we would make here is, on the surface, trivial, and yet it goes to the heart of many of the issues about censorship. One Afro-Caribbean male respondent felt that the censorship lobby was wrong because: 'Well, I think you need a little surprise in your life sometimes.' Where would television be without the 'little surprises': the glories of *The Singing Detective;* Sheila's rape in *Brookside* (and Sue Johnson's powerful handling of the role); the tenderness of *Pixote*; and the many other moments on British television which many of our respondents felt transported British television out of its mundane, ordinary existence. The fear that we unearthed is that 'surprise' will be stifled and killed. One of the firmest conclusions of the whole study was that the trend of thought represented by Whitehouse was deeply distrusted and disliked by the most of our respondents.

The vital issue for most people is choosing for oneself: a great many things will be sacrificed to individual choice. Even swearing, which apparently annoys people more than sex, is subject to the twin pressures of realism and individual choice. One group accept it because 'that is the way the world is', another group accept it because 'they want the choice to watch it if it suited them.' In neither case do they make hard and fast rules about swearing, although it should be stated that it is the most persistent worry of most of those who complained about moral standards on television. Time and again, however, the groups came back to the assertion of their basic rights and their basic common sense.

I'm very aware of what the programme is before I enter into it.
Group 14                                    [Male Over 35 BC1 Bristol]

Blue movies, gratuitous violence ... wouldn't affect me ... [I do not think] Oh, I must go and do that.

[But sex] shouldn't be allowed.

I mean you get different churches on you know, does it alter your faith?

You are what you are and you stay that way.

No, they can't change your mind, just make you a little more curious.
Group 10                              [Female Over 35 BC1 Birmingham]

I don't think people are swayed to such an extent.

I mean it's really down to you. I think you're the one that censors it, you switch it on or off.

And you've got the option.

Yes, you just don't watch it.
Group 10                                  [Female Over 35 BC1 Glasgow]

You make up your own mind on what's right.
Group 25                                           [Male Teenager]

You're not forced to listen are you?

Everything is better out in the open
Group 28                                [Female OAPs Nottingham]

Sex... it's late at night and they are catering for those that does.

You can tell your children to go to bed.

You can censor your TV.

So it's your choice if you are watching it really.
Group 33                                                                          [Female Afro-Caribbean]

Although the question of self-censorship is extremely important, one should not lose sight of the 'Carry On' element in British views of sex and nudity on television. Most people treat SDR films with a large pinch of salt. The woman who said that she must tune into C4 more because it is all bottoms and bosoms was only half joking; she was indicating that nudity on television is not that important. Similarly, given that young men are considered to be at risk from the corrupting influence of films, the following quotation from two lads in the Catholic group sums up the good-humoured way that they approach SDR films: 'If there's a bit of dirt on television, we say, let's turn it on and get a curry.' They found it difficult to believe that they could be too corrupt after an onion bhaji and a meat and mushroom Madras.

*(4) Evaluating Television*
People have an extremely sophisticated and complex set of rules for interpreting the effects and influence of television. In fact, they do not engage with the debate about television as it is commonly presented by the press, media commentators, academics and politicians. Contrary to these groups, the general public has a non-media centred view of reality. Ordinary people know that social reality is constructed by powerful forces, such as unemployment, the family, local culture and work, and therefore do not subscribe to the ideas of those who live by ideas alone. In other words, reality is their everyday lived experience, and it has a brute facticity unmatched by the symbolic world of television. This has profound implications for Channel Four's approach to television, which involves allowing the presentation of social reality, red in tooth and claw.

Whatever the level of tolerance toward televised nudity, individuals do not hold television responsible for any decline in sexual morality. People's understanding of the social world and causal agency is not television-centred. Television, so far as most people are concerned, is peripheral to social change. For example, while 69 per cent of people think that sexual morality has declined over the last twenty years only 18 per cent blame television. Given a list of causes for the decline in morals most people nominate easier contraception (35 per cent). This is by far the most important category, and much further down in people's perception are pornographic magazines (19 per cent), television (18 per cent), sexy advertising (6 per cent), simpler divorce (6 per cent) and sex education in schools (4 per cent) (Table 12).

To put this into even clearer perspective one quarter of the population claims that television is least responsible for the decline in sexual morality. This is the same among both women and men; indeed, women are more likely to blame easier contraception than men, indicating that they are more aware of

113

## TABLE 12

Which one of these do you think is most responsible for the decline in sexual morality?

BASE: All who think that sexual morality has declined in the last 20 years

| | Total | SEX | | AGE | | | | | CLASS | | | | CHILDREN | | | ETHNIC ORGIN | | | |
|---|---|---|---|---|---|---|---|---|---|---|---|---|---|---|---|---|---|---|---|
| | | Male | Fe-male | 16-20 | 21-24 | 25-34 | 35-54 | 55+ | AB | C1 | C2 | DE | U5 | 5-15 | None | White | Afro-carib | Asian | Miss C4 a lot |
| TOTAL | 675 | 282 | 393 | 57 | 33 | 91 | 235 | 259 | 141 | 172 | 166 | 196 | 74 | 133 | 497 | 658 | 72 | 82 | 99 |
| Easier contraception | 35% | 30% | 38% | 32% | 39% | 37% | 34% | 35% | 43% | 42% | 30% | 27% | 38% | 32% | 35% | 34% | 42% | 26% | 36% |
| Simpler divorce | 6% | 6% | 7% | 4% | — | 9% | 8% | 6% | 6% | 5% | 7% | 8% | 7% | 8% | 6% | 6% | 6% | 7% | 9% |
| Page 3 girls | 2% | 3% | 1% | 4% | 3% | 2% | 3% | 1% | 3% | — | 1% | 5% | 4% | 2% | 2% | 2% | 3% | 4% | 1% |
| Pornographic magazines | 19% | 18% | 20% | 21% | 21% | 13% | 19% | 21% | 9% | 15% | 22% | 30% | 15% | 20% | 19% | 19% | 21% | 21% | 21% |
| Television | 18% | 20% | 17% | 21% | 21% | 23% | 19% | 15% | 18% | 27% | 21% | 13% | 16% | 22% | 18% | 19% | 10% | 18% | 19% |
| Sexy advertising | 6% | 6% | 6% | 2% | 3% | 8% | 4% | 8% | 5% | 5% | 7% | 6% | 5% | 5% | 6% | 6% | 4% | 6% | 4% |
| Sex education in schools | 4% | 5% | 3% | 2% | 6% | 1% | 4% | 5% | 1% | 4% | 5% | 4% | 4% | 2% | 4% | 4% | 6% | 9% | 3% |
| Other | 5% | 6% | 3% | 5% | 6% | 5% | 6% | 3% | 9% | 5% | 3% | 3% | 5% | 4% | 5% | 5% | 4% | — | 3% |
| Don't know | 6% | 6% | 6% | 12% | — | 1% | 5% | 7% | 7% | 3% | 5% | 7% | 5% | 5% | 6% | 6% | 6% | 2% | 3% |

what affects their own sex lives. Age does not seem to affect the rank ordering of the causes of sexual decline; the older groups, who were most concerned with nudity on television, do not extend their worries to a concern with the effects of television.

Unlike the tabloid press and moral crusaders, people are unlikely to nominate television as an important factor in the increase in violent crime in the UK. When asked what has caused this increase respondents nominated lack of discipline in the home (41 per cent) and unemployment (25 per cent). Much further down in people's perceptions comes lack of discipline in schools (10 per cent), television (10 per cent) and poor housing (5 per cent).

Those who live at the sharp end of rising crime, namely the unemployed working class, are much more likely to nominate unemployment as the main cause of violence (32 per cent) than the middle class (19 per cent). The middle class blames individual and personal factors, namely lack of discipline in the home, rather than the structural factor of unemployment. People relate to this question out of their own experience; if someone suffers the result of structural change then they adopt sociological explanations – they blame the social world. Those for whom structural change is not a problem tend to blame individual morality or the home; the middle class in particular allocates responsiblity to bad parents and home-life for the rise in crime. Very, very few people adopt the radically individualist view that there is a causal relationship between television and crime. To do so would be to deny the very social reality of which they are part. As members of families, occupations, religions, political parties, gangs, or social movements people have some understanding of the sources of their behaviour. To deny this is to dehumanise people and, in some ways, to suggest that they are incapable of performing as full members of a democracy. If they are incapable of seeing what is in front of them in the empirical world, how could one trust them with the abstract world of political ideals?

Those who blame television for shifts in sexual or personal morality in the name of 'the people', do so at the expense of treating people as capable, rational beings. One of the great dangers of populism down the ages has been the tendency to treat 'the people' as if they are leaderless children in need of a parent. As our research has demonstrated overwhelmingly, in the particular case of television 'the people' claim that they have no need of a parent to tell them that they must be protected; most people think that it is ludicrous to ignore the social sources of their behaviour in favour of claiming that their attitudes and actions are formed by television.

If we see these explanations as types of social analysis we can say that the working class think like sociologists, the middle class like psychotherapists, and those who hold TV to be responsible for social change like mystics. Mystics argue that one can abandon oneself to the ineffable where the self becomes a vehicle for something or someone else. Those who extend this

115

## TABLE 13

Which one of these factors do you think is mainly responsible for the rise in violent crime?

BASE: ALL

| | Total | SEX | | AGE | | | | | CLASS | | | | CHILDREN | | | ETHNIC ORGIN | | | Miss C4 a lot |
| --- | --- | --- | --- | --- | --- | --- | --- | --- | --- | --- | --- | --- | --- | --- | --- | --- | --- | --- | --- |
| | | Male | Fe-male | 16-20 | 21-24 | 25-34 | 35-54 | 55+ | AB | C1 | C2 | DE | U5 | 5-15 | None | White | Afro-carib | Asian | |
| Total | 974 | 431 | 543 | 109 | 57 | 149 | 334 | 325 | 199 | 235 | 256 | 284 | 209 | 693 | 948 | 117 | 119 | 158 | |
| Unemployment | 25% | 26% | 24% | 50% | 39% | 32% | 21% | 15% | 19% | 20% | 26% | 32% | 30% | 30% | 23% | 24% | 42% | 45% | 28% |
| Lack of discipline in schools | 10% | 10% | 10% | 8% | 9% | 10% | 9% | 13% | 11% | 8% | 12% | 11% | 10% | 8% | 11% | 10% | 9% | 13% | 9% |
| Poor housing/poverty | 5% | 6% | 7% | 7% | 9% | 2% | 2% | 7% | 6% | 6% | 3% | 10% | 10% | 6% | 5% | 5% | 13% | 8% | 4% |
| Lack of discipline in the home | 41% | 42% | 41% | 20% | 32% | 35% | 48% | 47% | 47% | 49% | 36% | 36% | 36% | 39% | 43% | 42% | 25% | 17% | 35% |
| Television | 10% | 7% | 11% | 7% | 9% | 6% | 9% | 13% | 9% | 7% | 11% | 11% | 5% | 8% | 11% | 10% | 2% | 8% | 8% |
| Break up of old communities | 4% | 4% | 5% | 1% | 2% | 5% | 6% | 4% | 8% | 6% | 4% | 2% | 2% | 5% | 4% | 4% | 3% | 3% | 10% |
| The decline of religion | 3% | 3% | 3% | — | 2% | 1% | 3% | 5% | 4% | 3% | 2% | 2% | 2% | 2% | 3% | 3% | 6% | 5% | 3% |
| Other | 2% | 3% | 1% | — | 4% | 1% | 2% | 3% | 3% | 2% | 2% | 2% | 3% | 3% | 2% | 2% | — | 1% | 4% |
| Don't know | 3% | 3% | 2% | 1% | 2% | 1% | 3% | 3% | 2% | 3% | 2% | 3% | 1% | 2% | 3% | 3% | 6% | 3% | 2% |

type of analysis to television assume that there is a form of communion between tv and its viewer which undermines and obliterates the viewer's sense of self and community — almost as if viewers were like the Gadarene swine, taken over by demons and driven over the moral cliff. Just as casting out demons was a mystical response to mental illness, so greatly increasing the level of censorship of television is a mystic response to the decline of sexual morality (if such it be), and growing violence in the UK. This attitude to television is clearly not shared by the most of the UK population.

Importantly, although the adult world, as expressed through the newspapers, blames television for youthful violence, young people themselves do not. Half of the young people blame unemployment for rising violence, which is a great deal higher than any other group. Those at the sharp end of unemployment have an understanding of the problems they face similar to that adduced by sociologists. They are more likely to claim that the pressures and frustrations of unemployment produce intense anti-social reactions in a way that watching *Miami Vice* does not. They do not take the easy way out and blame television for forcing them to adopt behaviour which they would not otherwise do. Television is not used as a scapegoat. Only 7 per cent of young people adopt the mystic explanation connecting television with violence and, after all, as they are the ones committing most violent crime one would assume that their testimony must count a little more than that of a sub-editor at the Sun.

> I mean I watched tv as a kid, saw *Tom and Jerry* — I didn't end up throwing ironing boards at people, and dropping anvils on them; the way you are brought up in your family maybe makes all the difference; going out in the park and having to fight this man, instead of backing down — now that is very much part of your environment. Tv: I think that it happens too often, that we all turn around and say — there are evils in society, that thing in the corner is to blame.
> Group 37                                                    [Male Catholic Belfast]

Even those who consider television to be a malevolent force do not extend their dislike of television across all social dimensions. Those who think that television affects sexual morality, do not argue that it is the cause of an increase in violent crime. Similarly, only one fifth of those who think that television is responsible for the rise in violence also blame it for the decline in sexual morality. In other words, there is no blanket condemnation of television. Even though working class people are less likely to blame television for the rise in crime, they are more inclined to say that television has affected people's attitudes to violence. However, this is more a concern about crime as such than television; people worried about crime above all else will seek out every explanation for any perceived increase, and therefore will attribute responsibility to an important part of their social world — namely, television. Although it is important to recognise that the older working class fear the effects of television, as we pointed out above, they still think it much less important than unemployment as a contributory factor to the rise in crime. The middle classes, who are much more worried about morality than violent crime (which they seldom have to deal with), are more likely to express their dissatisfaction with television in moral-psychological terms: namely, that it has contributed to the decline in sexual morality.

A third area of concern for most people is swearing on television. Given that sexual morality and violent behaviour are such powerful factors in any society one would expect perhaps that most people would not nominate television as a cause of such behaviour and attitudes, but swearing is such an imitative phenomenon, and one where the sources of learning can be fairly easily identified, one could reasonably expect television to play a leading role. Yet, here again, people do not attribute as much influence to television (32 per cent) as they do to other children in school (51 per cent), family (37 per cent) or other children out of school (34 per cent).

Quite simply, people are again indicating that any reasonable person would recognise that most children spend most of their waking hours with their friends in and out of school, therefore they are bound to learn more from peer groups than from television. Peer group pressures are, as most studies of childhood show, infinitely more powerful in forming culture and values than the media. Therefore, it is not only the quantity of time spent with the peer group that matters but the quality of that time.

This is not to say that people do not object to swearing on television, rather that this is something different from people's perception of the imitative power of television. Those who object to swearing on television in all probability object to anyone swearing at all in their home. There are very strict rules about the use of 'bad' language in most households. These rules are concerned with the boundaries of acceptable behaviour but, perhaps more importantly, they express concern about the nature of relationships: if a grand-daughter swears in front of, or to, her grand-mother, then she is disrespectful. Even if people are on their own in the house they might be shocked by swearing, because they themselves would never use that language in the house (or even sometimes just in that room).

Language, as ever, is about social relationships as much as about the simple meaning of the words. If one believes that the home is somehow a place where 'good' behaviour is constitutive of what one means by being 'home', then swearing on television can be immensely disorienting. One's own identity is disturbed if one listens to (and therefore condones) swearing in one's own living room. Television crosses the boundaries of important social relationships when swearing occurs on a programme, therefore swearing worries people more than, say, topless female nudity. For this reason swearing is the only category where a large portion of the population is concerned about the effect television has on behaviour.

**TABLE 14**

Swearing is very common among young people today. Where do you think they pick it up from?

| | Total | SEX | | AGE | | | | | CLASS | | | | CHILDREN | | | TV VIEWING | | | |
|---|---|---|---|---|---|---|---|---|---|---|---|---|---|---|---|---|---|---|---|
| | | Male | Fe-male | 16-20 | 21-24 | 25-34 | 35-54 | 55+ | AB | C1 | C2 | DE | U5 | 5-15 | None | Light 1-14 | Med 15-27 | Heavy 28+ | Miss C4 a lot |
| TOTAL | 974 | 431 | 543 | 109 | 57 | 149 | 334 | 325 | 199 | 235 | 256 | 284 | 124 | 209 | 693 | 337 | 267 | 348 | 158 |
| Other children | 51% | 57% | 47% | 59% | 70% | 62% | 49% | 43% | 58% | 60% | 44% | 46% | 61% | 53% | 50% | 55% | 51% | 49% | 55% |
| Other children (outside school) | 34% | 37% | 32% | 40% | 40% | 42% | 33% | 29% | 39% | 31% | 35% | 32% | 36% | 39% | 32% | 36% | 34% | 32% | 32% |
| Family | 37% | 35% | 38% | 20% | 32% | 36% | 36% | 45% | 38% | 32% | 34% | 43% | 42% | 32% | 37% | 39% | 31% | 39% | 34% |
| TV programmes | 32% | 30% | 34% | 33% | 35% | 31% | 32% | 31% | 31% | 33% | 32% | 32% | 34% | 34% | 32% | 32% | 31% | 31% | 34% |
| Pop magazines | 2% | 2% | 3% | 2% | 2% | 3% | 2% | 3% | 3% | 3% | 2% | 2% | 1% | 1% | 3% | 3% | 3% | 2% | 3% |
| Cinema | 8% | 7% | 8% | 4% | 11% | 10% | 10% | 5% | 8% | 9% | 8% | 6% | 8% | 8% | 8% | 7% | 9% | 7% | 3% |
| Other people in the street | 25% | 25% | 26% | 44% | 25% | 34% | 21% | 20% | 21% | 24% | 28% | 27% | 26% | 23% | 25% | 24% | 24% | 28% | 26% |
| Other | 3% | 2% | 4% | 2% | 2% | 3% | 4% | 3% | 3% | 0% | 5% | 4% | 4% | 3% | 3% | 1% | 3% | 4% | 3% |
| Don't know | 3% | 3% | 3% | — | 2% | 2% | 4% | 5% | 2% | 3% | 4% | 4% | 2% | 3% | 3% | 4% | 3% | 2% | 3% |

To sum up then: the public has sophisticated techniques for understanding the relationship between television and the social world. People do not condemn 'the box in the corner' for crimes which they feel it has not committed; at worst it is regarded as a petty-criminal. Whitehouse and the Special Discretion Required symbol provoked discussion marked by the quality of the argument, and also by a kind of bluff good humour. Many people acknowledged that they had deliberately turned on an SDR film and stopped watching out of boredom rather than disgust. Films such as *Pixote* and *The Clinic* were praised because they were good films, whereas *Themroc* was criticised because it was boring. The films were judged, not the sex in the films. One antidote to counter the persistent claims of the excessive censors was humour. For example, one old lady who complained that in many programmes 'they've no sooner met than they're in bed', was put down by another pensioner who said: 'You're only jealous.'

## (4) Minorities: Rights and Representation

'Everybody's got a right to a say.'
[Female Under 35 C2D Glasgow]

Above all else, Channel Four is an actor in a social drama about human rights and cultural representation. This drama, played out on what Burke called 'the moral theatre of the world', took place in Britain in the 1970s. The middle and latter parts of this decade were characterised by a series of challenges to the cultural and political monopolies which had dominated the country in the post-war years.

The sense of Britain in the late 1970s was of a society where the rules of debate no longer held: consensus had given way to minoritarian zeal. One outcome of this was the call for more partisan minority and special interest television. Part of the resolution of this crisis in the drama involved the creation of Channel Four, whose brief was to serve those previously excluded by television. This challenge to the idea of a monolithic television culture helped re-establish the possiblity of cultural reintegration for those groups and interests which felt excluded from mainstream culture. It would appear from our research that the channel has either convinced most people that specialist and minority-oriented television is important, or that it has tapped into feelings about human rights and representation which pre-existed it. Either way, the channel has the backing of the majority of the public in its orientation toward new voices and experiences.

Just as drama ends with the re-establishment of order, or the resolution of conflict (albeit temporary), so Channel Four is now being regarded by the public from a position of a new social order. Most people have settled (albeit unwillingly) for a multi-ethnic society, and generalise about the effects of ethnic or minority television from the basis of their experience of such a society. That experience has led white people to be sympathetic to ethnic television — although of a very marginalised kind — and to ethnic and sexual minorities tempering their demands on television because of their realisation that television does not fundamentally change their lot.

We will be dealing with two themes in this section: the grounds which people adduce for advocating or tolerating minority and specialist television, and the complexity of the views of ethnic and sexual minorities about television. In particular, we will explore their reluctance to present themselves as part of a common cause. The rainbow coalition of minorities does not exist: Asians do not link themselves with Afro-Caribbeans; ethnic groups will not unite with gays; and lesbians are not happy identifying themselves with homosexual men.

### (1) The Grounds of Tolerance

The backdrop to the public's attitudes about minority television is its commitment to public service television (which inherently appeals to tolerance), and the range of special interests which people themselves have. By and large, the public is committed to experimental television, or, at least to the idea that programmes should be transmitted that might appeal only to a few people (Table 15). This philosophical ground for tolerance is supplemented by the range of special interests held by the public, which television exploits with only partial success.

Around two-thirds of the population claim to have watched a Channel Four programme because it was about their own special interest (Table 16). One reason for people's affection for the channel is that they watch specialist programmes; fully eight out of ten of those most committed to the channel claim to have done so. Furthermore, almost half of the population have untapped interests about which they would like to see television pro- grammes. The public's curiosity and range of interests has yet to be exhausted by Channel Four. This is especially the case for Afro-Caribbeans — almost two-thirds of whom claim to have special interests which they would like the channel to explore — and Asians, who likewise have substantial untapped interests. The channel's ethnic policy has clearly yet to satiate those for whom it was developed.

On the basis that most people have an acknowledged special interest, we can say that the public appreciates that everyone is part of some kind of minority. The fragmentation of taste is held to be acceptable if it contributes to the range of what is available on television; therefore, at one level at least, programmes for ethnic and sexual minorities are judged according to public service criteria: the politics of minority programmes feed on the principles of public service television.

The question of minority programmes is larger than that of public service broadcasting; it goes to the roots of tolerance in society. Attitudes to

121

## TABLE 15

How much do you agree or disagree with these statements?
If a programme is only watched by a very few people who really enjoy it, it should be replaced by something more popular?

BASE: ALL

| | Total | SEX | | AGE | | | | | CLASS | | | | CHILDREN | | | ETHNIC ORGIN | | | Miss C4 a lot |
| | | Male | Fe-male | 16-20 | 21-24 | 25-34 | 35-54 | 55+ | AB | C1 | C2 | DE | U5 | 5-15 | None | White | Afro-carib | Asian | |
|---|---|---|---|---|---|---|---|---|---|---|---|---|---|---|---|---|---|---|---|
| TOTAL | 974 | 431 | 543 | 109 | 57 | 149 | 334 | 325 | 199 | 235 | 256 | 284 | 124 | 209 | 693 | 948 | 117 | 119 | 158 |
| Definitely agree | 10% | 8% | 11% | 10% | 12% | 9% | 10% | 10% | 5% | 10% | 9% | 13% | 10% | 8% | 5% | 10% | 24% | 17% | 8% |
| Tend to agree | 34% | 35% | 34% | 38% | 33% | 36% | 30% | 37% | 25% | 33% | 41% | 36% | 35% | 36% | 33% | 34% | 32% | 35% | 30% |
| Neither | 5% | 5% | 5% | 7% | 5% | 7% | 6% | 2% | 5% | 6% | 6% | 3% | 5% | 4% | 5% | 5% | 7% | 9% | 4% |
| Tend to disagree | 35% | 33% | 37% | 37% | 35% | 39% | 37% | 32% | 40% | 38% | 32% | 33% | 38% | 40% | 33% | 35% | 23% | 27% | 35% |
| Definitely disagree | 13% | 16% | 11% | 6% | 12% | 9% | 15% | 15% | 24% | 11% | 9% | 10% | 10% | 10% | 14% | 13% | 12% | 9% | 22% |
| Don't know | 3% | 2% | 3% | 2% | 2% | 1% | 3% | 5% | 2% | 2% | 2% | 5% | 2% | 2% | 3% | 3% | 2% | 3% | 2% |

## TABLE 16

Have you ever watched a Channel 4 programme because it was about you own special interest, for example DIY, opera, fishing and so on?

BASE: ALL

| | Total | SEX | | AGE | | | | | CLASS | | | | CHILDREN | | | ETHNIC ORGIN | | | Miss C4 a lot |
| | | Male | Fe-male | 16-20 | 21-24 | 25-34 | 35-54 | 55+ | AB | C1 | C2 | DE | U5 | 5-15 | None | White | Afro-carib | Asian | |
|---|---|---|---|---|---|---|---|---|---|---|---|---|---|---|---|---|---|---|---|
| TOTAL | 974 | 431 | 543 | 109 | 57 | 149 | 334 | 325 | 199 | 235 | 256 | 284 | 124 | 209 | 693 | 948 | 117 | 119 | 158 |
| YES | 64% | 70% | 59% | 66% | 56% | 58% | 68% | 63% | 70% | 67% | 62% | 58% | 52% | 60% | 67% | 64% | 74% | 57% | 83% |
| No | 35% | 29% | 41% | 34% | 44% | 41% | 31% | 36% | 29% | 32% | 37% | 41% | 47% | 39% | 33% | 35% | 26% | 42% | 17% |
| Don't know | 1% | 1% | 1% | — | — | 1% | 1% | 1% | 1% | 1% | 1% | 1% | 1% | 1% | 1% | 1% | — | 1% | — |

## TABLE 17

Are there any special interests which you personally would like to see Channel 4 make programmes about?

BASE: ALL

| | Total | SEX | | AGE | | | | | CLASS | | | | CHILDREN | | | ETHNIC ORGIN | | | | |
| | | Male | Fe-male | 16-20 | 21-24 | 25-34 | 35-54 | 55+ | AB | C1 | C2 | DE | U5 | 5-15 | None | White | Afro-carib | Asian | Miss C4 a lot |
|---|---|---|---|---|---|---|---|---|---|---|---|---|---|---|---|---|---|---|---|
| TOTAL | 974 | 431 | 543 | 109 | 57 | 149 | 334 | 325 | 199 | 235 | 256 | 284 | 124 | 209 | 693 | 948 | 117 | 119 | 158 |
| Yes | 42% | 47% | 38% | 48% | 35% | 34% | 49% | 38% | 49% | 43% | 43% | 36% | 36% | 43% | 42% | 42% | 62% | 52% | 55% |
| No | 51% | 47% | 53% | 46% | 58% | 57% | 47% | 51% | 45% | 50% | 52% | 54% | 58% | 52% | 49% | 51% | 32% | 40% | 37% |
| Don't know | 7% | 6% | 8% | 6% | 7% | 9% | 4% | 10% | 6% | 7% | 5% | 10% | 6% | 5% | 8% | 7% | 6% | 8% | 8% |

programmes about racial and sexual minorities are as much a reaction to the minorities as they are to special interest television. Racial hatred spreads to views about the appearance of ethnic minorities on television; if someone considers West Indians to be a cultural blight he is hardly likely to sanction television programmes by, or about, West Indians.

Few people express such extreme reactions to the idea of West Indian programmes. Indifference, a more common form of racism, however, leads to a very precise notion of 'representative television'. Positive discrimination in television, which would give more air-time to ethnic minorities than their size deserves, is not favoured by the public. Most people, including the ethnic minorities, argue that each minority should be allocated TV time on the basis of its proportion of the population.

> It isn't really minority groups it's specialist groups. Minority groups implies that they are a minority in everything.
> Group 14                                             [Male Over 35 BC1 Bristol]

> Minority programmes shouldn't be as peak viewing, it shouldn't be on at times where ... if you're interested in that kind of thing you're going to sit and watch it, but it really shouldn't be peak viewing ... because the vast majority of folk wouldn't be interested.
> Group 3                                             [Female Under 35 C2D Glasgow]

> TV should cater for all kinds of people. We have an on and an off switch - something like that [an ethnic programme] wouldn't appeal to me, we just wouldn't watch it. But there must be people who find it interesting.
> Group 17                                             [Female Under 35 BC1 Woking]

> If they're in England, well they have the right to a little bit of say. As long as the don't try to rule the world.
> Group 28                                             [Female Pensioners]

> I think that they should do it on a proportional basis, you know, I mean if there is very few of a particular minority, well I mean, you don't give them that much time, and you don't do it all that often.
> Group 27                                             [Male Pensioners]

This principle of proportionality is central to people's views of Channel Four, but it is moderated by another principle, that of cultural integrity. This second principle states that only those minorities which have a recognisably coherent and distinctive culture should be allowed access to television.

According to the principle of proportionality: 'everyone has got to have a say'. Television has to cast its net sufficiently wide and capture the range of attitudes, opinions and beliefs of the British population. When this principle is extended to specific minorities, these must have cultural integrity. The public separates legitimate minority groups who have distinctive values, experiences and cultures, from illegitimate groups who are not considered to have a 'real' culture, ie one which is sufficiently different from that of the mainstream.

Ethnic groups qualify for TV airtime on two counts: they are part of the population and qualify therefore under the proportionality principle; furthermore, they have recognisably distinctive cultures, which qualifies them under the principle of cultural integrity. According to the first principle homosexuals have certain rights — although it is difficult to discover what proportion of airtime they would deserve as no-one knows the size of the homosexual population — even though many people exclude homosexuals on the basis that they do not qualify under the cultural integrity principle. Their culture is not uniform nor sufficiently distinctive to afford them a voice. Futhermore, the perceived social difficulty of allowing the homosexual voice on television is not offset by their rights to representation. A male OAP summed up this position when he argued: 'We've got so many blacks and Asians, and if they've got to have their own point of view I suppose, and don't get me wrong, I'm against it, but that's beside the point, there's so many of them now that they've got to have their own point of view and I suppose you've got to let them do it. And if I don't want to watch it I turn the thing off. I can accept it for the Asians and your coloureds and all that, but when it comes to your bloody queers and God knows what, you know sorry, not for me.'

Homosexuality is at the cutting edge of tolerance. Gay programmes are simply unacceptable to over half of the British population; when asked with what regularity homosexuals should have a programme on Channel Four, six out of ten said: 'None' (see Table 18). This is not the result of simply disliking minority programmes — only one-fifth of the population objects to television programmes for Asians or Afro-Caribbeans — it is an anti-gay response and poses some difficult questions for Channel Four (Tables 19/20). It should be noted though that only one-fifth of the population would object to a programme about gay rights.

In order to understand why half the population are unwilling to allow certain interest groups, such as the Communist Party, to appear on television, while at the same time 80 per cent are prepared to accept the principle that Afro-Caribbeans should have such access, we have to explore the wider aspects of social tolerance, which are the philosophical grounds of television tolerance (see Table 21).

Those who are socially tolerant are more likely to accept the need for television to explore areas in which they themselves are not interested. We can see this from the public's acceptance of public demonstrations and moral education. The former tells us about attitudes to the public expression of

## TABLE 18

For each of the following groups, do you think they should have regular/occasional/no programmes on Channel 4? *Homosexuals*

BASE: ALL

| | Total | SEX | | AGE | | | | | CLASS | | | | CHILDREN | | None | ETHNIC ORGIN | | | Miss C4 a lot |
|---|---|---|---|---|---|---|---|---|---|---|---|---|---|---|---|---|---|---|---|
| | | Male | Fe-male | 16-20 | 21-24 | 25-34 | 35-54 | 55+ | AB | C1 | C2 | DE | U5 | 5-15 | | White | Afro-carib | Asian | |
| TOTAL | 974 | 431 | 543 | 109 | 57 | 149 | 334 | 325 | 199 | 235 | 256 | 284 | 124 | 209 | 693 | 948 | 117 | 119 | 158 |
| Regular | 3% | 3% | 3% | 5% | 4% | 3% | 4% | 1% | 3% | 1% | 3% | 5% | 3% | 3% | 3% | 3% | 9% | 6% | 5% |
| Occasional | 32% | 30% | 34% | 53% | 49% | 53% | 34% | 11% | 38% | 31% | 32% | 29% | 48% | 39% | 28% | 32% | 32% | 27% | 45% |
| None | 61% | 63% | 59% | 40% | 47% | 39% | 59% | 82% | 56% | 64% | 60% | 62% | 44% | 53% | 66% | 61% | 57% | 63% | 47% |
| Don't know | 4% | 4% | 3% | 2% | — | 5% | 3% | 5% | 4% | 3% | 4% | 4% | 4% | 5% | 4% | 4% | 3% | 4% | 3% |

## TABLE 19

For each of the following groups, do you think they should have regular/occasional/no programmes on Channel 4? *West Indians and Africans*

BASE: ALL

| | Total | SEX | | AGE | | | | | CLASS | | | | CHILDREN | | None | ETHNIC ORGIN | | | Miss C4 a lot |
|---|---|---|---|---|---|---|---|---|---|---|---|---|---|---|---|---|---|---|---|
| | | Male | Fe-male | 16-20 | 21-24 | 25-34 | 35-54 | 55+ | AB | C1 | C2 | DE | U5 | 5-15 | | White | Afro-carib | Asian | |
| TOTAL | 974 | 431 | 543 | 109 | 57 | 149 | 334 | 325 | 199 | 235 | 256 | 284 | 124 | 209 | 693 | 948 | 117 | 119 | 158 |
| Regular | 13% | 13% | 13% | 18% | 12% | 14% | 15% | 10% | 17% | 14% | 11% | 13% | 15% | 16% | 12% | 13% | 41% | 37% | 22% |
| Occasional | 62% | 60% | 64% | 63% | 67% | 66% | 64% | 57% | 63% | 66% | 63% | 58% | 62% | 59% | 63% | 62% | 53% | 57% | 59% |
| None | 21% | 24% | 19% | 17% | 21% | 17% | 19% | 27% | 17% | 20% | 20% | 26% | 22% | 21% | 21% | 22% | 6% | 3% | 18% |
| Don't know | 3% | 3% | 3% | 1% | — | 3% | 2% | 6% | 4% | 1% | 5% | 3% | 2% | 4% | 3% | 3% | — | 3% | 1% |

**TABLE 20**

For each of the following groups, do you think they should have regular/occasional/no programmes on Channel 4?
*Asians*

BASE: ALL

| | Total | SEX | | AGE | | | | | CLASS | | | | CHILDREN | | ETHNIC ORGIN | | | | Miss C4 a lot |
| | | Male | Female | 16-20 | 21-24 | 25-34 | 35-54 | 55+ | AB | C1 | C2 | DE | U5 | 5-15 | None | White | Afro-carib | Asian | |
|---|---|---|---|---|---|---|---|---|---|---|---|---|---|---|---|---|---|---|---|
| TOTAL | 974 | 431 | 543 | 109 | 57 | 149 | 334 | 325 | 199 | 235 | 256 | 284 | 124 | 209 | 693 | 948 | 117 | 119 | 158 |
| Regular | 13% | 13% | 13% | 17% | 11% | 14% | 15% | 10% | 17% | 14% | 11% | 11% | 15% | 16% | 12% | 12% | 27% | 47% | 22% |
| Occasional | 62% | 60% | 64% | 62% | 68% | 64% | 64% | 58% | 63% | 65% | 63% | 59% | 60% | 60% | 63% | 62% | 63% | 49% | 61% |
| None | 22% | 24% | 20% | 20% | 21% | 19% | 18% | 27% | 18% | 20% | 21% | 27% | 23% | 20% | 22% | 22% | 9% | 2% | 17% |
| Don't know | 3% | 3% | 3% | 1% | – | 2% | 2% | 6% | 3% | 1% | 5% | 3% | 2% | 3% | 3% | 3% | 1% | 3% | 1% |

**TABLE 21**

Are there any minority groups which you would not like to appear on Channel 4?

BASE: ALL

| | Total | SEX | | AGE | | | | | CLASS | | | | CHILDREN | | ETHNIC ORGIN | | | | Miss C4 a lot |
| | | Male | Female | 16-20 | 21-24 | 25-34 | 35-54 | 55+ | AB | C1 | C2 | DE | U5 | 5-15 | None | White | Afro-carib | Asian | |
|---|---|---|---|---|---|---|---|---|---|---|---|---|---|---|---|---|---|---|---|
| TOTAL | 974 | 431 | 543 | 109 | 57 | 149 | 334 | 325 | 199 | 235 | 256 | 284 | 124 | 209 | 693 | 948 | 117 | 119 | 158 |
| NO | 46% | 40% | 51% | 59% | 61% | 66% | 40% | 37% | 46% | 43% | 52% | 43% | 59% | 49% | 43% | 46% | 52% | 44% | 45% |
| YES – CND | 6% | 7% | 5% | 5% | 4% | 3% | 5% | 9% | 5% | 9% | 3% | 6% | 2% | 5% | 7% | 6% | 3% | – | 2% |
| Friends of the Earth/Greenpeace | 4% | 4% | 4% | 1% | 2% | 1% | 4% | 6% | 3% | 4% | 3% | 5% | 3% | 4% | 4% | 4% | 2% | – | 2% |
| Anti-abortionist | 5% | 5% | 5% | 2% | 5% | 2% | 5% | 7% | 6% | 6% | 4% | 5% | 2% | 5% | 5% | 5% | 2% | 5% | 3% |
| National Front | 30% | 34% | 26% | 28% | 26% | 27% | 32% | 29% | 28% | 30% | 27% | 33% | 28% | 29% | 30% | 29% | 33% | 34% | 28% |
| Pro-abortionist | 6% | 6% | 6% | 2% | 2% | 4% | 7% | 8% | 6% | 6% | 5% | 6% | 5% | 5% | 6% | 6% | 6% | 8% | 3% |
| Gay rights | 24% | 26% | 22% | 13% | 16% | 9% | 28% | 32% | 26% | 26% | 20% | 26% | 15% | 24% | 25% | 24% | 13% | 21% | 21% |
| Communist party | 17% | 18% | 16% | 6% | 14% | 13% | 16% | 23% | 13% | 19% | 13% | 21% | 10% | 14% | 18% | 17% | 9% | 13% | 14% |
| Pro-Censorship | 5% | 6% | 5% | 3% | 5% | 2% | 5% | 9% | 4% | 8% | 4% | 5% | 2% | 4% | 6% | 5% | 4% | 3% | 5% |
| Anti-apartheid | 5% | 5% | 5% | 2% | 4% | 2% | 5% | 9% | 6% | 6% | 4% | 6% | 4% | 4% | 6% | 5% | 4% | – | 4% |
| Any other | 7% | 10% | 6% | 3% | 4% | 3% | 12% | 8% | 15% | 7% | 7% | 3% | 2% | 5% | 9% | 8% | 8% | 3% | 9% |
| Don't know | 9% | 8% | 10% | 4% | 4% | 2% | 8% | 16% | 5% | 9% | 9% | 13% | 6% | 7% | 11% | 9% | 4% | 12% | 7% |

political and cultural minorities, and to the rights of free speech; the latter about the range of views to which people are willing to expose their children.

Although one can discern broad social patterns among those who are prepared to accede to the public expression of political differences, these are neither consistent, nor necessarily coherent. Those who argue strongly for the right of free speech often wish to restrict that right to those who express palatable views. Certainly, they are unwilling to extend the right to those who would deny free speech to others. This is the classic case of complex tolerance which, as we shall see, deeply affects attitudes to television tolerance.

We can see this in the public's attitude to street demonstrations. We know, for instance, that many supporters of National Front-type views on race are drawn from the older working class, and yet this group are the most adamant that the Front should not be allowed to demonstrate in public, or to have a television programme reflecting their views. On the other hand, those who are not held to be sympathetic to formal racism are more willing to allow the Front to demonstrate. Six out of ten middle class people do not object to even the most controversial of interest groups holding a public demonstration, compared with only three out of ten in the lower working class.

Extended to television we discover that less than one third of the population are unwilling to allow even the most controversial groups to appear. Therefore, to cater for these viewers, British television would have to offend the vast majority of the British population. This would be like banning public demonstrations because one in ten of the population disagreed with them. One cannot destroy the fabric of democracy in both public life and television on the basis of the prejudices of a minority.

Education is the key to debates about tolerance. Children are regarded as being particularly vulnerable to propaganda and therefore their parents fear those groups and attitudes which might sway them. But, more importantly, what a society teaches its children is the mirror of what that society believes about itself. The morals of the nation are expressed in every classroom, and the tensions surrounding the toleration of other races, classes and political groupings emerge in those classrooms.

There is an important distinction between being taught about controversial beliefs and being addressed, in school, by people who hold those views. Most people seem willing to allow contentious and difficult issues to be raised in a formal educational context. Indeed, when asked whether children should be taught about homosexuality, sexually transmitted diseases, drug addiction, contraception, abortion and euthanasia, only five per cent dissented. Clearly some issues were more difficult to deal with than others: nine out of ten were willing to see drug addiction discussed, presumably as an attempt to prevent

## TABLE 22

Do you think that any of these groups should be banned from holding demonstrations in public?

| | TOTAL |
|---|---|
| TOTAL | 974 |
| None, none/all allowed | 42% |
| YES:- | |
| CND | 4% |
| Friends of the Earth/Greenpeace | 4% |
| Anti-abortionist | 6% |
| National Front | 31% |
| Troops out of Ireland | 14% |
| Pro-abortionists | 7% |
| Gay rights | 26% |
| Communist Party | 17% |
| Pro-censorship | 4% |
| Anti-Apartheid | 8% |
| All should be banned | 11% |
| Don't know | 1% |

Are there any minority groups which you would not like to appear on Channel 4?

| | TOTAL |
|---|---|
| TOTAL | 974 |
| NO | 46% |
| YES:- | |
| CND | 6% |
| Friends of the Earth/Greenpeace | 4% |
| Anti-abortionist | 5% |
| National Front | 30% |
| Pro-abortionist | 6% |
| Gay rights | 24% |
| Communist Party | 17% |
| Pro-censorship | 5% |
| Anti-Apartheid | 5% |
| Any other | 7% |
| Don't know | 9% |

## TABLE 23

Do you think that pupils in their final year at secondary school should be taught about any of these ?

| | Total | SEX | | AGE | | | | | CLASS | | | | CHILDREN | | ETHNIC ORGIN | | | | Miss C4 a lot |
|---|---|---|---|---|---|---|---|---|---|---|---|---|---|---|---|---|---|---|---|
| | | Male | Female | 16-20 | 21-24 | 25-34 | 35-54 | 55+ | AB | C1 | C2 | DE | U5 | 5-15 | None | White | Afro-carib | Asian | |
| TOTAL | 974 | 431 | 543 | 109 | 57 | 149 | 334 | 325 | 199 | 235 | 256 | 284 | 124 | 209 | 693 | 948 | 117 | 119 | 158 |
| Yes:- | | | | | | | | | | | | | | | | | | | |
| Drug addiction | 93% | 93% | 92% | 96% | 91% | 95% | 94% | 89% | 96% | 90% | 93% | 92% | 95% | 96% | 91% | 93% | 89% | 82% | 92% |
| Homosexuality | 72% | 72% | 73% | 72% | 67% | 81% | 75% | 67% | 82% | 72% | 69% | 68% | 79% | 76% | 71% | 72% | 73% | 56% | 69% |
| Sexually transmitted diseases | 88% | 87% | 88% | 86% | 81% | 94% | 91% | 83% | 94% | 85% | 89% | 85% | 94% | 93% | 86% | 88% | 89% | 71% | 89% |
| Abortion | 75% | 74% | 76% | 79% | 72% | 82% | 80% | 66% | 84% | 74% | 72% | 72% | 81% | 80% | 73% | 76% | 74% | 56% | 77% |
| Contraception | 85% | 86% | 85% | 86% | 86% | 91% | 90% | 77% | 91% | 86% | 86% | 80% | 92% | 94% | 82% | 85% | 85% | 64% | 86% |
| Euthanasia | 63% | 64% | 63% | 72% | 56% | 65% | 67% | 57% | 74% | 63% | 63% | 56% | 63% | 68% | 62% | 64% | 56% | 39% | 63% |
| None of these | 5% | 4% | 5% | 2% | 7% | 4% | 3% | 7% | 3% | 6% | 3% | 6% | 2% | 1% | 5% | 4% | 6% | 17% | 4% |
| Missing data | 1% | 0% | 1% | — | 2% | — | — | 1% | 1% | 1% | — | 0% | — | — | 1% | 1% | — | — | 1% |

experimentation, whereas this drops to seven out of ten happy with homosexuality as a subject matter.

People are generally willing to allow difficult issues to be aired; but there seems to be a hardcore group unwilling to let children become aware of any contentious, and possibly confusing, issue. When asked which religious group should not be spoken of at a religious morning assembly, fifty per cent said: 'The Moonies'. This only dropped to twenty-seven per cent when the same group were asked if they would still object if the children were taught that the faith was wrong. Some people simply will not tolerate the public airing of social differences, regardless of whether it is done in an illiberal or liberal context.

**TABLE 24**

Are there any religious faiths which you think should not be talked about at a secondary school assembly?

|  | TOTAL |
|---|---|
| TOTAL | 617 |
| Jewish | 8% |
| Moslem | 10% |
| Church of England | 1% |
| Mormons | 29% |
| Jehovahs Witnesses | 38% |
| Roman Catholic | 5% |
| Moonies | 50% |
| Baptist | 4% |
| Hindu | 11% |
| Rastafarian | 23% |
| All of them | 5% |
| None of them | 40% |

Would you still object to these religious faiths being discussed if children were told that this faith was wrong?

|  | TOTAL |
|---|---|
| TOTAL | 617 |
| Jewish | 3% |
| Moslem | 5% |
| Church of England | 0% |
| Mormons | 13% |
| Jehovahs Witnesses | 21% |
| Roman Catholic | 2% |
| Moonies | 27% |
| Baptist | 2% |
| Hindu | 5% |
| Rastafarian | 12% |
| All of them | 1% |
| None of them | 68% |

These educational tensions are mirrored to a lesser degree in people's attitudes to television. People are basically happy, in principle, with minority programmes on Channel Four (see Table 1). Those viewers who might never watch a programme designed for a specific racial or sexual minority are adamant that such a programme is a necessary part of British television. Moving from general principles to specific programmes is nevertheless a difficult process, and many of our respondents fell into inconsistencies at this point.

It's up to them, give them a spot on telly, they don't get any other chance to talk do they really?

Because they are living here just like you are so they have got just as much right to be on television as white people, because they live here don't they?

Oh I could imagine Wednesday night at 7.30 and an Asian programme comes on.

Yes, there would be a riot

Oh God, yes.
Group 42                                                    [Female 16-20 Oldham]

I like watching the one at 11 o'clock on a Monday night, they have a coloured programme and the money programme. They wouldn't appeal to quite a lot of people, but I find it interesting.

I've no objections so long as it's just over a short period. I wouldn't expect it to take up all viewing time.
Group 4                                              [Male Over 35 C2D Edinburgh]

Why should they have their own programmes when, if you went out there you wouldn't get an English programme if they had TV.

They are not on at peak times.
Group 10                                          [Female Over 35 BC1 Birmingham]

What about *Black on Black?*

If they don't like it over here they can bloody well go back where they came from.

I used to watch *Black on Black*.

I think you should have a fair balance. One who's preaching once, and you should have one preaching on the other side. I think you should have a fair side of everything. I don't think there should be any biased argument without someone who's going to put someone else's point. If you've got someone who is like that you should have someone who is not like that to give a fair opinion, not just a biased.

[Why don't you want a programme by racists?] Because we don't preach, the coloureds do.

But I think if it is only one channel like C4 that are doing it, it don't really matter ....

If you had a white programme on they would be the first to complain.
Group 13                                              [Females Under 35 BC1 Southampton]

Can you imagine India having a programme *White on White*?

How many of them are saying what they believe? Ninety-five per cent of them are saying what they have been told to believe. It's giving them more of a chip on their shoulder, I would have thought, to have a programme like *Black on Black*.
Group 16                                              [Female Over 35 C2D Southampton]

There is a need for, there are, there's definitely a need for minority outlets, I wouldn't say minority politically but certainly in minority areas and things like that. And certainly ethnic groups you know Rastas you know they classify themselves as an ethnic group as far as I am concerned they are of West Indian origin. They've just turned a little soft in the head because they're on drugs but it's the slot in, I think if you want, if you are interested in your own minority group, why have prime-time. The thing is to look for prime-time to hit the market.

Even a minority programme to cater for them would not be watched by them. It's the same with the majority of West Indian type of people in this country, they're all brought up in this country and they know as much about *Coronation Street* as a white bloke, you know, and they're not really bothered about a minority situation covering Rastas and things like that. Because they are a minority the majority of coloured type of people will be drinking in the same pub as the white bloke.
Group 11                                              [Male Over 35 C2D Nottingham]

I'm not against [ethnic programmes] but it must cost quite a lot of money to put over a programme like that and you're limiting your viewing aren't you.
Group 15                                              [Male Over 35 BC1 Bristol]

I don't think [black people] have enough programmes on, you know, about their culture.

If you are British I think that programmes should be geared for British people. I wouldn't expect to land in a foreign country and expect them to show British films for me.

I don't think we cater for [other religions].

It's the same with the handicapped.
Group 2                                    [Females Over 35 BC1 Glasgow]

It is interesting that the white's definition of a white programme is of a racist counterweight to black shows. For many, black programmes were by definition propaganda, and the whites did not want 'white' television because they, unlike the ethnic minorities, did not propagandise. Consequently, there was very little support for racist programmes.

Young people, in particular, seem to be the most tolerant of ethnic minorities, perhaps because they are the heirs to a functioning multi-ethnic society. The young discussion groups were sympathetic to the problems of ethnic minorities and wanted to see blacks represented in 'normal' television.

You never see any programme, they don't, I mean no channel have the things that they should do, everybody should know that there are all different people and different colours in England, I mean ... it's British ... and they should know that, I mean they should have them on all channel and they don't, I haven't seen anything on ITV and BBC1 or BBC2.

They've started to do more programmes with coloured people.

Soap operas never have black people in nowadays.

There's only one coloured family in *EastEnders*.

There's only one Asian family.

One vital component of the exposure of these young people to black culture is that they like situation comedies, and feel somewhat aggrieved that *No Problem* was taken off. All enjoyed *The Cosby Show* and *Differn't Strokes* because they broke away from the stereotypes of black people offered to them by the other media.

Some things, nearly all programmes are white, or mixed, or mostly if they're mixed it's only a couple of black people or Asians or whatever and mostly all white, and they don't do anything say just black, white or ... they always do white. *No Problem* was good because they had one ... name of her, she's a social worker in *EastEnders* now, she used to talk in a very posh up-market way and I mean most people think all blacks are ... speakers or Rastafarians, and they think they're ... I've seen lots of people about here that have a very posh accent, and people don't associate them with with an accent. They always associate them with... [black accents].

If changes in the scheduling of ethnic programmes would destabilise support for C4, changes in provisions for homosexuals would blow it apart. There was no more controversial subject in the discussion groups than films and programmes aimed, if only in part, at the homosexual community. The small minority prepared to accept programmes specifically made for homosexuals had two reasons for doing so: the principle of proportionality was resorted to but, more to the point, they had an interest in a realistic understanding of problems like AIDS and how homosexuals fitted into British life.

Well it might be [important] to the queers wouldn't it? I mean it's a valid point that they should have a half-hour programme once a week.

I mean let's face it, whether we like it or not, it's with us.

C4 are doing the right thing.
Group 27                                                          [Male Pensioners]

Gays [are fine] in small doses, we have got to learn about these things, but you know you don't want it everyday.
Group 16                                  [Female Over 35 C2D Southampton]

We all know it's going on and it's been going on for years and years and years and it's never been brought out, so why is it so terrible that it's been brought out?
Group 10                                     [Female Over 35 BC1 Birmingham]

Homosexuals [make me] uncomfortable but I accept they have a right to their programmes.

Homosexuality: actually you make your own mind up. But if there is just one person's point of view you might be led to believe that he is right — you can't think of anything else.
Group 12                                  [Female Under 35 C2D Birmingham]

There are loads of programmes on AIDS on all channels, particularly later at night, one particularly good one presented by a load of homosexuals which got my back up a bit, but they presented it in a such a way that it was educational and started watching it. Afterwards I actually learned something which all other programmes about it did not, they were way above my head. For a minority group presenting something, they presented it in a balanced way.
                                                          [Male Under 35 C2D Newcastle]

Homosexuals have a right to a voice on British TV. I don't think they should make out they're normal though on telly.
Group 12                                        [Female Under 35 C2D Birmingham]

I would apply the same standards to homosexuals, as I would to Gerry Adams — let them have their say, they exist, so therefore, they have a right to be heard. Everyone, as I say, owes it to themselves to make their own decisions on what is presented to them, from the point of view of their comments.

Yes, they deserve a percentage of time, but they don't deserve sort of over-coverage.

Something has just occurred to me... People who watch *Open University*, have to actively seek out in the early hours, that programme. I've to get out of bed at six o'clock in the morning just to watch it; and it suddenly occurred to me, that it wouldn't be a bad idea instead of going on for longer hours (to accomodate homosexual programmes), instead you've got to get up in the middle of the night to watch it! So, that's my right-wing — coming out now.
Group 37                                                    [Male Catholic Belfast]

The idea that programmes for homosexuals should be treated like the *Open University* may seem very anti-homosexual, but it is a picture of reason compared to the outbreak of hostitilty that programmes for homosexuals elicited in many respondents. As the following remarks show, homosexuality evokes disgust among most people.

I'd turn it off.

Poofs, no.

I'd definitely turn it off.

There is a difference between Asians, blacks and homosexuals. That is a belief, a religion, but homosexuals is not a belief or religion. The dirty mac brigade, they have to go out to the cinema. You don't see those types of films on TV.
Group 31                                                [Male C4 Heavy Viewers]

Gays, no need for it.

Makes me uncomfortable.

It's depressing I think really.

It's a deviation isn't it encouraging it by showing it.
Group 12                                    [Female Over 35 BC1 Birmingham]

Should there be programmes for psychopaths, showing why they mash people to bits.

It would be interesting to see the reaction of the press if C4 showed an hour long documentary to try and prove that homosexuality was a mental illness, for example, they wouldn't be likely to show that, they would show it the other way, but a documentary showing that sort of thing probably wouldn't be allowed on television at all.
Group 17                                        [Male Under 35 BC1 Esher]

We want less films on gays.

Well, there is a way of doing things, there is always a way of doing things isn't there, and that doesn't mean that it is always the right way of doing things, there is a nice way you can put something forward, and there is a nasty way.
Group 16                                   [Female Over 35 C2D Southampton]

The debate between those holding the 'realist' view that gays are part of life, and those disgusted by homosexuals, and appalled by the idea of gays on television, was fascinating. On two occasions group members challenged the anti-gay consensus and caused some consternation among the rest of the group as they attempted to justify their position.

Homosexuality and lesbianism, I don't see why we should have to watch that on television.

You don't have to watch it.

Well it's life.

I pay my licence, I have a right to watch four channels.

No you don't. C4 and ITV are paid for by ads.

I don't think that they should show that sort of thing.

Well I do... it's spoken about and you are reading about it everyday, so why should it not be on television. I know you're saying you don't like it, you see I would let my children watch that if they particularly wanted to, if I was there with them, because you could then answer the questions.

I think the more you know about the subject the less likely you are to be afraid of it.
Group 2                                                          [Female Over 35 BC1 Glasgow]

This is a fascinating exchange. Initially, someone attacks gays only to discover someone else weighing in with a 'realist' defence of such programmes: 'that's life', the attacker argues. The anti-gay respondent comes back with the 'I pay my licence fee' gambit, which is undermined by the other replying that C4 is paid for by ads and therefore does not owe the complainant anything. In the face of continued 'disgust' the realist shifts into the 'education' defence, arguing that children have to face up to the realities of the social world, and that she values knowledge gained through television because it reduces fear.

The second debate is interesting because it shows the value of strong narrative lines in winning people over to previously unacceptable issues.

The last time I watched C4 it was a homosexual film − just turned it on and there it was − there was just two men and that dirty, sleeping bedroom types.

Oh! Was it where they, his father found out that he was homosexual.

I didn't watch it that long, about three minutes that was all.

I watched that − [voices agreeing].

I thought it was good. It was really good − I like things like that. It doesn't offend me or anything like that.

No it doesn't me, but I just sit there and think − oh you know how boring.

It was a good film, I watched it, but it was a bit slow.
Group 5                                                    [Female Under 35 BC1 Manchester]

Although there was a strong anti-gay tendency in the groups, few people argued that homosexual programmes had any effect on their own sexuality. Many did worry about the effects on young people even though the same people earlier argued that young people should be in bed when these programmes were on.

If you are gay, you are gay, if you watch a homosexual programme you don't think you want to be one.
Group 7                                                      [Male Under 35 C2D Newcastle]

There are a lot of lesbians about and they have all got televisions, they want something....

Just like we are all young, we like music.

Programmes like that are all on at night anyway, if you don't want to watch it you turn it off.

There are four channels

You sit there and watch it just to complain about it, why don't they just turn it off.

They make up their own minds later on in life whether they watch programmes like that or not anyway.
Group 42                                                    [Female 16-20]

If you get a teenager watching these sorts of things then it's a case of they have to try it.

It doesn't alter my opinion

It's not entertainment.

It's not educational really.
Group 10                                    [Female Over 35 BC1 Birmingham]


Even those who are pro-gay programmes are somewhat apologetic, not wanting to offend anyone because of their interest in the subject. One very English apology went along the lines of:

Well, I think I must be in the minority here, but I hope you don't think this is a horrible thing to say. I feel that I've watched a homosexual programme. I don't know anything about it and I must say my mind is very curious.
Group 10                                    [Female Over 35 BC1 Birmingham]

The real difficulties of building a coalition of minorities in television terms becomes apparent from the defence of homosexuals by the Afro-Caribbean males (Asian and Afro-Caribbean females were as rabidly anti-gay as the rest). One man pinpointed the problem:

What people are afraid of is that they think the minorities might come on and try and brainwash them into thinking that it is the right way to be. And the way they are is the wrong way to be, that is what they seem to be afraid of. They don't want to be told that being homosexual is right

**TABLE 25**

If racial minorities do have programmes on Channel 4 at what time of day do you think they should be on?

BASE: ALL

| | | TV TOLERANCE | |
|---|---|---|---|
| | TOTAL | TOLERANT | INTOLER-ANT |
| TOTAL | 974 | 376 | 588 |
| Any time | 21% | 29% | 16% |
| Before 4pm | 17% | 16% | 18% |
| 4-6 | 3% | 2% | 3% |
| 6-8 | 8% | 10% | 7% |
| 9-10 | 9% | 10% | 8% |
| 10-12 | 22% | 20% | 23% |
| After midnight | 18% | 9% | 23% |
| Don't know | 3% | 5% | 2% |

And if homosexuals or lesbians have programmes on Channel 4, at what time of the day do you think they should be on?

| | | TV TOLERANCE | |
|---|---|---|---|
| | TOTAL | TOLERANT | INOLER-ANT |
| TOTAL | 974 | 376 | 588 |
| Any time | 3% | 6% | 1% |
| Before 4pm | 4% | 3% | 4% |
| 4-6 | 0% | 0% | — |
| 6-8 | 1% | 2% | 1% |
| 9-10 | 7% | 14% | 3% |
| 10-12 | 28% | 39% | 21% |
| After midnight | 52% | 32% | 64% |
| Don't know | 6% | 5% | 7% |

> and heterosexual is definitely wrong.
> Group 21                              [Male Afro-Caribbean]

His fellow discussants also accepted the importance of programmes for homosexuals, but wanted to push them into the fringes of the viewing day, just as the whites wish to push ethnic programmes to the fringes. A coalition of the under-represented would inevitably flounder with defenders who argue:

It should be very late at night to cater for a few freaks, if I'm allowed to say freaks − at seven o'clock kids are easily impressed.
Group 21                                                               [Male Afro-Caribbean]

Programmes for homosexuals are even more marginalised by time than those aimed at the ethnic minorities (Table 25). Over half of the population wanted gay programmes to be scheduled after midnight, and less than one in ten were happy to see them appear at any time.

Those who are tolerant of what appears on television, and who are committed to Channel Four are less likely to want to marginalise minority programmes. Around half of those whom we identified as being tv tolerant were willing to allow gays on between nine o'clock and midnight compared to only one quarter of those tv intolerant − fully 64 per cent of the latter insisted that homosexual programmes should be on after midnight.

The reason behind the marginalisation of homosexuality is quite clear: people see it as a deviant form of sexuality which should not be encouraged. For instance, when asked whether tv plays should reflect homosexuality as a normal way of life, 64 per cent say no. And yet, despite this, people do not want to discriminate actively against homosexuals. They think that homosexual couples should be treated with the same courtesy and respect as heterosexual couples. In short, they make a distinction between the expression of homosexuality as normal behaviour and mistreating homosexuals because of their sexuality.

Tolerance is not a uniform social quality. For instance, there are large age differences among those who are prepared to accept plays which show homosexuality as a normal way of life. Half of those between sixteen and twenty are prepared to accept such a play compared with slightly less than one in six of those over fifty-five. But one should be wary of simplistic explanations based on age; young adults, aged between twenty-one and twenty-four are in fact much more anti-homosexual than the succeeding age group: 33 to 42 per cent.

Young adults are consistently more conservative on every indicator of sexual tolerance on television than the age groups on either side. They are more unwilling to accept gay programmes on C4 (16 per cent compared to 9 per cent of twenty-five to thirty-four); couples making love (58 per cent to 48 per cent); and nudity (30 per cent to 25 per cent). If ageing involves exluding those groups and thoughts which challenge established cultural codes, then, according to our survey the twenty-one to twenty-four year olds are undergoing a process of re-evaluation which leads some of them to reject groups which challenge their sexual identity. But not only are young adults sexually conservative, they are also much more fixed in their political and moral views. Again, this is revealed by their attitude to moral education. This

## TABLE 26

If a TV play had scenes which showed that two people of the same sex were in love with each other, should the play also show that homosexuality is a normal way of life? In a documentary about couples, should a homosexual couple be treated in the same way as a heterosexual couple?

BASE: ALL

|  | | SEX | | AGE | | | | |
|---|---|---|---|---|---|---|---|---|
|  | Total | Male | Female | 16-20 | 21-24 | 25-34 | 35-54 | 55+ |
| TOTAL | 974 | 431 | 543 | 109 | 57 | 149 | 334 | 325 |
| Play showing homosexuality as a normal way of life | | | | | | | | |
| Yes | 27% | 26% | 28% | 50% | 33% | 42% | 25% | 14% |
| No | 64% | 67% | 62% | 42% | 60% | 46% | 65% | 78% |
| Don't know | 9% | 7% | 11% | 8% | 7% | 11% | 10% | 8% |
| Homosexual couple be treated same as heterosexual couple | | | | | | | | |
| Yes | 43% | 42% | 43% | 61% | 51% | 60% | 46% | 23% |
| No | 47% | 49% | 46% | 34% | 44% | 29% | 44% | 65% |
| Don't know | 10% | 9% | 11% | 5% | 5% | 11% | 10% | 12% |

group are the most nervous of contentious groups or the discussion of problematic moral issues. They are not committed conservatives, but confused and a little tense about social reality.

If this is the case then Channel Four has a problem. This age-group who most people in the discussion groups assumed were the channel's natural

## TABLE 26 (A)

In *EastEnders* there is a homosexual couple shown as living together. Which one of these answers on this card best describes your feelings towards this type of relationship being shown on *EastEnders?*
BASE: All who watch *EastEnders* nowadays

|  | | SEX | | AGE | | | | |
|---|---|---|---|---|---|---|---|---|
|  | Total | Male | Female | 16-20 | 21-24 | 25-34 | 35-54 | 55+ |
| TOTAL | 601 | 238 | 363 | 89 | 45 | 118 | 203 | 146 |
| Approve a lot | 12% | 9% | 13% | 26% | 20% | 15% | 8% | 3% |
| Approve a little | 24% | 18% | 27% | 25% | 16% | 29% | 23% | 22% |
| Neither | 26% | 31% | 23% | 28% | 27% | 31% | 28% | 18% |
| Disapprove a little | 21% | 17% | 23% | 17% | 24% | 16% | 20% | 27% |
| Disapprove a lot | 17% | 24% | 13% | 4% | 13% | 8% | 20% | 30% |
| Don't know | 1% | 1% | 0% | — | — | 1% | 1% | 1% |

audience, and who the channel itself might imagine are open to, and supportive of, experimentation and radicalism, are in fact unwilling partners in the project.

In general, people are reasonably tolerant of minority television as long as it does not impinge on their viewing time. There is little evidence that black, Asian or gay programming has broken out of the ghetto and changed anyone's mind on a subject. Furthermore, most people talk of minority broadcasting in ghetto terms; they are happy with it's existence but have no desire to watch it.

When it comes to the minorities themselves, most are ambivalent about the potential of television and, incidentally, of Channel Four's contribution to the maintenance of their culture. Their attitudes to the channel, and rules they apply to evaluate the channel, are as complex and as inconsistent as those of the mainstream culture.

### (2) The Rainbow Coalition?

Should Channel Four be happy with satisfying the majority of whites that programmes for ethnic minorities can be integrated into the television schedule without disturbing the day's schedules? Not according to the ethnic groups themselves. Most people in the ethnic discussion groups were grateful to the channel for initiating ethnic programming, but there was a distinct feeling that the revolution had stopped and that things were back to normal. One damning comment was: 'The only black face you see on C4 at the moment is in American football.'

> All this C4 idea right at the beginning ... cater for the ethnic minorities, that's what I saw them doing at the beginning. And eventually they were sort of drifting off and right now I think they don't know where they want to go.

> Yes, I mean they used to have *Black on Black* and then they had *Eastern Eye,* and then they all just went. And then, there's not as much black programmes on C4 at the moment. I mean it's all sorts of documentaries about this and that, you know, people and Africa and all this. I mean what we want to know is, you know, what's going on in England.

> The only black face you see on C4 at the moment is in American football.

> That's about it, but it's completely gone down. But, I must admit when it first came, when it first started broadcasting I used to watch it all the time, because it was good to switch on a black face, any coloured face and I mean it's really just gone.
> Group 25                                                    [Male Afro-Caribbean]

The American shows are always better presented than the English ones. They tend to give them menial tasks here don't they in these programmes but in America they show them in a highlighted area rather than a menial task.

Kelvin [in *EastEnders*] was shown as a nice normal boy, and afterwards he sort of changed his hair.

Your children identify with things like that don't they?

Some coloured kids aren't like that — some are, but not many.

The media shouldn't present that to your children.

And the times they put them on tv — *Black on Black* is 11:30 you can't get to see it, its shocking.

I think it was *No Problem*... That was the only one where they really didn't put you down.

I think television is anti-black anyway — it's just that C4 is a bit more for blacks.

If they ever have a show it's always about the slavery days, it's never up to date about the black people.

In a serial — it could be like *Coronation Street* — but show black people right there, as part of the spectrum, rather than people out of work and that. There are rich blacks.

C4 did promise everyone would have a voice so how come the programmes have been axed with nothing to replace them. What's happening?

Yes, these programmes do come on — American programmes which present blacks which are good, but it's always too late at night people are in bed.

You hardly see any black dancers on the telly — there is loads of black ballet but you never see it.

You get some black shows on C4 but they are still not doing enough.

I think *Black on Black* should come back.

It should — the was the only black informative programme.

*Black on Black*, people... should be on say from eight in the evening whereby everybody can watch it.
Group 33                                                    [Female Afro-Caribbean]

(We recruited eight ethnic groups. The process of selection was the same as for the other groups: the recruiters asked people in the street if they would like to attend a group to discuss television.)

By and large the ethnic minorities rejected the notion of proportional television. Many, although by no means all, felt that they needed more television time; furthermore, they were deeply unhappy about the time that most ethnic programmes were scheduled, which they regarded as being not only off-peak but off the mountain altogether.

There's one thing though, why doesn't an ethnic minority programme like *Ebony* or *Black on Black* get some high peak time viewing. Why is it always shoved back to about nine to ten o'clock. Like Mum and Dad, right, they work, they would not stay up until ten o'clock to watch nothing if they were starting early the next morning.

I must say I'm going to be controversial now, I'm not totally in favour of anything that's put on specifically for any one group at all. I don't mind, I like the news [from *Black on Black*] and I like to get all that news, but I'm quite happy to see that once a fortnight, and I'm happy to see it at an off-time as well.
Group 21                                                     [Afro-Caribbean Males]

I think that one or two programmes a week is enough, because I think more than that would be.....

Yes.

Right.

Or even once a week.

And not put on at a ridiculous time they used to at 11.30.

And you know you're sort of half asleep and... because I used to love that programme [*Eastern Eye*].
Group 39                                               [Female Asian Nottingham]

*Eastern Eye*, I looked at it as entertainment and information, it was lovely and it has been taken off.

It was really great.

I mean why should we do this. The English, their programmes are always on at the right time.

We want an Asian magazine.

When I was approached for this and was asked whether you watched Asian programmes or something, I automatically said 'yes on C4,' and when I thought about it, there weren't an awful lot, there is only probably about one or two, and I though that was quite bad really, when it is catering for minorities it ought to have more programmes.

It's 'keep you happy', that's how I see it.

It's not just Asian, it's Chinese, everything − they like the one token gesture but that's it, it should be like a programme every night, just so everybody's got the choice.

We need some kind of consistency.
Group 24                                              [Female Asian]

And also I think, speaking for the Asian community, when I think Channel 4 was the only one that started bringing some programmes for the Asian community, and that's how big, that became popular. And now it's all stopped.
Group 39                                              [Female Asian]

These respondents feel that something has gone badly wrong with C4's ethnic provision, and that the move away from the high profile flagships of *Black on Black* and *Eastern Eye* (which even the whites knew), to more diffuse and varied programmes and series, has deprived the channel of any focus to its ethnic programming policy. But, as we saw earlier, any change in ethnic provision, or foregrounding of that provision, would be bound to upset those in the middle ground who currently support the channel. Somewhere in there is a real structural problem for C4 and the organisation of its schedules (see Tables 19/20).

One key question concerning tolerance is the degree to which the various minorities tolerate one another. There is no rainbow coalition. In particular, Afro-Caribbeans and Asians are deeply ambivalant about homosexuals and minority voices which might be directed against them. One-fifth of Asians objected to gays appearing on Channel Four. Indeed, when asked a further question concerning the regularity of gay programmes, fully three-fifths said that there should not be any gay programmes, and only 6 per cent said that gays should have regular programmes (Table 27). Asians are the most conservative of the racial groups in our sample. They are most reluctant to allow television to explore difficult moral and political issues, and share little common feeling with other minority voices (Table 28).

**TABLE 27**

For each of the following groups, do you think they should have regular/occasional/no programmes on Channel 4?
*Homosexuals*

|  | ETHNIC ORIGIN | | |
|  | WHITE | AFRO-CARIB | ASIAN |
|---|---|---|---|
| TOTAL | 948 | 117 | 119 |
| Regular | 3% | 9% | 6% |
| Occasional | 32% | 32% | 27% |
| None | 61% | 57% | 63% |
| Don't know | 4% | 3% | 4% |

When asked about regularity of programmes about and for ethnic minorities, the Afro-Caribbeans and the Asians were not one hundred per cent behind one another. Only around one-quarter of Afro-Caribbeans wanted regular programmes for Asians, and slightly more than one-third of Asians wanted regular programmes for Afro-Caribbeans (see Tables 19 and 20). One of the Afro-Caribbean respondents summed up the problem when he said:

> I think the difference in character is too vast... for a black person to appreciate an Indian film in its own language, you know it's like asking a blind man to ride a bike.
> Group 21                                                    [Afro-Caribbean Males]

Having a great deal of regular access to television is not particularly important to most Blacks and Asians: less than half wanted regular programmes aimed at their ethnic group. Television is not seen as a crucial medium for the maintenance of their culture and not too much weight is put on the benefits which they might gain from it. Furthermore, they are unhappy about forcing themselves on the mainstream culture in case they alienate it. Indeed, they seem to regard television as essentially a medium of entertainment that should occasionally be exploited for the advancement of black issues. This is not to say that they wish to be ignored hence they want occasional programmes. (Interestingly, whites who are high on our tv tolerance index are more likely to say that blacks should be on television at any time than the blacks themselves.)

One, perhaps major, problem for the channel is that Afro-Caribbeans do not perceive the channel as sufficiently distinct from ITV. In fact, more Afro-Caribbeans think that C4 is like ITV than do white people. In terms of Channel Four's stated aim of serving ethnic minorities this seems disasterous. And yet, when pressed to describe Channel Four, Afro-Caribbeans identified many differences between the two channels. One possible explanation for this is that their general attitudes to television are formed by their social class rather than their ethnicity. Their opinions are much closer

**TABLE 28**

Would you object to any of these groups appearing on Channel 4?

BASE: ALL

| | Total | SEX | | AGE | | | | | CLASS | | | | CHILDREN | | | ETHNIC ORIGIN | | | |
| --- | --- | --- | --- | --- | --- | --- | --- | --- | --- | --- | --- | --- | --- | --- | --- | --- | --- | --- | --- |
| | | Male | Fe-male | 16-20 | 21-24 | 25-34 | 35-54 | 55+ | AB | C1 | C2 | DE | U5 | 5-15 | None | White | Afro-carib | Asian | Miss C4 a lot |
| TOTAL | 974 | 431 | 543 | 109 | 57 | 149 | 334 | 325 | 199 | 235 | 256 | 284 | 124 | 209 | 693 | 948 | 117 | 119 | 158 |
| No. all should appear | 21% | 19% | 22% | 29% | 26% | 23% | 22% | 15% | 19% | 20% | 22% | 22% | 27% | 24% | 18% | 21% | 30% | 12% | 27% |
| **Yes** | | | | | | | | | | | | | | | | | | | |
| Repatriation of coloured immigrants | 21% | 24% | 19% | 15% | 28% | 26% | 22% | 20% | 25% | 23% | 18% | 21% | 27% | 22% | 21% | 20% | 34% | 47% | 19% |
| Marijuana | 45% | 43% | 46% | 39% | 42% | 45% | 45% | 47% | 39% | 49% | 46% | 44% | 44% | 45% | 45% | 45% | 25% | 45% | 39% |
| Sexual consent | 45% | 43% | 45% | 28% | 32% | 42% | 48% | 50% | 46% | 45% | 44% | 44% | 45% | 46% | 45% | 45% | 38% | 43% | 37% |
| Homosexual couples | 33% | 34% | 32% | 21% | 19% | 19% | 32% | 48% | 28% | 32% | 34% | 37% | 23% | 30% | 35% | 33% | 28% | 40% | 26% |
| Smoking | 25% | 26% | 24% | 27% | 21% | 25% | 24% | 25% | 26% | 23% | 27% | 23% | 25% | 25% | 25% | 25% | 21% | 30% | 20% |
| Birch | 11% | 9% | 12% | 13% | 12% | 9% | 10% | 11% | 9% | 10% | 12% | 12% | 11% | 9% | 12% | 10% | 17% | 18% | 12% |
| All of them | 10% | 10% | 11% | 5% | 4% | 5% | 11% | 15% | 14% | 9% | 9% | 11% | 5% | 6% | 13% | 11% | 10% | 10% | 8% |
| Don't know | 6% | 5% | 6% | 3% | 2% | 5% | 6% | 8% | 6% | 3% | 5% | 8% | 6% | 4% | 6% | 6% | 2% | 8% | 3% |

147

to those of working class whites than to middle class Asians. The working class were also more likely not to say that Channel Four and ITV were similar, and then proceed to identity a range of differences between the channels. It is likely that they seldom watch Channel Four and therefore have no idea what the channel shows; or, if they watch the channel it is likely to be something like *Brookside* or *Hill Street Blues*, which are no different from what they might see on ITV. The differences which they identify when asked to describe that channel are the result of the channel's public profile, as refracted through the press and public discussion, rather than their own viewing habits. It is not illogical to hold that one's experience of Channel Four is the same as that of ITV if all one watches are soap operas etc., but also to argue that the channel is different from ITV in many respects. The former is based on personal viewing, the latter on public profile.

This class- rather than ethnicity-based analysis of Afro-Caribbean attitudes to the media is borne out by our study of community radio, conducted for the Greater London Council in 1985. In that research we discovered that Afro-Caribbeans were less likely to demand a culturally distinctive radio station than Asians. Firm evidence emerged that Asians felt that they had deep cultural differences with the host nation, and wished to express their religious, linguistic, musical and dramatic differences on a separate station. Afro-Caribbeans, on the other hand, because most share a common religion, language and culture with the host nation, had too many things in common to develop an image of a culturally distinctive station. The most widespread and important cultural marker for Afro-Caribbeans was music, and most turned the demand for community radio into a request for a black music station: the music was the message.

The majority of whites are perfectly happy with the idea of occasional programmes for blacks and Asians, but they have no wish to extend the idea of positive discrimination to a fundamental organising principle of television. They want to marginalise black programming into 'educational' ghettos outside peak time – particularly between ten and midnight. Blacks, on the other hand, want their programmes to be on during what they regard as peak time. Their reason for this is apparently simple: people who work tend not to stay up to eleven o'clock at night to watch television. This simplicity, however, disguises an extremely complex evaluation which goes to the heart of the problem of cultural marginalisation. The ethnic minorities are claiming that they wish to have the right to see their programmes on in the heart of evening's schedules. As a member of one of the groups stated above: 'why doesn't an ethnic programme like *Ebony* or *Black on Black* get some high peak-time viewing?' The general feeling was that such a programme would imply a commitment to, and a normalisation of, black programmes as 'ordinary' television.

The worries ethnic groups expressed about tokenism and marginalisation were also articulated by homosexuals. Gays were cautiously grateful for

Channel Four's contribution, a view summed up by someone who said: 'Channel Four should go a lot further than they do.'

The nature of the debate within the gay groups was fascinating. Some argued that they should not expect representation in television, others that they did not want to draw attention to themselves, and yet others said that they were being ghettoised into the late hours − traditionally a morally suspect time-slot. They seemed confused on the precise nature of the types of programme they wanted. Those looking for early evening slots wanted programmes which addressed the general public and which broke away from the homosexual ghetto. Those willing to accept the late night slot did so because they wanted 'gay' entertainment, and realised that such programmes would inevitably shock many heterosexuals. They wanted proportional, ghettoised television, because it allowed programmes to be more explicit in their address to the homosexual community.

On balance, there was not a massive outcry for more television time from the gay men in our groups. They did not watch much television, and when they did it tended to be movies or soap operas. Most were not interested in the politics of the gay movement, and had many other cultural resources within the gay community where they would rather spend their time − television was peripheral to their lives and their attitudes reflected this.

> There was a series of gay films on just recently. I didn't watch it, but maybe − of course it was put on at say twelve o'clock ... everybody else is going to be in bed. Why can't − that's what I mean about the censorship coming from the media. You know people think it's a nasty programme for nasty people if its shown at that time. Maybe if they brought it down to six o'clock or whatever so a family could watch it.
>
> You'd get an outcry then.
>
> But, if it's on before a certain time, people will think that you are pushing it down their throat.
>
> They don't have to watch it. It's like us we don't have to watch a woman and a fella having sex.
> Group 29                                                    [Homosexual Males]
>
> The best shows on Channel Four are on folks in America, the best comedy I have seen on Channel Four for ages is *Brothers*.
>
> I think films that they are for entertainment not necessarily sexual .... but something like that, other people would find it interesting as well.
>
> Gay-bashing. It happens, its part of life, I wouldn't mind it being on.

I don't want to see explicit sex on television.

If you are watching a film and two people climb into bed, its just normally part of the film, you are only sat for ten minutes watching them do things to each other, it's got nothing to do with the story, I think sex is private and personal, and should be kept in the boundaries of your own home.

It would also seem like gays are pushing, well we are in a way, we like to be accepted but there is a limit.

They don't want gays rammed down their throat.

Not forced on them.
Group 41                                                    [Male Homosexual Glasgow]

(The gay groups were recruited by asking around in gay clubs and bars, or by finding some contact with the gay community and asking them for the names of friends.)

The extraordinary complexity of minority attitudes to the channel can be seen from the lesbian group's dislike of 'the homosexual mafia', which they presumed dominated C4's gay programming. They accepted that:

Channel Four is the only channel with anything for us. Other channels have changed their output slightly because of the influence of C4, but homosexuality is very controversial for the public and the white middle class men running television.
Group 30                                                         [Homosexual Females]

Although they respected what C4 was trying to achieve in its attempt to screen gay programmes, many gay men, but especially lesbians, felt betrayed by *In the Pink*, the season of gay films. Many of them felt the films in this season had pandered to male gay 'sado-masochist fantasies', rather than normal gay life.

Gays are very much more voluble than lesbians but the image of gay men is very camp. It portrays stereotypes rather than ordinary people with different sexuality.
Group 30                                                         [Homosexual Females]

There was little in the way of a unified gay front in these attitudes, gay men were still men, committed to power for its sake, and interested only in themselves. The women felt very strongly that many of the *In the Pink* films did not advance the cause of 'enlightening' the general public; indeed, they have caused more harm than anything else. The lesbians wanted the general public to be more aware of the idea that homosexuals were normal people, and wanted television to legitimise gay sexuality.

I'm not saying there should be lesbian cookery programmes and lesbian news, but we're here, we exist and we are here to stay, so they shouldn't pretend we don't exist in the vast majority of programmes.
Group 30                                                                    [Homosexual Females]

[What type of people do you think appear on Gay television programmes?]

I think usually the extremes.

Yes.

And some are very extreme.

You get the really outrageous ... Being on tv saying that I'm gay. They're normally outrageous things aren't they.

The nearest we got to (normality) was during that week of AIDS where you did actually see other people.

Other people who, well ... they did actually look like normal people before they looked, before it was known that they were gay or whatever.

Mostly they are quite flamboyant the men that they have.
And the women can sometimes appear to be really heavy.

Yes

And not the sort of woman you'd like to meet.

They portray the sort of masculine side, they come across terribly butch.

Remember that silly episode on *Brookside* where the boy who is playing the gay fart with his triangle, do you remember?

Yes.

I mean that was farcical as well.

It was wasn't it?

The only decent portrayal that we've had of that is Colin on the *East-Enders.*

Yes, he's great and Barry.

151

And Barry, yes.

I mean they are not outrageous, queens or anything.

No, I mean they're normal run of the mill.

But again there was an awful lot of input from America, which is what I thing seems to be coming out, everything that ... in America, So I think also what's sadly lacking is anything from this country.

Well if somebody is strongly political and a film maker and a lesbian they're going to make a film about.....they're not going to go out and research other aspects.

Channel Four are more positive than negative because at least they're attempting to give a viewing, an airing to a subject which is very much taboo on other channels.

But, then again, they put it on sometimes too late at night for anybody to watch it.

Yes, and you're so tired you just you know.

It's a shame, it's always has been documentaries that we've been talking about, and it's a shame that that's the only form at the moment that we're talking about.
Group 40                                                    [Female Homosexual]

Several of the lesbians in one of the groups had children, and this dominated their attitudes to sex and violence on television more than their sexuality. They were wary of the effects of television in these areas, but attempted to wrap up their concerns in humour; one woman claimed that she did not want to see heterosexual sex on television because 'there is enough comedy on television already'. These worries demonstrate the naivity of assuming that people's attitudes to television emerge from one source; motherhood and sexuality combine to produce attitudes very different from the male homosexuals, and one would also expect homosexuality to be undercut by the tensions of class, age, political affiliation etc. in much the same way as heterosexuality. The attitudes of minorities to television cannot be understood simply by isolating the characteristics that make them a minority.

The difficulties of extending the range of programmes, keeping the majority satisfied, whilst also promoting minority programmes are legion. This section has identified the main principles with which the majority operate in relation to minorities. But it has also shown that the level of provision currently on offer to those minorities is unacceptable to them. This problem is probably unresolvable in the present climate but, on the positive side, the various minorities accept that Channel Four is at least trying to do something about resolving this dilemma.

One perfect expression of the middle way put it:

> Homosexuality should not be portrayed as being the normal way of life, because it isn't. They are very much a minority, but I do not think people should get very uptight about it either.
> Group 2                                              [Female Over 35 BC1 Glasgow]

To sum up: the principles of social tolerance are extended to television. The rights of free speech are the heart of the matter, followed by the right of cultural expression. But the ethnic and sexual minorities, while concerned with the quantity of programmes aimed at them, seem more worried about their representation on mainstream television. Many would give up a black specialist programme for a decent, realistic version of black life on *East-Enders*. Similarly, the lesbians were happier with Barry and Colin than with the *In the Pink* series. Although the whites and the heterosexuals thought that the minorities wanted television programmes which propagandised or were ghetto broadcasting, most people in the minority groups were unhappy with the overly serious tone of minority programmes; they wanted entertainment as much as, if not more than, education. Television is firmly located in the realm of pleasure rather than politics.

Minority programmes were seen as adding to the balance of British television, which brings us on to a key problem for Channel Four, namely does the public accept that Channel Four is politically balanced across its output?

## (5) Bias and Balance

'We are the ones balancing things, not television.'
[Male under 35 BC1]

Channel Four has made great demands of the public's ability to discern political or cultural bias in television. The channel's assertion that it seeks to balance programmes over its output rather than within individual programmes assumes a politically and television literate audience capable of not confusing fact and value. Or, more precisely, with the ability to suspend judgement on the presentation of facts until, and unless, they watch a balancing programme at some later date.

On the evidence of our research the channel has the competent audience which it requires. The public is, however, developing its views about balance on television in ways which even Channel Four will find surprising. We have discovered that the public is happy with the idea of television which is assertive or strident, and feels that arguments should be put cogently and forcibly. Therefore, it has moved away from the simple belief in the meticulous balancing of one argument by its opposite. On the other hand, it is not at all happy with the notion that someone with contentious views should be allowed to make unchallenged assertions. The public wants television to own up to the complexity of the world; in particular, it requires a range of views on a particular topic to be aired. The troubles in Northern Ireland provided a test case for this as we see below. The Northern Irish wanted television to acknowledge that not all Catholics were Nationalists, and not all Protestants were Orangemen.

Other people pointed to the debate around AIDS as one of the few occasions where they could remember seeing gays presented as ordinary people. The homosexual groups pointed out that they were unhappy with militant or extreme gays dominating debates, and they would rather see gays who were quite conservative in dress and attitude, or indeed appear as just ordinary people, rather than another example of left-wing gays. The public requires television to present the inconsistencies and complexities of people's decisions and wants comments on these positions also to reflect the ambiguities and uncertainties people have. Channel Four's recent strand of late night chat shows, *UK Late* and *After Dark*, conform to the notion that a range of people, who do not represent any cause, should be allowed to debate controversial issues in such a way as to bring out a range of difficult questions and anwers.

What we are dealing with in the discussion of C4's policy on balance is the public's view of democracy. When someone makes an assertive television programme he assumes a readiness on the part of the viewer to understand the programme-maker or presenter's arguments and justifications for a position. For his part, the viewer has certain background assumptions about how arguments should be presented; principally that the programme is sincere, intelligible and aims to be true. If a programme-maker breaches these rules then the viewer has to work extremely hard to sort out the status of the assertions in the programme. The fear that the rules of discourse can be breached is at the heart of the public's worries about Channel Four's policy. Although people are satisfied that the channel treats them as adults capable of evaluating complex arguments they want the rules of debate to be underpinned by challenges to assertions made in programmes. The public wants Channel Four to continue to experiment with ways of presenting unmediated controversial views on television, but it is yet to be convinced that the form of such presentation is adequate.

One of the great problems in trying to evaluate the success or failure of Channel Four is that we do not have a benchmark of previous public opinion about television bias (particularly from the late 1970s) against which to measure the current attitudes of the public to Channel Four's policy on bias. We have to entertain the strong possiblity that people may have changed their minds about the nature of bias on television as new rules for debating social and political issues were established in mid-80s Britain. The sense that politcs involved assertion and not dialogue, so prevalent at the end of the 1970s, has been replaced with a feeling that discussion is possible again, and that decent arguments might change minds rather than brainwashing them. The third term of Thatcherism has challenged the idea that all the opposition has to do is to shout long enough and hard enough and the voters will change their minds. There is a great deal of evidence building up from the counter-reformation in the Labour Party, the new 'realism' in the Trades Union movement, and the merger of the Liberals and SDP, that politics is about convincing people with evidence and debate rather than assertion and brute-ideology. The point of this speculation about such changes in the political parties' dialogue with the public is that there is evidence from our discussion groups that the public does think of televised debate as an extension of its views about the correct nature of public debate.

The groups demonstrate that a large minority of people are prepared to accept 'extremist' programmes. But even those who argue for balance within programmes do so from the perspective that they are able to make up their own minds. Few felt that television could radically alter their political or social views, but most did not want to have to sit through a programme to which they were going to take great exception. The principles of tolerance and proportionality were brought into play. People felt that biased programmes should be broadcast if they did not harm anyone (the debate on the National Front was particularly interesting in this respect); but if programmes were going to be contentious airtime must be allocated in proportion to the pressure group's size.

The major problem with discussions of political and social bias is that large numbers of people do not care about politics. As one young women put it:

> Yes, we read enough in the papers about politics; I don't think that we should come home and have to sit and watch politics. I think that it is the older generation that tend to take a lot of notice of politics, but the younger generation like me, I couldn't care less about it.
> Group 12                                     [Female Under 35 C2D Birmingham]

This attitude while extensive is not universal, and another young woman attacked television because it treated people as if they did not care about politics:

> I hate the way they make as though you're stupid ... they'll say 'and the Tories — that's the Conservatives'. It really is, it's abysmal. They think you know nothing.
> Group 3                                        [Female Under 35 C2D Glasgow]

Those who did accept the idea of balance across the schedules did so because they disliked the boredom of traditional documentaries, and felt that they were perfectly capable of sorting out truth from bias. The challenge of assertive programmes excited many people; indeed, one woman argued that the rest of her group accepted the notion of balance because they had been 'brainwashed' into it by television itself.

> I think there is a lot to be said for documentaries that are controversial and except from the bias viewpoint, it certainly arouses the interest and the emotions in the viewers more than a straight-forward suited man from the BBC would do giving both sides of the argument all the time.

> It would be sensible to provide a balance.

> C4 counterbalance the other channels.
> Group 17                                    [Males Under 35 BC1 Esher]

> Well I haven't identified any political bias and I don't think there should be either.
> Group 27                                           [Male Pensioner]

> National Front ... I think most people have their minds made up which way they're going anyhow, they don't need it.

> I'd rather hear that in a documentary where they can hopefully put both sides.

> We're so brainwashed with that though aren't we?
> Group 10                          [Female Over 35 BC1 Birmingham]

> I wouldn't watch a programme with one point of view − you would be shouting at the TV set your point of view.

> It all depends on how strong your point of view is. Some have a very strong opinion. I presume that a strongly opinionated person would be on TV, therefore if you didn't agree with that you would turn over thinking that he was talking a load of garbage, unless of course you agreed with him.
> Group 12                           [Female Under 35 C2D Birmingham]

> Channel Four tends toward the extemes, they are either talking about the left-wing or the right, extreme right.

> It's a little to the left I would have thought.

> If I was a journalist working for Channel Four and I felt strongly about something in South America for instance why the hell should I put forward other people's arguments.

> *Question Time* − it's a circus.

There should be an activist sort of channel.

They do do in fact, I'm very much into ... I don't know enough about this so I dipped in the other day and found a lady on the screen talking to me about the prison system and the fact that she'd been to prison − it was only on for about five minutes and I thought this was great they were using − I mean, she'd been there and she said what she thought was wrong and I thought that that was a good thing and probably in its own way quite as effective as say a series of three or four documentaries on another channel.

[Which channel was that on?]

That was Channel 4.

[You recognised it as Channel 4?]

Well, yes...

It sounds as if it came in with the news. They have from seven to eight the news and broad comment and then they have an individual talking.

I'm sure that was it, I'm sure you are right. And I thought again that it was very refreshing, you know, you get ... idea of what television has got to be − it tends to flow from one thing to another and it was very nice to see an ordinary person, OK they were sitting there listening to them on the screen, but there they were, no props, talking about something they knew about for just a short period of time and yes it came across quite strongly.

Group 9                                         [Male Under 35 BC1 Nottingham]

[Most documentaries are] middle of the road, wishy-washy, need someone with a very strong viewpoint.

Group 31                                         [Male C4 Heavy Viewers]

I think I like the idea of them trying to do something different.

In the extremes, well, as long as it's in good taste then I don't mind it being extreme.

I think as long as they declare their interest that is fair enough.

I don't think you necessarily reject the provocative programmes providing you know that a person is putting their own point of view.

The danger is television gives it sanction.

And I don't see why Channel Four should be given licence to do, it certainly should have the same licence as others, there should be certain standards set and nobody should go beyond that.
Group 6                                                    [Male Over 35 BC1 Newcastle]

Despite the popular press's harangue, Channel Four is not perceived by the public as being particularly left wing. Although one in five consider it to be so, this is only around 7 per cent more than those who think ITV and BBC left-wing. In other words, the channel is considered left-wing by those who think that television as such is oriented to the left (Table 6).

The public is satisfied that the channel is not unduly biased; but, more to the point, it does not want the channel to sacrifice committed television on an altar of obsessive issue or minute counting. Six out of ten people regard Channel Four as 'daring'. Compared to BBC1, whom less than one in ten consider 'daring', Channel Four is generally regarded as a channel where anti-establishment voices can be heard: over one-third of the population describe C4 as 'anti-establishment', compared to less than one in ten who so regard BBC1. In other words, Channel Four allows for committed and experimental programmes which are not necessarily balanced in the traditional manner.

The public's approval of minority programmes demonstrates that it requires television to explore methods of presenting issues which do not necessarily conform to the *Question Time* approach to political balance. Although most people approved of *Question Time*, because it had representatives from the three main political groupings, they felt that some arguments required the expression of more complex positions. Having said that, there is no doubt that the idea of balance is deeply rooted in people's perception of public debate on television. Almost nine out of ten of the population agree that if someone or some organisation wishes to make a controversial case, it should be challenged by others who do not hold these views (Table 29).

This should not be taken at face value. It does not signify a return to a desire for 'safe' mediated television. The public remains willing to tolerate extremely controversial programmes made by groups from the far right and the far left. For example, over a quarter of the population are prepared to accept a National Front programme about the repatriation of coloured immigrants, and around one-third a Communist Party programme about compulsory nationalisation of private companies (Table 30).

Tolerance is issue-specific. For example, only around one-third of young people are prepared to accept the National Front whereas half will sanction a programme by the Communist Party. Free speech is tempered by other values, such as concern for minorities, or anti-violence, though this does work both ways. Afro-Caribbeans, whom one would expect to be extremely anti National Front, are as willing to allow them access to television as the population as a whole: one-quarter claim that the National Front should be

158

## TABLE 29

If television showed a programme about the privatisation of British Coal should they be required to show the case for and against in the same programme?

If television showed a programme which argued for privatisation of British Coal should they be required to show another programme soon after which was against it?

BASE: ALL

| | Total | SEX | | AGE | | | | | CLASS | | | | CHILDREN | | | ETHNIC ORIGIN | | | |
| --- | --- | --- | --- | --- | --- | --- | --- | --- | --- | --- | --- | --- | --- | --- | --- | --- | --- | --- | --- |
| | | Male | Fe-male | 16-20 | 21-24 | 25-34 | 35-54 | 55+ | AB | C1 | C2 | DE | U5 | 5-15 | None | White | Afro-carib | Asian | Miss C4 a lot |
| TOTAL | 974 | 431 | 543 | 109 | 57 | 149 | 334 | 325 | 199 | 235 | 256 | 284 | 124 | 209 | 693 | 948 | 117 | 119 | 158 |
| **Show for and against in the same programme** | | | | | | | | | | | | | | | | | | | |
| Yes | 88% | 87% | 89% | 92% | 93% | 93% | 88% | 84% | 88% | 90% | 88% | 86% | 93% | 91% | 87% | 88% | 83% | 79% | 87% |
| No | 7% | 9% | 5% | 6% | 5% | 5% | 7% | 8% | 11% | 5% | 7% | 6% | 4% | 7% | 8% | 7% | 6% | 5% | 10% |
| Don't know | 5% | 3% | 6% | 2% | 2% | 2% | 4% | 8% | 1% | 5% | 5% | 8% | 3% | 2% | 6% | 5% | 11% | 16% | 3% |
| **Show programme soon after which was against it** | | | | | | | | | | | | | | | | | | | |
| Yes | 83% | 84% | 82% | 84% | 89% | 87% | 87% | 76% | 87% | 82% | 83% | 81% | 87% | 85% | 82% | 83% | 82% | 77% | 84% |
| No | 10% | 11% | 9% | 10% | 9% | 9% | 8% | 12% | 9% | 9% | 11% | 10% | 7% | 9% | 10% | 10% | 9% | 8% | 11% |
| Don't know | 7% | 5% | 9% | 6% | 2% | 4% | 5% | 12% | 4% | 9% | 6% | 9% | 6% | 6% | 8% | 7% | 9% | 14% | 6% |

159

## TABLE 30

Should the National Front be allowed to make a television programme about the repatriation of immigrants?

Should the Communist Party be allowed to make a television programme about compulsory nationalisation of private companies?

BASE: ALL

| | Total | SEX | | AGE | | | | | CLASS | | | | CHILDREN | | | ETHNIC ORGIN | | | Miss C4 a lot |
| --- | --- | --- | --- | --- | --- | --- | --- | --- | --- | --- | --- | --- | --- | --- | --- | --- | --- | --- | --- |
| | | Male | Fe-male | 16-20 | 21-24 | 25-34 | 35-54 | 55+ | AB | C1 | C2 | DE | U5 | 5-15 | None | White | Afro-carib | Asian | |
| TOTAL | 974 | 431 | 543 | 109 | 57 | 149 | 334 | 325 | 199 | 235 | 256 | 284 | 124 | 209 | 693 | 948 | 117 | 119 | 158 |
| **National Front** | | | | | | | | | | | | | | | | | | | |
| Yes | 26% | 29% | 24% | 35% | 32% | 28% | 27% | 20% | 40% | 26% | 23% | 20% | 32% | 30% | 24% | 26% | 25% | 17% | 32% |
| No | 65% | 65% | 64% | 60% | 67% | 63% | 62% | 70% | 54% | 68% | 67% | 68% | 63% | 59% | 67% | 65% | 73% | 73% | 61% |
| Don't know | 9% | 5% | 12% | 6% | 2% | 9% | 11% | 10% | 7% | 6% | 10% | 12% | 5% | 11% | 9% | 9% | 3% | 10% | 7% |
| **Communist** | | | | | | | | | | | | | | | | | | | |
| Yes | 31% | 38% | 25% | 49% | 32% | 32% | 36% | 19% | 44% | 33% | 29% | 21% | 37% | 37% | 28% | 30% | 39% | 25% | 37% |
| No | 61% | 58% | 64% | 46% | 65% | 60% | 54% | 73% | 51% | 62% | 62% | 67% | 55% | 55% | 64% | 61% | 54% | 62% | 54% |
| Don't know | 8% | 4% | 11% | 6% | 4% | 7% | 10% | 8% | 5% | 6% | 9% | 12% | 8% | 8% | 9% | 8% | 7% | 13% | 8% |

allowed to make a programme about the repatriation of immigrants. This is not quite matched by the Asians — only 17 per cent would accept a programme by the National Front — but it should be pointed out that the Asians are the most conservative group throughout the survey, and this low response appears also in their attitude to the Communist Party. They do not appear to want television to enter controversial areas and confront issues head-on (Table 31).

**TABLE 31**

Would you object to any of these groups appearing on Channel 4?

BASE: ALL

| | ETHNIC ORIGIN | | |
| --- | --- | --- | --- |
| | WHITE | AFRO-CARIB | ASIAN |
| TOTAL | 948 | 117 | 119 |
| No, all should appear | 21% | 30% | 12% |
| YES | | | |
| Repatriation of coloured immigrants | 20% | 34% | 47% |
| Marijuana | 45% | 25% | 45% |
| Sexual consent | 45% | 38% | 43% |
| Homosexual couples | 33% | 28% | 40% |
| Smoking | 25% | 21% | 30% |
| Birch | 10% | 17% | 18% |
| All of them | 11% | 10% | 10% |
| Don't know | 6% | 2% | 8% |

Along with allowing television to act as a medium for the expression of controversial political views, the public expects television to allow for non-political groups to express contentious views. Only one in ten wants a total ban on all types of controversial programmes. Although most people were prepared to tolerate programmes about the legalisation of marijuana, advocating the benefits of smoking or the re-introduction of the birch for young offenders, it is equally true that most had one sticking point — mainly lowering the age of sexual consent.

It is a measure of the complexity of the arguments about tolerance that the most tolerant people are also the most likely to sanction a programme which advocates the restoration of the birch. At first sight it is puzzling that the birch should elicit such a low negative response, after all more people are willing to accept such a programme than one extolling the virtues of smoking, which one would have thought less contentious. The pro-birching response probably indicates that those who are socially intolerant are more inclined to accept controversial programmes which represent their point of view, and although those who are tv tolerant might object to birching on principle, their overriding concern is with free speech on television. The birch is an example of an issue where all groups agree but do so for widely varying reasons, indicating that tv intolerance is, in some ways, issue-specific rather than a question of general principles (Table 32).

**TABLE 32**

Would you object to any of these groups appearing of Channel 4?

BASE: ALL

|  | | TV TOLERANCE | |
| --- | --- | --- | --- |
|  | TOTAL | TOLERANT | INTOLER-ANT |
| TOTAL | 974 | 376 | 588 |
| No, all should appear | 21% | 37% | 11% |
| **YES** | | | |
| Repatriation of coloured immigrants | 21% | 13% | 26% |
| Marijuana | 45% | 26% | 56% |
| Sexual consent | 45% | 30% | 53% |
| Homosexual couples | 33% | 7% | 49% |
| Smoking | 25% | 16% | 29% |
| Birch | 11% | 6% | 13% |
| All of them | 10% | 3% | 15% |
| Don't know | 6% | 9% | 4% |

The middle class is the most committed to the ideals of free speech on television. Middle class people are twice as likely as those from the lower working class to allow the National Front and the Communist Party to present their views. Whereas half of the middle class fit our television tolerance profile, only one in three of the working class do so (see Table 33). The middle classes are, it seems, much more prepared to accept a range of opinion on television. It is conceivable that they are secure in their beliefs and are unafraid of alternative points of view. They are also more likely to have benefited from further education, which allows them to explore ideas for their own sake, rather than seeing them as a direct challenge to be repulsed. The working classes are less prepared to tolerate challenges to their world view; they seem unprepared to accept the world of ideas divorced from its social and political consequences. The National Front, or its neo-Nazi offshoots, is not a marginalised, disembodied idea for people living in housing estates. Neo-Nazis are the living embodiment of political conflict and uncertainty. People living in areas with racist graffiti and skinheads are not likely to see the expression of these ideas, contained on television, as the harmless, and perhaps idiosyncratic, expression of marginal groups.

It is striking that those who fit our TV tolerance profile are much more willing to accept assertive, essentially unbalanced, programmes. Over half are willing to accept the National Front and almost six out of ten the Communist

Party. On the other hand, over eight out of ten of those who are TV intolerant are unwilling to accept programmes from these two groupings.

**TABLE 33**

| | CLASS | | | |
| --- | --- | --- | --- | --- |
| | **AB** | **C1** | **C2** | **DE** |
| TOTAL | 199 | 235 | 256 | 284 |
| **TOLERANCE** | | | | |
| Tolerant | 54% | 44% | 41% | 40% |
| Intolerant | 46% | 56% | 59% | 60% |
| **TV TOLERANCE** | | | | |
| Tolerant | 47% | 39% | 38% | 34% |
| Intolerant | 53% | 60% | 61% | 65% |

Having established that a significant minority of the population are prepared to accept contentious assertive television, we can now move on to explore the public's view about the appropriate channel for such programmes. One in four of the population think that all television channels should have contentious programmes, but, of those who nominate a particular channel, 49 per cent say Channel Four, 42 per cent choose BBC2, 17 per cent BBC1, and, finally, ITV squeezes in a poor last with 8 per cent. Young people seem more committed to the idea that Channel Four is the natural home for controversial political programmes: 58 per cent nominate Channel Four as opposed to the 31 per cent who say BBC2. The other age groups tend to suggest that both channels have the same level of resonsibility for such programming. Despite the general feeling that BBC2 and Channel Four share common duties, most people still think that C4 is more likely to fulfil these responsibilites. Almost half claim that Channel Four is more likely to show sensitive political programmes, compared to only 23 per cent who nominate BBC2 (Table 35).

**TABLE 34**

Should the National Front be allowed to make a television programme about the repatriation of immigrants?

| | | TV TOLERANCE | |
| --- | --- | --- | --- |
| | **TOTAL** | **TOLERANT** | **INTOLER-ANT** |
| TOTAL | 974 | 376 | 588 |
| **National Front** | | | |
| Yes | 26% | 51% | 11% |
| No | 65% | 31% | 86% |
| Don't Know | 9% | 18% | 4% |

**TABLE 35**

And which channel do you think would be most likely to show such programmes?

BASE: All who think there should be television programmes by the Communists/National Front

| | Total | SEX | | AGE | | | | | CLASS | | | | CHILDREN | | | ETHNIC ORGIN | | | Miss C4 a lot |
|---|---|---|---|---|---|---|---|---|---|---|---|---|---|---|---|---|---|---|---|
| | | Male | Fe-male | 16-20 | 21-24 | 25-34 | 35-54 | 55+ | AB | C1 | C2 | DE | U5 | 5-15 | None | White | Afro-carib | Asian | |
| TOTAL | 346 | 183 | 163 | 54 | 21 | 53 | 129 | 89 | 99 | 86 | 80 | 81 | 50 | 86 | 230 | 336 | 47 | 35 | 67 |
| BBC1 | 8% | 10% | 6% | 7% | — | 6% | 7% | 12% | 6% | 3% | 8% | 15% | 6% | 6% | 8% | 8% | 17% | 23% | 6% |
| BBC2 | 23% | 22% | 25% | 30% | 14% | 21% | 28% | 17% | 27% | 23% | 24% | 19% | 22% | 28% | 23% | 24% | 15% | 17% | 24% |
| ITV | 9% | 9% | 10% | 9% | — | 8% | 8% | 15% | 8% | 10% | 10% | 9% | 4% | 7% | 10% | 10% | 11% | 6% | 9% |
| C4 | 49% | 53% | 45% | 61% | 71% | 55% | 47% | 38% | 46% | 52% | 51% | 48% | 66% | 58% | 45% | 48% | 49% | 46% | 57% |
| Any | 13% | 14% | 12% | 6% | 10% | 11% | 14% | 19% | 18% | 14% | 9% | 11% | 6% | 12% | 15% | 14% | 4% | 14% | 15% |
| Don't know | 5% | 3% | 7% | — | 10% | 8% | 5% | 6% | 4% | 6% | 6% | 4% | 6% | 3% | 5% | 5% | 6% | 3% | 1% |

The public sees Channel Four as having a responsibility to explore issues in a different and controversial manner; but there can be little doubt that overall it is concerned that television retains its commitment to balance, whether over time or within a programme. Perhaps balance is the wrong word; it appears to want a range of people with many different voices to explore issues in a variety of ways. Controversy is applauded as long as everyone has a say.

Although there is a strong surface commitment to experimentation with unbalanced programmes, the deep fears about the effects of such program- mes will not disappear. The argument that Channel Four does not have a special dispensation to allow controversial programmes emerges out of fears about the effects of one-sided programmes. Underneath the veneer many people were afraid that they might be swayed by information. However, despite this fear, the majority of discussants felt that although programmes might affect you at the time, when you wake up in the morning you are still yourself, with your background and beliefs intact.

> As long as you hear both sides OK, and that leaves the individual to make up his own mind. I mean I wouldn't want somebody forcing one side of an argument down my throat, without knowing the other side, so that you could then, you know, make your own decision as to what was right and what was wrong.
> Group 9                                    [Male Under 35 BC1 Nottingham]

> No I would say you've always got to have an equal. Even if they had one programme that gave one point and they said tomorrow night we'll have the opposite view.

> I like discussion programmes, it gives everybody's point of view and they at least let you make up your own mind.
> Group 3                                    [Female Under 35 C2D Glasgow]

> Waking up the next morning. I mean you are going back to being yourself, but I think when you are actually watching something you think they might be right.
> Group 2                                    [Female Over 35 BC1 Glasgow]

> One programme that shows both points of view is better than two programmes, one on each side.
> Group 13                                   [Female Under 35 BC1 Southampton]

Most people appreciated that *Channel Four News* was attempting to provide in-depth coverage of major issues, and judged it on the basis of their own ability to cope with this level of coverage.

> I must admit I never watch the news on Channel Four because they

have it on there for a full hour and I can't be bothered to go into that sort of depth.
Group 16                                    [BC1 Female Over 35 Southampton]

Most people fixed on programmes about racism as an example of the type of programme of which they were afraid. It is here that the complexity of their views emerges. For instance, some Asians and blacks recognised that any form of political or cultural censorship might well affect their programmes and were prepared to put up with racist programmes to keep the television channels open (it should be said that this is a minority viewpoint). Others within the ethnic communities were interested in what the National Front actually had to say, wanting to know what they had against them, and thought that television would be a useful forum in which to find out. Some of the homosexual groups also recognised the problem of censorship, and were prepared to tolerate the National Front even though they disagreed with it.

The problem for most people was the classic liberal dilemma of tolerating free speech from people who would not allow them the same freedoms; the extraordinary thing was the number of people who were prepared to bite the bullet and let the National Front appear.

[National Front]: My immediate reaction is to say no, don't allow them to show it. But it comes down to freedom of choice again. You always have the option to turn it off.

They are a minority group, so they couldn't have been at peak period time.

They are very dangerous ... I would rather it wasn't shown.

Two minutes if you relate it to the rest of the population.
Group 31                                          [Male C4 Heavy Users]

I mean the National Front has had party political broadcasts in the 1974 elections and they were responsible in the presentation of their policies, I mean, I can't say that I agree with one iota with them, but I think it's healthy to actually listen to them as a member of society.

Even over a period of time, by the time you come to the week after you have forgotton all about it.

[Draw the line] at racism because it is against the law of the land to have these people ... now the guidelines for me would be things that are against the law and to mention the communists in the same breath is a totally different thing that peole want to know about. If they want to

know about communism, then they can listen to it, but not about racialism.
Group 5                                    [Female Under 35 BC1 Manchester]

Fascists [have no rights].

You can't let in extremes.

I find that sort of [question] kind of hard to answer actually.

I've never heard their views openly, you know, what they find so negative about us.

It should never become one-sided bias programmes for they change all the viewers views as well and that would be a danger.

South Africa — I'm afraid that has to be one-sided, doesn't it?
Group 23                                                    [Asian Males]

There are communists in this country ... There is, but I think the more these people have their say they'll end up running the country.

I don't think that at all.

I mean there are communists, so I think they should be allowed to go on television if they want to, we don't have to listen to them.

But it's a free country we don't want to change it do we, people are allowed their own opinion.
Group 2                                            [Female Over 35 BC1 Glasgow]

No to the National Front. Hidden views and attitudes.

You've got to have someone there to say stop.
Group 21                                              [Male Afro-Caribbean]

[National Front] I would to an extent. I would give them airtime to pose their opinion. I think that everyone has the right to use the media that's available to the general public, and if you stop them, I think you only make them more insidious, and more powerful in their own way, because everybody goes — well, what are these people saying? I think that it's good to have it out in the open, so that people can discuss, sort of with object, or agree — and everybody who is going to agree, will agree already.
Group 37                                              [Male Catholic Belfast]

National Front. They could be really offensive.

Yes, but if other people are given a chance to speak out, I think everybody should have that right.

Yes, if one is given then everybody should.

I think that it could be dangerous. If they're live ones, then I mean if it's pre-recorded obviously you can edit it afterwards and that is different.

I think they should cover every single issue. It might be degrading but at least we should hear what the other people have to say.

But do they say it, why bring it out in public. I mean you're not there to answer the questions but ask the questions, it's only one view.

But if there are whites and Asians in the audience you've got quite a good discussion.
Group 39                                              [Females Asian Nottingham]

I say as much as we want the entitlement to have a gay film they should be able to show their political point of view.

[Should there be censorship?]

None whatsoever. I'm looking at it from my point of view that if I want to see a gay film and somebody else doesn't they turn off. Now somebody that is a member of the National Front they've got as much entitlement to watch a film on the movements of the National Front of the policies or whatever and if it offends me, which maybe it would do, I would turn it of. I wouldn't phone up Channel Four and say, 'come on look we shouldn't be seeing this, you shouldn't be screening that type of thing' − no.
Group 29                                                    [Homosexual Males]

Thus far we have established that the public wants assertive television; that it is unafraid of the effects of such television on attitudes and values; that television, and particularly Channel Four, should explore extremely difficult moral issues; but that all this should be done with due regard for the rules of debate and argumentation. The principle being that television should allow for the full complexity of issues to emerge. The Irish troubles are a perfect site to explore this.

I just don't know, it's just that I get so sick of this one attitude getting across all the time, why don't they make, that were all the same as it's like when they make other programmes of Northern Ireland, with other things going on in the province apart from the troubles − I know there are lots of things going on, but you don't always want programmes about it − because I think that there are lots of things going on in the province – good things, interesting things, little babies for instance, there are lots of things going on here.

I would say that the extremists on both sides have a voice.

But the ordinary, the majority of people.

Yes, the majority of people don't, you know.

About it being slanted towards one side of the wall, it is very hard to show one side – I just don't think that you can.

[There is] no such thing as representation: you see every Catholic is not a nationalist, people don't understand it, every Catholic is not a nationalist and every protestant is not an Orangeman, you know.

You would need, I don't know what you would need – probably people who would be speaking for the majority, who could speak for the majority, as you say who don't get a word in edgeways, they would just be shouted down, because...

They would be too reasonable to be listened to.
Group 35                                         [Female Catholic Belfast]


It is always the worst part, it is always a family in a small house, lots of arguments, lots of problems, it never ends in a nice sort of ordinary family.

They are always showing wee back streets in Belfast, they never show the nice parts of Northern Ireland.

I suppose – we see enough of it.

I like, I like the documentaries that come out and spotlight, and half the things in Belfast and Northern Ireland, and I would disagree with half of them, they just show you really the bad side.

Well I think that if you've a programme about the wee show, if you had a topic, you know, sort of black against white – and have the ones, they are all sort of degrees of, you know, racial prejudice and then have families that are mixed, and are black –now why can't they do something like that here? You know; there is a problem of religion in areas that aren't there are certain degrees of it, why can't they show it to you?

You would have to get the right balance though...

There are middle class everywhere, we don't have problems.

Well I think − I don't like to hear either side about the IRA, I don't like them...

[But do they have the right to voice it on television?]

I don't see why not.

People are entitled to make up their own minds to what they think.

You've just got to show that the majority aren't that bad, that's why I think it is a good thing if you are having a documentary, going through the majority. I would say that the majority of people are not, you know, that politically conscious as in, you know Catholic and Protestant. I mean they are just content to make their friends, and take what they become on their own merits, and I think they just have to get the balance, and I would've said, the balance is that most people, the majority of people in Northern Ireland, you know, are just quite contented you know, as they are, and they don't want this violence.

I think that it's a mistake. It's very difficult to show it on television.

Well, I think when they did the AIDS programme, I thought it was well thought out, you know, and they didn't choose their audience, they let the audience just put across − they had a lot of kids in early teens, up to adults, up to old men, everything in the studio, and they interviewed all of them. It was like as if the audience was being interviewed, and I thought that it came across very well, to get everyone's point of view, and it was, very funny, because some of the people were so naive, and so thick, and some of them were so clever.
Group 36                                    [Female Protestants Belfast]

IRA/UDA... They are propaganda outfits I think, all of them are, all the three mentioned are propaganda outfits − and their reactions would be certainly to get publicity, but I disagree with that, because I think that at the end of the day what Kieran says is right, because you are a right-minded person, but if you see it on television, or hear it on the radio, or read it in your newspapers or not, you are a right-minded person, you are ultimately going to seek them out, or they are going to seek you out, one of the two... I honestly don't think that Gerry Adams getting up on TV − I think if anything people are going to sit down and say − what is this man talking about.

See that trouble is, I was going to say, is that left-minded people are watching that − and they are going to be influenced by their so-called leader.

But, there are too many other influences that can come to bear, if that fertile mind is being brought up in an environment which will more than applaud Gerry Adams, they don't go by whether he is on the box or not. If they are in the environment where everything that a man like that would do would be abhorrent, however clever he may be he is never going to turn their minds to facts.

You should put Gerry Adams on the television, but you should equally put the opposite, yes the opposite opinion to that, and then perhaps try to do your best to form a neutral stance on it, and give both particular points of view, so that you are giving the general viewing public, all aspects of a situation.

(Male Catholic Belfast)

[Do you think of yourself as a minority?]

No.

I don't want to be like a minority.

The majority of Northern Ireland can be classed as a minority.
Group 36                                    [Female Protestants Belfast]

The Irish groups do not want to return to the idea of the silent majority, as if this was a monolithic group; rather, they are concerned with the range of silent voices. They feel that the extremes in their society already have a voice, and impose a spurious unity on their arguments. The right of free speech is not impugned by the groups; the Protestants, with reservation, were willing to bite the bullet over the IRA, and the Catholics likewise the Protestant militants. But this is not enough for them; they want the debate to enter into complex areas where religion, politics and class fragment, and where real debates take place. The ritual of assertive spokesmen bellowing at one another is unacceptable.

This model is important. It preserves the gains which the public sees in Channel Four's policy of allowing assertive television, but also takes seriously the public's desire for proper debate and dialogue. Trust people seems to a rather simplistic solution to the problem of censorship and bias on television, but it seems to be the solution preferred by most of our discussants. If the intellectual level of debate is anything to go by the public deserves to be trusted. The viewers of television are actively participating in the creation of the meaning of a television programme. This simple but vital fact is often ignored by the censorship lobby as well as increasingly by many in television.

It's not just for young people on Channel Four. I think it's for everyone. It's only the young things like sex or the music thing that hit the

171

headlines about Channel Four. It certainly has got a myth that everyone thinks that Channel Four's about... I think if it's on Channel Four it gets hit anyway, if it's wrong or right it's going to get picked on.
Group 4                                    [Edinburgh Male Over 35 C2DE]

Where did the image come from?

Has it not come from the late night films?

Yes and that is always what you read about in the papers.

Never any fuss about BBC2's film corner.
Group 31                                        (Male C4 Heavy User)

Throughout this book we have been exploring the images of Channel Four held by the British public. Along with these images people have a sense of Channel Four's target audience; some of course think that Channel Four is for other people and not them, but the stereotypes seldom work as the following remarks show.

You don't get older people watching it.

[A young person]

It's an old person's channel.

[A pensioner]

In a sense the greatest compliment paid to the channel is that it demands alert, attentive viewing. Several respondents said:

If I was just idly thinking about watching TV Channel 4 would be my fourth choice to be honest.
Group 15                                        [Male Over 35 BC1 Bristol]

I think that I tend to be more selective with C4 than with the others. I can sit and let it wash over me, but not with C4. If I watch C4, it is a deliberate act on my part rather than just let it waffle on.
Group 31                                        [Male Heavy C4 user]

You start with BBC1 and then BBC2, and then if BBC1 is good you leave it on, and if not, then BBC2, and if you don't like anything that's on ... if you still don't like it, then Channel Four.
Group 39                                        [Female Asian Nottingham]

To sum up then: there is general approval of the idea of specialist/minority programmes. However, a principle of proportionality is at work, by which we mean that the prevailing opinion among the public is that groups should be apportioned broadcasting time according to their relative size and cultural distance from something which might recognisably be defined as mainstream British culture. Ethnic groups and gays are unhappy with the channel and feel that it has gone backwards in the past two years. In particular, ethnic groups miss the flagship programmes such as *Black on Black* and *Eastern Eye*. Although the public is prepared to accept, and, indeed condone minority or specialist interest television, a strong anti-homosexual current runs through the public's attitudes, even among those who seek to articulate in the abstract the rights of such groups and individuals.

We demonstrated that the public does not blame television for changes in sexual morality, indeed that it has a rather sophisticated understanding of sex on television, based on the viewer's right to choose. The SDR symbol was highly approved of, and many wanted it extended to all programming with classifications similar to those of the cinema. Whilst many recognised the need to protect children through some kind of regulation of both schedules and programme content, there was an overwhelming feeling that the opinions espoused by people like the National Viewers and Listeners Association were unrepresentative and, on balance, did more harm than good.

This leads us to our final and most significant conclusion. If there was a single thread unifying what ostensibly were differences of opinion within and across the groups it was what one might call the 'adult citizen' syndrome. This is that attitude of mind which recognises that there are programmes which may delight, others which may offend, but which feels that the audience – as mature adult members of a mature political democracy – should be allowed to make its own judgements about what it does or does not watch.

Throughout this study we have tried to elicit from the public its view of the responsibilities of television, therefore let us give the last word to the viewers. Under the impression that we had some influence over Channel Four's programming policy we were often offered advice, perhaps the most heartfelt of which was:

Tell Channel Four not to bother with black and white Japanese films.

Bung 'em back in the archive.

# Conclusion

Is Channel Four a success or a failure? Too extreme or not extreme enough? An extension of the public service tradition in broadcasting or its deathknell? These questions are impossible to answer in some ways. Those with extremist politics will probably claim that the channel bears no resemblance to the OBA and has had no real impact on British television. Others, from a different political standpoint, may claim that the channel undermines the consensus of values, culture and politics which, they argue, is essential for the country's continued stability. For those who believe in the value of monolithic public broadcasting organisations, the channel's encouragement of independent producers has undermined the fabric of the British public service tradition. Others, on the other hand, argue that the only way to preserve the tradition in an age of increasing competition is to encourage the development of public service values in the independent production sector.

We have no simple answers to these questions. What we have shown, however, is that three important groups of people judge the channel a qualified success. The public wants the channel to continue in its present form, and would be deeply unhappy if, as a result of government policy, the channel became simply a pale imitation of ITV. Television, the public tells us, should continue to be adventurous and experimental; it should attempt polemical programmes while respecting the public's right to know the full story; and, finally, it should be properly, but not overtly, cautious in the areas of sex and morality.

The independent producers are, by and large, happy with Channel Four. Even David Graham, the 'prince of darkness' as far as conventional broadcasters are concerned, feels that Channel Four is the best that regulated television has to offer. Most independents complain about technical aspects of the channel: the slowness and inconsistencies of the commissioning process, the budgetary constraints, the lack of consultation on scheduling, the occasional timidity. However, despite all that, the majority of independents interviewed for this book felt that the channel remains adventurous and reasonably open to new ideas. (It is not insignificant that those who complained most vigorously about the channel still had a significant number of commissions for programmes.) There is a pervasive feeling that the bureaucrats might take over once Isaacs has left and erect barriers against adventurous programmes but that, despite this, the present crop of commissioning editors are committed to what one might call the 'project of Channel Four'.

On a broader level, the channel appears to have fulfilled the ambitions of its creators. Tony Smith, its intellectual parent, claims that 'the reform of the BBC is the real objective for the institution of Channel Four' and, in that, it has been successful: 'it has opened the sluice gate' to change. Of the future, Smith added: 'I don't think anyone else is going to take on Channel Four's remit ... no-one else wants to take it on. It adds something to the life of this society which is extremeley beneficial, I mean not just to television. The sense of opportunities, recognition of groups and communities, sense of involvement in television among people who are otherwise outside the discourse of television as a whole. It is immensely valuable as a source of patronage: it is the second Arts Council in this country.'

William Whitelaw, the channel's political parent, feels that it has succeeded in his terms: 'I think on the whole that it has lived up to what it was asked to do. It has given new outlets. It has popularised different sports, it has given a different type of news programme and on the whole it has given a slightly different slant in the field of music and the field of drama. It hasn't been as adventurous as some people would like but I think it has been sufficiently adventurous to have an identity of its own.'

The worst thing about a channel dedicated to challenging and transforming conventional television is if it succumbs to complacency. The public, and the broadcasting industry, believes that Channel Four has an important contribution to make to British culture and society. It would be disastrous then if the channel settled into the rhythms of the past five years. Staying one step ahead or, more precisely, one step slightly ahead and to the side, is a major task, and only the channel's tenth anniversary will tell us if it succeeded.

# Technical Appendix

## Discussion Groups:

Overall, we ran forty-four discussion groups, distributed as follows:

| | | Scotland | | North Eng | | Midlands | | South West | | London | |
|---|---|---|---|---|---|---|---|---|---|---|---|
| | | M | F | M | F | M | F | M | F | M | F |
| ABC1 | 16−34 | 1 | | 1 | | 1 | | | 1 | 1 | |
| | 35−60 | | 1 | 1 | | | 1 | 1 | | | 1 |
| C2DE | 16−34 | | 1 | 1 | | 1 | 1 | | | | 1 |
| | 35−60 | 1 | | 1 | | | | 1 | 1 | 1 | |
| Afro-Carib | | | | 1 | 1 | | | | | 1 | 1 |
| Asian | | 1 | | 1 | | 1 | | | | 1 | |
| Teenagers | (12−16) | | | | | 1 | | | | | 1 |
| Young Adults | (16−20) | | | | | | 1 | | | 1 | |
| OAP | | | | | 1 | | | | | 1 | |
| Gay | | 1 | | 1 | 1 | | | 1 | | | |
| C4 Heavy Users. | | | | 1 | | | 1 | | | | |
| (plus four groups from Northern Ireland split by sex and religion) | | | | | | | | | | | |

Controls

At least half of the repondents in each of the main groups had children under the age of 16.

Respondents watched at least two hours a week of television, and viewed C4 at least one hour in the previous month.

The Heavy C4 viwers were those who had watched at least four news, current affairs, documentary, or feature [films] on C4 in the previous two weeks.

177

*List of Groups*

General

Group 1 : Male 16−34 BC1 Scotland
Group 2 : Female 35−60 BC1 Scotland
Group 3 : Female 16−34 C2D Scotland
Group 4 : Male 35−60 C2D Scotland
Group 5 : Female 16−34 BC1 North of England
Group 6 : Male 35−60 BC1 North of England
Group 7 : Male 16−34 C2D North of England
Group 8 : Female 35−60 C2D North of England
Group 9 : Male 16−34 BC1 Midlands
Group 10: Female 35−60 BC1 Midlands
Group 11: Male 35−60 C2D Midland
Group 12: Female 16−34 C2D Midlands
Group 13: Female 16−34 BC1 South West England
Group 14: Male 35−60 BC1 South West England
Group 15: Male 35−60 C2D South West England
Group 16: Female 35−60 C2D South West England
Group 17: Male 16−34 BC1 London
Group 18: Female 35−60 BC1 London
Group 19: Female 16−34 C2D London
Group 20: Male 35−60 C2D London

Specialist

Group 21: Male Afro-Caribbean North of England
Group 22: Female Afro-Caribbean London
Group 23: Male Asian London
Group 24: Female Asian North of England
Group 25: Male Teenager North of England
Group 26: Female Teenager London
Group 27: Male OAP London
Group 28: Female OAP
Group 29: Male Homosexual North of England
Group 30: Female Homosexual South West of England
Group 31: Male C4 Heavy Users North of England
Group 32: Female C4 Heavy Users Midlands
Group 33: Male Afro-Caribbean Midlands
Group 34: Female Afro-Caribbean London
Group 35: Male Asian Scotland
Group 36: Female Asian Midlands
Group 37: Male Protestant Northern Ireland
Group 38: Male Catholic Northern Ireland
Group 39: Female Protestant Northern Ireland
Group 40: Female Catholic Northern Ireland
Group 41: Male Homosexual Scotland
Group 42: Female Homosexual Midlands
Group 43: Male 16−20 London
Group 44: Female 16−20 North West

178

We administered two questionnaires, the first prior and the second subsequent to the discussion: the initial questionnaire contained 26 attitude statements on a five-point scale 'agree strongly' to 'strongly disagree': respondents were also allowed a 'don't know' category. These attitude statements were factor analysed, and subsequently formed the basis for a cluster analysis. The second questionnaire was used as a check for any major shift in attitudes as a result of the discussion; a small shift toward a more conciliatory opinion of C4 was discovered.

## Factor Analysis

Four factors were discovered, explaining 44% of the variance.

Variable Loading Statement
Factor One

| 18 | 0.7120 | C4 caters for trendy lefties. |
| 13 | 0.6769 | Television News is too biassed against the Conservatives. |
| 16 | 0.6093 | C4 is being run badly. |

(The following variables do not contribute strongly to the factor and should be interpreted with caution.)

| 23 | 0.4979 | C4 should show the right-wing point of view more often. |
| 8 | 0.4962 | C4 News is too left-wing. |
| 11 | 0.4123 | C4 should be just like ITV and BBC1. |
| 4 | 0.3978 | Government should exercise more control over C4's programmes. |
| 12 | −0.3560 | Like programmes show point of view on issue not commonly aired. |
| 17 | 0.3227 | C4 is the only station that has decent programmes for young people. |

Factor Two

| 24 | 0.7342 | C4 should not show programmes made by homosexual groups. |
| 21 | 0.6468 | Programmes about homosexuals make me uncomfortable. |
| 14 | 0.6211 | Programmes about homosexuality should not show it as normal sexual practice. |
| 3 | 0.5872 | There shouldn't be programmes with explicit sex scenes on television. |

(The following variables do not contribute strongly to the factor and should be interpreted with caution.)

| 5 | −0.4755 | Rastafarians' programmes reflect their religion's positive views about marijuana. |
| 20 | 0.4701 | Never watch film which had Special Discretion Required symbol. |
| 19 | −0.4540 | British TV shows more programmes for political minorities eg National Front, Communist Party, Green Party. |
| 15 | 0.4290 | Ethnic minorities should not expect special treatment from television. |
| 4 | 0.4122 | Government should exercise more control over C4's programmes. |
| 2 | −0.3575 | Don't mind hearing swearing on C4 as I would on BBC1 or ITV. |

Factor Three

| 25 | 0.739 | Documentaries should always try to show both sides of the story. |
| 1 | 0.6680 | Programmes about race relations should always show all points of view. |

(The following variables do not contribute strongly to the factor and should be interpreted with caution.)

| 12 | 0.4370 | Like programmes show point of view on issue not commonly aired. |
| 7 | 0.3650 | Best things show programmes wide variety minority sports like cycling and baseball. |
| 5 | −0.3041 | Rastafarians' programmes reflect their religion's positive views about marijuana. |

Factor Four

| 9 | 0.6242 | Without C4 black people would not have a voice on British television. |
| 6 | 0.5927 | Like programme makers to always make their political positions clear. |
| 12 | 0.5411 | Like programmes show point of view on issue not commonly aired. |
| 22 | 0.5402 | British TV does not produce decent programmes for pensioners. |

(The following variables do not contribute strongly to the factor and should be interpreted with caution.)

| 10 | 0.4886 | Think more women and young people should make television programmes. |
| 15 | −0.4108 | Ethnic minorities should not expect special treatment from television. |
| 5 | 0.3981 | Rastafarians' programmes reflect their religion's positive views about marijuana. |

*Four Cluster Solution*

Cluster Profiles

|  | 1 Cluster | 2 Cluster | 3 Cluster | 4 Cluster |
|---|---|---|---|---|
| 1. F1 | XXXXXXXX. | .XXXXX | X. | .XXXXX |
| 2. F2 | XXXXX. | .XXXXXXXXXXX | XXX. | |
| 3. F3 | XX. | XX. | .XXXXXXXXX | XXX. |
| 4. F4 | XXXXX. | XXXXXXX. | .XXX | .XXXXXX |

SALIENT STANDARD DEVIATE

| Cluster 1 (Size 66) | 1. F1 | −0.818 | 4. F4 | −0.623 |
|---|---|---|---|---|
|  | 2. F2 | −0.462 | 3. F3 | −0.188 |
| Cluster 2 (Size 42) | 2. F2 | 1.094 | 4. F4 | −0.736 |
|  | 1. F1 | 0.481 | 3. F3 | −0.170 |
| Cluster 3 (Size 47) | 3. F3 | 0.934 | 4. F4 | 0.332 |
|  | 2. F2 | −0.267 | 1. F1 | −0.126 |
| Cluster 4 (Size 87) | 4. F4 | 0.648 | 1. F1 | 0.456 |
|  | 3. F3 | −0.280 | 2. F2 | −0.034 |

# 2. Survey

*THE SAMPLE*

The survey was based on a probability sample, in 90 constituencies across Great Britain. All constituencies were stratified according to region, urban/rural mix, and social breakdown. From this stratified list 90 constituencies were selected with a probability proportional to size. In each constituency a polling district was selected at random, and 18 electors were selected for interview (20 in London constituencies), on the basis of selecting every fifteenth name on the electoral register after a random start point.

In addition to the selected, who was always interviewed if possible, if there were any people aged 18 and over at the same address but who were not listed on the register, then one of these was selected for interview.

This provided a sample representative of the population as a whole, but it was also necessary to achieve enough interviews with Afro-Caribbean and Asian respondents to enable them to be analysed separately. Two booster quota samples were used. Using Census and other survey data, 25 constituencies were chosen which had a high proportion of Afro-Caribbean residents, and a further 25 with a high proportion of Asian electors. In each constituency four people were interviewed, with quotas set for age.

*FIELDWORK*

Interviewing took place between July 16th and 24th. On the main sample 974 interviews were conducted, in addition to which there were 110 quota interviews with Afro-Caribbeans and 102 with Asians. Including those interviewed as part of the main sample, this produced total sub-samples of 117 Afro-Caribbeans and 119 Asians.

Allowing for ineligible names in the main sample, such as vacant or non-residential addresses, the total of 974 main sample interviews represents a contract rate of 62%.

*ANALYSIS*

Because of their differential chances of selection, the quota respondents were not included in the main analysis. They appear only in a specific crossbreak cell for ethnic origin. Thus in the tables the 'total' column, and the crossbreak cells such as age, sex and class include only the respondents from the main sample.

The questionnaire provided the basis for statistical analysis of the range of attitudes unearthed in the discussion groups. In particular it allowed us to explore the nature and limits of the public's general social tolerance as compared to its acceptance of the rights of minority groups to have their voice represented on television, and its understanding of the need for television to innovate. As part of the analysis a number of composite variables were created. These scores were calulated on the following basis.

*TOLERANCE SCORES*

+1    for 'Made to attend Christian Assembly' at Q2
+1    for wanting 2 or 3 of Moslem, Hindu, Rasta not talked about at Q3
+1    for wanting 2 or 3 of Mormans, Jehovah's Witnesses, Moonies not talked about at Q3

+1    for wanting 2, 3, or 4 of Jewish, Cafe, RC, Baptist not talked about Q3
−1    for wanting 2 or 3 of drug addiction, STD, contraception talked about at Q5
+5    for not acceptable to have black headmaster at Q6a
+1    for wanting 3−5 of groups at Q7 banned
+2    for wanted 6−8 of groups at Q7 banned
+3    for wanting 9/10 of groups at Q7 banned
+5    for very offended by doctor with earring at Q8
+1    for fairly offended by doctor with earring at Q8
+5    for very offended by conductor with earring at Q9
+3    for fairly offended by conductor with earring at Q9
+3    for tend to disagree that libraries should stock Asian books at Q10a
+5    for definitely disagree that libraries should stock Asian books at Q10a
+5    for definitely agree that immigrants must learn English at Q10b
+2    for tend to agree that immigrants must learn English at Q10b
−1    for wanting 2/3 of ethnic minorities, groups, feminists, punks and anti nuclear to have radio programmes at Q11
−2    for wanting 415 at Q11

Range = −3 to +30
Tolerant = less than 7


*PUBLIC SERVICE BROADCASTING (PSB) SCORES*
−1    for choosing Channel X as best for population as a whole
−1    for choosing Channel Y as best for population as a whole
+3    for definitely disagree to replacing minority programmes at Q25a
+2    for tend to disagree to replacing minority programmes at Q25a
+3    for definitely agree to experimental programmes at Q25b
+2    for tend to agree to experimental programmes at Q25b

Score of 4 or more counts as committed to PSB


*TV TOLERANCE SCORES*
+2    for not allow National Front at Q29a
+2    for not allow Communist at Q29b
+1    for disapprove a little of C4 minority policy at Q3b
+2    for disapprove a lot of C4 minority policy at Q3b
+1    for 3−5 groups not to appear on C4 at Q37
+2    for 6−8 groups not to appear on C4 at Q37
+3    for 9/10 groups not to appear on C4 at Q37
+1    for 3 groups not to appear on C4 at Q39
+2    for 4/5 groups not to appear on C4 at Q39
+3    for 6 groups not to appear on C4 at Q39
+1    for 2 of Irish, Chinese, Asian, Afro−Caribbeans not on C4 at Q41c
+2    for 3/4 of Irish, Chinese, Asian, Afro−Caribbeans not on C4 at Q41c
+1    for homosexuals not on C4 at Q41a
+1    for lesbians not on C4 at Q41a
+1    for disapprove a little of gays on Eastenders at Q52
+2    for disapprove a lot of gays on Eastenders at Q52

Score 0−4 = Tolerant: Score 5+ = Intolerant

The questionnaire contained fifty-six questions and each interview lasted between 25 and 35 minutes. The first eleven questions are concerned with tolerance of minority voices; the following five questions put the social power of television into perspective by asking people to rank the reasons for changing sexual morality, increasing crime and the spread of swearing; questions seventeen to twenty are concerned with the amount of time people watch C4; twenty-one to twenty deal with public service values; and, finally, twenty-nine to fifty-two explore what we call television tolerance. (The last four questions asked about voting and religious behaviour.) As with all our research we used National Opinion Poll's social reseach department (Director, Nick Moon) for the field work, but undertook the design and detailed analysis ourselves.

## 3. History of C4's Mandate

Interviewees

Commissioning Editors:

| | |
|---|---|
| John Cummins | (Commissioning Editor, Youth) |
| Farukh Dhondy | (Commissioning Editor, Multicultural programmes) |
| Alan Fountain | (Commissioning Editor, Independent Film and Video) |
| Michael Kustow | (Commissioning Editor, Art) |
| Adrian Metcalfe | (Senior Commissioning Editor, Sport) |
| Gywnn Pritchard | (Commissioning Editor, Education) |
| John Ranelagh | (Commissioning Editor, Documentary Series and Ireland) |
| Robert Towler | (Commissioning Editor, Religion and Open College) |
| Peter Ansorge | (Commissioning Editor, Drama Series and Serials) |
| Elizabeth Forgan | (Deputy Controller of Programmes) |
| Mike Bolland | (Assistant Deputy Controller of Programmes) |
| Seamus Cassidy | (Commissioning Editor, Light Entertainment) |
| David Rose | (Senior Commissioning Editor, Fiction) |
| Naomi Sargant | (Senior Commissioning Editor, Education) |
| Caroline Thomson | (Commissioning Editor, Industry and Finance) |
| David Lloyd | (Commissioning Editor, Current Affairs) |
| Nick Hart-Williams | (Commissioning Editor, Single Documentaries) |
| Jeremy Isaacs | (Controller C4) |

Independent Producers:

| | |
|---|---|
| David Graham | (Diverse Productions) |
| Mark Lucas | (After Image) |
| Joan Shenton | (Meditel) |
| Peter Montangon | (Antelope) |
| Rob Burkitt | (Birmingham Film and Video Workshop) |
| Alan Lovell | (Birmingham Film and Video Workshop) |
| Don Coutts | (After Dark) |
| Sebastiane Cody | (After Dark) |
| Ann Skinner | (Skreba) |
| Michael Darlow | (Try – Again Ltd.) |
| Paul Styles | (IPPA) |
| John Ellis | (Large Door) |

The independents represent a broad range of opinion about C4, from those who think that it has sold out, through to new people who have just been given their first chance, and are still full of enthusiasm.